Wind in my Sleeve

✿ *The Enchantress* ✿

Books by Han Suyin

AND THE RAIN MY DRINK ✓
3— BIRDLESS SUMMER ✓
CAST BUT ONE SHADOW •
CHINA IN THE YEAR 2001 •
1— THE CRIPPLED TREE ✓
DESTINATION CHUNKING ✓
THE ENCHANTRESS ✓ (x)
FOUR FACES •
LHASA, the Open City •
A MANY SPLENDORED THING ✓
1. Mao ——— THE MORNING DELUGE ✓
2— A MORTAL FLOWER ✓
THE MOUNTAIN IS YOUNG •
4— MY HOUSE HAS TWO DOORS ✓
TILL MORNING COMES •
2. Mao ——— WIND IN THE TOWER ✓
WINTER LOVE •

5— Phoenix Harvest ✓

Wind in my Sleeve ✓
A Share of Loving ✓

HAN SUYIN

Wind in my Sleeve

*

CHINA
AUTOBIOGRAPHY
HISTORY

JONATHAN CAPE
LONDON

First published 1992
© Han Suyin 1992
Jonathan Cape, 20 Vauxhall Bridge Road, London SW1V 2SA

Han Suyin has asserted her right
under the Copyright, Designs and Patents Act, 1988
to be identified as the author of this work

The photographs are from the author's collection
Endpaper painting by Zhang Junguo

A CIP catalogue record for this book
is available from the British Library

ISBN 0-224-03496-0

Printed in Great Britain by
Butler & Tanner Ltd, Frome and London

This book is dedicated to the people of China. To the Four Generations who make up that billion of human beings whose attempts to free themselves from the miseries of the past have not ceased.

The First Generation, who were the young students of the early twentieth century: they fought and created a new China in 1949, free of the exploitations of the past. They have ruled for four decades, and history will give them their due, for they accomplished much. But every revolution breeds its own weaknesses, and history has taken on another amplitude.

The Second and Third Generations, among them my contemporaries, my schoolmates, my friends, members of my family in China, who have struggled in so many ways, and have suffered so much, to find a road to China's future.

The Fourth Generation, the young; inheritors of whatever has been accomplished, for good or ill. They will make new breakthroughs, and in the end will discover that they strangely resemble the First Generation, even if today they are loud in condemnation of it, and impatient to see it disappear.

Han Suyin,
summer of 1991

One

JANUARY 1977. A bitterly cold afternoon though the sun glints fitfully from a sky struggling with the fumes of the city, fumes of a million stoves burning coal in the huddled grey houses of Beijing. I stand on the marble bridge facing Tiananmen Square, square of Heavenly Peace, and watch it become awash with colour. Wreaths and garlands of roses, fuchsia, baskets of convolvulus and peonies, explosions of colour most of them made of paper, for fresh flowers in the long arctic winter of North China are hard to find, and expensive. Especially in this winter, just two months after the Cultural Revolution has ended, because there has been a ban on all flowers as 'bourgeois' imposed by that unimaginative, and strangely paranoid woman, Madame Mao, also known as Limpid Stream, translation of her name, Jiang Qing.

One hardy florist has started again, confident that times are changing, have changed, but his shop is small, and hundreds of thousands of hands have therefore confected bright paper emblems of love and remembrance. Love and remembrance for the Beloved, the late Prime Minister, Zhou Enlai, who died exactly a year ago, on 5 January 1976.

In solemn procession the hundreds of thousands come, swarm to lay their offerings, heaping them round the monument to the heroes of the Revolution, in the centre of the square. For there is no stele, no monument, no grave to commemorate Zhou Enlai. As he had willed it, his ashes were scattered over the mountains and rivers of his land. But the inscription on the monument is in his handwriting,

I

precious calligraphy, all that is left of him for public view. The colourful mementoes to him will stand untouched till 15 January when the square is restored to wide emptiness, save for strollers with their muffled children. This unhindered demonstration of love is also a political statement, a demand that the man who took over many of the duties during the last years of life of the cancer-gnawed Zhou, should return from obscurity and disgrace.

Deng Xiaoping. Xiao Ping. Two characters meaning small and even. A name that lends itself to a homonymous pun, 'small bottle'. Deng Xiaoping is short, five foot two, square and square-faced, not handsome or elegant, but he is the man the people want, for they identify him with Zhou, and with Zhou's unrelenting struggle to maintain order, to push China forward in her modernization, throughout the decade of the Cultural Revolution.

Twice since the Cultural Revolution began in 1966 has Deng Xiaoping been toppled from leadership. The first time in 1967, when he was targeted as a 'capitalist roader'. But Mao seems to have nurtured grudging affection for the little man who so stubbornly defied him. While Liu Shaoqi, President of China, vice-chairman of the Party, died in jail, Deng Xiaoping was sent to a small town, and his family was allowed to join him. This was due to Zhou Enlai as well as to Mao. Zhou had joined the group round Mao, all the better to thwart their plans for a power takeover, and to safeguard the intellectuals, as well as the Party members under attack. He made sure that Deng Xiaoping was safe from assault by the roving bands of Red Guards which rampaged at will throughout the land, all in the name of 'great democracy'. For this was what the Cultural Revolution was meant to promote.

By 1971 Mao knew that his dream of renovating China by launching China's youth against his own Party had turned into a blistering catastrophe. A new era began when in February 1972, President Richard Nixon flew from Washington to Beijing, abolishing twenty-two years of hostility. In April

1973 Deng Xiaoping reappeared at a banquet in the Great Hall of the People in honour of Prince Norodom Sihanouk of Cambodia. I remember that evening, for I saw him amble in, a security guard behind him. He walked briskly, and at the end of the reception I heard him say to his guard, 'I know, I know,' in that Sichuan province accent of his which reminded me of my father. He was to leave by the back door, not yet allowed to leave the reception through the main entrance with the other guests. However within a fortnight he was attending State Council meetings under Zhou Enlai, and in April 1973, a year later, he was in New York at the United Nations, to deliver a major speech on China. By 1975 he shouldered all the routine work of the desperately ill Prime Minister.

During the last months of Zhou's life, the battle between him and the faction gathered round Limpid Stream, Mao's wife, became an open clash, a major struggle for power. Mao's faculties declined. He was almost blind, afflicted with hours of stuporose, catatonic inertia. Nevertheless, he was determined not to hand power over to his wife, for he knew well her overvaulting ambition. He called her, and her supporters, the 'Gang of Four', a derisive nickname. And despite his affliction, took measures against her.

Zhou Enlai died on 5 January 1976, and in April, on the feast of Sweeping the Graves, demonstrations took place in Tiananmen Square to mourn him. Half a million of Beijing's inhabitants marched to the square, brought blossoms, declaimed poems. In thirty other cities of China similar demonstrations took place. The Gang of Four dubbed these demonstrations 'counter-revolutionary' and Deng Xiaoping was accused of having organized them. He was arrested, but once again Mao prevailed, and Deng Xiaoping was allowed to leave for Guangdong province, in South China, there to be protected by an important army commander. Then Mao died, on 9 September, and a month later, on 8 October, his wife and her followers were arrested.

They were arrested because, just before dying, Mao had

3

foiled his wife's ambition, by appointing as his successor a burly laconic man from his own province of Hunan. The man was Hua Guofeng, almost an unknown, but who had been head of security in China for the past eighteen months.

Millions of people now vented their hatred of Limpid Stream and her acolytes. Posters appeared on the walls of every city, caricaturing the Gang of Four. Limpid Stream was a favourite target. She was imaged as a grotesque she-devil, giving interviews to an American Sinologist, a woman who had inadvertently been there in 1972–73, and who was writing a book about her. Mao had become known to the world through *Red Star Over China*, by the American Edgar Snow. Mao's wife now wanted her own pet writer. The crowds in China jeered, 'That white-boned demon ill-treated anyone who had relatives or friends abroad, but she spent weeks babbling to a foreign woman.'

Scientists, writers, artists, were returning to their posts. Back from shadowland, those May 7 schools, as the special camps for intellectuals were called. Others merely from stagnating at home with salaries paid (though reduced) and no work. For a good many of them, reintegration was immediate, but others had to wait, their offices still occupied by appointees of the Gang of Four. However, their salaries were restored, and all the moneys owed to them from cuts given back. This created a sensation of euphoria among many, a feeling that the wrongs they had suffered would be righted. Hua Guofeng, the new chairman, was not popular with them, but neither was he resented. However, everyone knew that his hold was precarious, for it was uniquely based on Mao's personal approval. He was, therefore, bound to continue upholding Mao's dicta and declared, 'We must continue to criticize Deng Xiaoping.' But his weakness was evident, for the tide had turned and by mid-February criticism of Deng Xiaoping had vanished from the newspapers. By March Deng was back in Beijing, looking fit and energetic. In the six weeks preceding his return one met daily on the

4

streets of Beijing dozens of young men, and not so young men and women, dangling little bottles filled with red ink, or bicycling with red-filled bottles fixed to their handlebars. The red ink meant that Deng, 'Little Bottle', was a true revolutionary.

Within the Party Deng had a solid phalanx of supporters, all the Long Marchers, for he belonged to the same generation as Mao Dzedong and Zhou Enlai, the First Generation. This generation of the Chinese Revolution created the history of contemporary China. It was the generation which had created the communist Party, fought the Japanese, fought the military dictator Chiang Kaishek, and set up after the Long March those peasant guerilla bases which had wrested final victory. The First Generation had established the People's Republic of China in October 1949. Despite Mao Dzedong's attempt to unsaddle many of his colleagues and contemporaries, they had survived, they were back. Deng Xiaoping was one of them. Today, in the China of 1991, it is still Deng Xiaoping, and what remains of the First Generation, all of them in their eighties, in whose hands power and authority lies.

I met Deng Xiaoping on 24 September 1977.

It was Yingchao, the widow of Zhou Enlai, who arranged the meeting. Vibrant, energetic, despite her diminutive size, I had known Yingchao since that day in June 1956 when she and her husband, the Prime Minister, had received me in their home, the private pavilion within that area called Middle and Southern Sea, where the leaders lived and worked. It is an immense park, dotted with Ming dynasty buildings, bordering a central lake, hence its name of 'middle and southern sea'. It is in the middle of Beijing's Forbidden City, enclosed by purple walls capped with golden tiles.

In that June of 1956 I met the couple, and we talked for hours. After that my life had been irrevocably changed, although it took me some years of doubt, hesitation, to realize that indeed this had happened. Today, thirty-five years

5

later, the bond which was then forged has proved enduring, unbreakable. It has been an all-fulfilling commitment, not to a political creed, but to China, and to her people, who are also my people. Never was it a political adherence, and always Zhou Enlai admitted my freedom to differ, to hold sceptical and contrary views. But it was he and his wife Yingchao who reinforced in me that passion and dedication which has made me what I am.

Far from interfering with my private life, or lives, this new amplitude reinforced all other loves, made caring for not only China, but all the peoples of the world, coherent, evident. It never came into conflict with my love for Vincent my husband, who loves his India with similar passion, and understood me wholly, so that acceptance of each other's involvement became the basis of our happiness and enriched beyond measure our lives.

I had seen and talked with Zhou Enlai altogether ten times since that meeting in June 1956. But when Zhou was unable to see me, during the Cultural Revolution, Yingchao came alone, several times, to my hotel room, in her hands a bouquet of her home-grown roses. Yingchao loftily ignored the ban on the 'bourgeois' love of flowers. Chatting agreeably, she never betrayed the fact that her husband was desperately ill, his cancer discovered three months after Nixon's visit in February 1972. And I was not so stupid as to ask, 'How is the Premier?' I knew better, though my stomach constricted with desolation. We chatted, pleasantly, every word airy, and neither of us uttered an imprudent remark. For always there might be ears, eyes, to report every word, every gesture. One of Madame Mao's most important supporters had accused me of being an agent of the CIA, and this was a pretext to find fault with Zhou Enlai, to accuse him of being incompetent and bourgeois-minded, talking to an American spy.

In 1973 I had exacted a small revenge. Yingchao had turned up at a tea party I had given for my daughter Yungmei and my granddaughter, both coming to China from the United States in the wake of the Nixon visit.

There were around one hundred guests, many of them 'ghosts', intellectuals back from limbo, and restored to their offices by Zhou Enlai. The tea party was also, therefore, a political statement.

Now in 1977, I saw Yingchao again. She held out both hands to me. Her face was seared with grief. My heart wept and tears came welling up. For Zhou Enlai. I would never see him again. His doctor, George Wu, a friend of mine since our days together in Belgium as students, in the late 1930s, had related to me Zhou's agonizing final months. 'The pain . . . the pain was unbearable, but the beloved Premier refused to take pain killers because he wanted to remain lucid. The cancer ate up his body. We did fourteen operations on him . . . the last time, when we opened him up, it was a mess . . . every organ in his body had cancer in it.' And George Wu had cried, cried, punching the wall with his fists in frustration, as he remembered the horror of Zhou Enlai's final agony.

Now, a year after his death, I too was weeping . . . as I continue today, when I think of him, to weep inside myself. 'Oh elder sister, elder sister, such sorrow, such sorrow . . . ' But Yingchao is a woman warrior. When grief wears no mourning garb then is sorrow crystal pure. 'Do not weep. Enlai thought a great deal of you, and all you did to help,' she said. 'You have made a contribution to the Chinese people under difficult circumstances.' Then the consummate politician in her returned. 'Alas, there is a far greater, far greater loss upon us . . . it is the passing of Chairman Mao . . . that is incommensurable grief for us all.'

Silence.

I did not exclaim, move, because I could not, could not find an apt phrase. Mao's death had not touched me emotionally, though I respected his genius. Uneasy and dangerous silence spread around us, and around us were the usual cohorts of protocol officials and secretaries and newsmen. They waited. Among them too was my very dear friend, that great ambassador and ablest of Zhou Enlai's

7

trained men, Wang Bingnan. Wang had been, since 1955, ambassador in Warsaw, and had carried on secret talks with the American state department from 1955 till the arrival of Nixon in Beijing. He now grunted, sighed, Hrrumph . . . sighed again, sounds full of sorrow, to fill the void and to help me. Yingchao alertly took up the conversation, breaking the dangerous pause. 'Last year you gave an interview to the French press, after we correctly arrested the Gang of Four. In the interview you said that you hoped the true spirit of Mao Dzedong Thought would once again prevail, free of distortion . . . this showed your love for Chairman Mao, and I gave your interview to many western friends to read who were temporarily deluded by the Gang of Four . . .'

Some Frenchwomen had indeed greatly admired Limpid Stream. She appeared to them a role model for ultra-feminist assertion. When she was arrested they held a protest meeting in front of the Chinese embassy in Paris. Yingchao now continued by asking about the book purporting to be a biography of Madame Mao, soon to be published in the United States by the American Sinologist who had interviewed her at length during several weeks, being taken from splendid mansion to even more resplendent ones, and given an escort of deferential 'secretaries'. Zhou Enlai had tried to stop the publication when he had heard of the project, but in vain.

Mao Dzedong had been enraged by his wife's indiscretion, for as a Party member she was supposed to have Party permission before giving any interview. She ignored the ruling, neither had she consulted her husband. Mao had then refused to see his wife again and she had been ordered to move out of their pavilion in Middle and Southern Sea (Zhong Nanhai) to No. 17 Fisherman's Terrace, the imposing assembly of guest houses for heads of state paying visits to China. 'She is only waiting for me to die, so that she can become Party Chairman,' the embittered old man had said. Yet there had been love and passion between them, when they had met in the guerilla base of Yenan, amid the caves scooped out of yellow earth, way back in 1937 . . .

I told Yingchao of my own minor encounter with the author of the book, entitled *Comrade Jiang Qing*. 'I think that Madame Mao will play a most important role in the future of China,' the American Sinologist had said to me. I was a little surprised by her naïveté, but she was young and sincere. 'The Chinese people do not like her, so do take care,' I told her. Yingchao nodded when I told her the story. 'Enlai always cared for Chairman Mao, for his comfort, his health . . . He only took action against the book because of the Chairman.' Yet despite Zhou's devotion to Mao, a devotion which was obvious, but which was at times difficult to explain, Mao had never, all through the months that Zhou lay dying in hospital, bothered to come to see his Premier . . .

Yingchao arranged for me to see Deng Xiaoping. He was now vice-premier, politburo member, and member of the military commission. A car took me to the Great Hall of the People. Yingchao was there to introduce me. 'Here is comrade Xiaoping: Both he and I have the same family name, Deng, although we are not related.' Stolid, unmoving as a chunk of rock, a rock of particularly enduring composition, Deng Xiaoping shook my hand. He filled the space round him with massive singleness. His head was too large for his small body. His right eyelid drooped slightly. He had prominent cheekbones, like a Mongol or a Tibetan. He immediately started talking, with startling directness, eschewing the ritual of courteous preliminary phrases. 'I have no time for frills, you must take me as I am,' his demeanour implied. He was supercharged with the sense of all that had to be done, eager to pour it all out. He had no time for questions, he supplied the answers before any question could be asked. He spoke with logic and coherence, delineating the plans for economic reform, and still managing to smoke and occasionally to spit in a conveniently placed porcelain spitoon.

I wrote up a summary of the interview which was published by *Der Spiegel* in November that year.

There was a major difference between Deng Xiaoping and Zhou Enlai. Zhou revelled in digression, in comments, in discussing fine points. He relished disagreement. His eyes would shine with happiness if I said, 'I don't agree . . . ' It was a spur to him for further explanation. Not so Deng Xiaoping. He knew what he wanted to say and he said it and no one could stem the flow of his words. He brooked no interruption, and I doubt that he took contradiction well. He was already notorious for the pithy sentences he used, excoriating those he disagreed with. He possessed a formidably earthy vocabulary, which he exhibited when irked, and he irked easily. Now he referred to Madame Mao as 'the most wicked woman that ever lived'. He outlined the aftermath of the Cultural Revolution, mentioned a famine in North Sichuan which I had not heard about. There must be change, fundamental reforms. The most important thing was to raise productivity, to carry out the four modernizations already announced by Zhou Enlai in his last major public speech in January 1975. China could no longer afford the luxury to dawdle, to indulge in political struggles. There must be unity and stability. China must catch up with the West. Much precious time had been lost. 'We cannot go on slapping our own cheeks to make them swell and say: "Look how well fed I am",' said Deng Xiaoping.

Deng hinted at a Party shake-up. 'We must put our own house in order before anything can be attempted.' There was incompetence, a low level of performance and education among a good many Party cadres. I knew that millions of members had been recruited during the Cultural Revolution, and among them probably a considerable number secretly regretted the Gang of Four. He then switched to China's need for very large numbers of scientists and trained personnel. 'We must send many young people abroad to study . . . many thousands . . . ' I had heard from an official that the number contemplated would be something like 80,000 in the next ten years. I interrupted Deng, which was difficult, for Deng Xiaoping's flow of words is unquenchable.

'Sending students abroad is a good thing, but they should not be sent too young, without any experience of their own country and its needs . . . they have no mental preparation for the western world.' I saw Wang Bingnan, who as president of the Friendship Association, my host in China, was present, make a note on a small pad, but without a flicker Deng went on with his discourse as if he had not heard. Perhaps he was truly deaf, as I had been told, perhaps, as others hinted, conveniently deaf when he simply did not wish to listen. He now went on to say that many books must be written, all kinds of books. 'No one should sit on other people's brains, nor brandish threatening clubs at them when they voice unpleasant truths, and the practice of making people wear hats must be given up,' said he. Wearing hats means labelling politically someone as anti-Party, or counter-revolutionary or a 'capitalist roader', as Deng himself had been labelled. It has always been the proclivity of Party cadres to thus label real or imagined dissidents, people who held slightly different opinions. During the Cultural Revolution, putting 'hats' on suspects was almost a full-time occupation. I agreed – during the brief interval of Deng lighting up a cigarette – that indeed many books must be written, and that it was essential to allow many ways of writing. I then mentioned science-fiction, it should be encouraged in China, as it was good for children to read SF, stimulating their interest in science. Again I saw Wang Bingnan nod approval and jot something in his notebook, but Deng went on as if he had not heard.

The idea seemed to have taken hold, for shortly after that science fiction associations began, until there were, within the next four years, some forty such groups in China. However, by 1984, an ill wind blew for the SF writers. It was frowned upon as 'spiritually polluting', bringing back superstitious beliefs in ghosts or demons . . . I had some heated arguments, including letters published in the press, concerning the role of science-fiction. But it remains, as a writer was to say aptly: 'the Cinderella of Chinese literature'.

The usual photograph was taken, and I went back to my hotel room and lay flat on my bed. Here was the man who would now have to shape the future of China. He was from my province. Throughout the years, I had always refused to make any judgment on Deng Xiaoping. Now, though I was convinced that he had energy and intelligence, I felt a vague reserve. Why this reticence? Because of the sweeping assertion to send many thousands of youths abroad, unprepared, disoriented, perhaps unable to fit what they studied with what China required. This was happening in other Third World countries. And there would be an inevitable brain drain, the best and the brightest electing to stay in the West . . .

Deng Xiaoping is not Zhou Enlai, I reasoned with myself. Stop comparing everyone with Zhou. Deng 'Little Bottle' has a more daunting, infinitely more complicated task in front of him than Zhou had. In Zhou's time the Party was a wonderfully well-honed machine, whereas now it is disparate, it has lost morale and spirit . . . But the little man had courage. Enormous courage. He had a programme in mind. He had a plan. The people wanted him. They expected all things from him. Perhaps they expected too much . . .

With hindsight, I blame myself today for not having, there and then, taken up the subject of including in his reform programme the setting up of needed structures for the *participation* of young people in China in an active, positive manner. Why did I not do it? I was already aware of the confusion, what can be termed a crisis of faith, among the young. But I was only beginning to delve deep among the younger generation, I did not feel qualified to speak on the subject.

In that September there was hope, there was joy, there was a buoyancy among the intellectuals, a sensation of freedom hovered about their gatherings. 'Let a Hundred Flowers blossom once again, a hundred schools of thought contend with no fear,' wrote the newspapers. 'There is an intellectual renaissance,' said the eminent sociologist Fei

Xiaotong, the leader of the Democratic League, one of the eight non-communist parties of China, which grouped over a hundred thousand prestigious intellectuals. Many intellectuals assumed that democratization of the government and Party structure would come, almost automatically, with the economic reforms promised by Deng Xiaoping.

In the years 1977 to 1979 I had a number of encounters with large numbers of youths at universities, teachers' colleges, and middle schools. Not only in Beijing but in several provinces. Suddenly I was much in demand as a lecturer, because I could speak in Chinese, also because I was partly foreign, therefore 'different'.

'Talk about anything, anything you wish . . . China, the West . . . ' said the Party secretaries. 'They do not always believe us, and it is difficult for us to talk,' said more forthright professors back from limbo.

There had been too many drastic changes, too many reversals, in too short a time. There was bewilderment, discouragement. What did one say to the young? To the best of my recollection, I talked of the quirks, contradictions, which formed part of China's history. I mentioned confusion and doubt as natural. 'One need not be ashamed if one is confused . . . I am confused myself,' I said, and this set the tone of equality, not of submission and unwilling deference to the lecturer.

Far too often, indeed almost always, the students did not dare to contradict the lecturer, did not dare to ask questions. I was to change that in my lectures. 'We have come together to discuss as equals . . . I am learning more from you than you will learn from me.' There were nervous titters, but it worked. At first it was very difficult to get the audience to ask questions. My first hurdle was the professors, the Party secretary in charge. When I told them, 'I want the students to ask questions after my lecture,' I was told that this was not the custom. No questions. The Party secretary explained at length that lectures should last two hours, and after that the

13

lecturer should take a well-earned rest. I shook my head. 'Excuse me, but I shall lecture for forty-five to fifty minutes at most, then I expect questions for about forty minutes. I shall answer the questions.'

Consternation. The Party secretary said this was a problem which should be studied. 'There is nothing to study, it is the way lectures are conducted in the West. It promotes dialogue, understanding. This is how I have lectured in other countries.' The Party secretary kept a brave smile on. The professors smiled. After all, things were changing . . . perhaps it was possible to admit *some* questions. 'The best way is that the students hand in written questions to us . . . we shall sort them out and . . . ' 'Excuse me, but I will not answer any written questions. I want the young to stand up and ask their own questions. Even if the questions are not appropriate, they should be welcome . . . how else will you know what doubts, what problems, agitate the minds of the young?'

I won. Not only the first time, but every time, and today no one objects when, after the lecture, the students stand up and query some point or other, or bring in new themes. The sky has not fallen, the earth has not cracked, and the Party has survived (even when unpleasant questions are asked), I used to say, in conclusion, poking a little fun at the proceedings.

In those early years the questions were almost identical. No one, not one of the students, referred to the Gang of Four, or to Mao, directly. They would stand up and say: 'There is confusion in our minds . . . we have many doubts in our hearts . . . we do not quite know what to believe or not to believe . . . in the past few years, we have many times been told to believe this or that, and then, a few months, a few years later, to believe just the opposite . . . how is it that something is found good and correct today and wrong tomorrow?'

What they were asking for, of course, was an explanation of the Cultural Revolution, and this was still a taboo subject in the Party, except for a vague assertion that Mao's grandiose ideas had been distorted, twisted, by ambitious 'counter-revolutionary plotters'. Even among small groups picked from the Communist Youth corps the same words recurred. And no amount of verbal placebos would fill the void within these young souls . . . it must be filled by something else.

When I told them that confusion and hesitancy were normal and understandable, in view of the mistakes that had been made, and that No Man, No Party, was Infallible, there was an almost audible stir. The most important thing now was to try to understand what had happened, and 'to have the right to voice one's own opinion'.

A little later, it was possible for me to bolster my appeal to 'using one's own brain' by quoting Deng Xiaoping: 'Emancipate the Mind, Explore New Ideas, Seek Truth from Facts.' That is what Little Bottle was saying.

However, I had to warn, there must be no anarchy. Anarchy, overthrowing everything, had been practised by the Red Guards during the Cultural Revolution. It solved no problems, but only brought new ones. 'I hope that young people will be able to participate in the discussion and rethinking of many problems.'

This was to be my leitmotiv for many years. I talked with the professors, with the Party cadres in charge. 'There is a vacuum of trust, of belief . . . the young must not only be reassured, but they want some good, common sense answers. Mutual trust must be re-established. They no longer trust the older people . . .'

The professors sighed. Some of them told me, shaking their heads: 'They are not as we were when we were young'.

Of course they were not. How could they have the same impulses, the emotions and the ardour which had carried the Revolution forward? The patriotism which had led many non-communist intellectuals to sacrifice themselves for the country, to accept suffering and denial of their own personalities . . . how could one ask this to exist among the successors?

'There must be new ways of talking with young people . . . a new vocabulary . . . the doctrinal phrases used appear to them void of any reality . . . they are almost grotesque in the new context.' I find this in a notebook I kept at the time.

And the hope, the renewed confidence among those in my generation – which is reckoned to be the Second Generation – was also puzzling, for it was among us that the greatest number of victims of the last thirty years were to be found. But also, the greatest number of achievers.

Marshal Ye Jianying, Long Marcher, great friend of the late Zhou Enlai, invited me to tea.

Ye Jianying came from a well-to-do Hakka family. When Zhou Enlai returned to China from France in 1924, he and Ye had created the first army corps of the future communist army. They had been together in many battles, and of course during the Long March. Ye had survived the Cultural Revolution, despite his open disagreement with it. And everyone in China knew that he was the man who had engineered the swift and bloodless arrest of the Gang of Four in October 1976. 'Marshal Ye never gives interviews, but he would like to meet you, he says you are not a foreigner,' Wang Bingnan told me as he took me to see the prestigious Ye. Not a foreigner . . . sometimes a foreigner . . . not quite a foreigner . . . maybe a foreigner . . . a perpetual humming-bird hover for me . . . I have never felt torn by inner conflict, by doubt as to who I was or where I belonged. The difficulties, the disapproval, the rejections, had come from outside of myself, from others . . . but I had never let them submerge my own assurance that it was an asset, not an inferiority, to be multi-cultural, to be the world of the future. I had discovered way back in 1938 that my Chinese side came first, but the foreigner in me was a blessing, a boon, for it enabled me to perceive the limitations of Chinese tradition. And I guessed that Ye Jianying probably had many Overseas Chinese among his relatives, so that he knew what it was like to have to integrate several modes of thought and behaviour into oneself. During the Cultural Revolution, being a Eurasian and having 'overseas' connections, I was a walking time bomb to my relatives and friends. Their knowing me could be used against them. Now another dispensation was upon the land, and to be a foreigner even partly, or an Overseas Chinese, was a good thing . . . almost a superiority.

'Welcome, welcome, *tungxiang*.' The resonant, easy baritone of Marshal Ye greeted me as I walked into the room. *Tungxiang* means member of the same village, county, province. 'Your family is Hakka, and so am I . . . your family originally came from Meixian, and so do I. You wrote about the Hakka people in a book of yours. I read it. Tell me, do you speak Hakka?' 'Alas no, Marshal, only standard Chinese, and also Sichuan dialect.' Ye nodded. 'Many of the people in Sichuan were Hakka some centuries ago . . . we are fighters, we the Hakka. We fear not death nor hard work. Your father worked for China, he built railways, and you too have made contribution to the ancestral land.' 'The Marshal overpraises me . . . it is heroes like yourself, like late regretted Premier Zhou, and so many others who gave their lives for China who have inspired my generation . . . I have done so little, far too little . . . ' Having thus established the appropriate tone and ambiance, we settled to relaxed, cheerful talk, and spent a delightful hour. Ye Jianying was now old, over seventy, but had retained the handsomeness of his youth. He remained erect, unshrunk, and sprightly. I remembered how, in the photographs of the 1930s and 40s, he managed to convey elegance and dash, even when clad in padded grey guerilla pants and uncouth jacket. He had loved to dance, as did Zhou Enlai, and they, together with another dashing and debonair companion of Zhou, Ho Lung the Dragon, were known to love waltzing. Ye Jianying talked of the Cultural Revolution. 'My secretary (he pointed to the young man seated near us) was harshly treated because he refused to fabricate crimes I was supposed to have committed,' chuckled Ye. The secretary blushed. 'It is Marshal Ye who restored hope to our land,' said he. 'Indeed, I know a little of this, sir,' I said. Ye laughed, well pleased. He had evolved the plan to arrest the Gang of Four by getting the man who ran the élite pretorian unit, the 8341 regiment in charge of the safety of the leaders, to co-operate. On 7 October this man had sent a message to the three male colleagues of Limpid Stream, that their presence was required at a meeting in the Great Hall of the People. The three trusted him, and unsuspectingly turned up, to be arrested by the 8341. Mao's wife was arrested in her own house.

The Marshal talked joyously, remembering how he had brawled with Limpid Stream's supporters way back in 1967, and in anger slapped his hand so hard upon the table that he had broken a bone. But he said not a word against Mao Dzedong. 'We must now unite, all of us unite . . . there is so much to do . . . ' His voice lowered. 'We have many problems. Our coffers are empty. Now the Albanians are angry with us . . . did you know that? And also the Vietnamese . . . because our coffers are empty, and we can no longer help them . . . we have given more than 20 billion US dollars to Vietnam.'

On 1 October, anniversary of the People's Republic, Ye asked for me and I was led into the reserved enclosure to shake hands with Hua Guofeng, the new chairman. Hua was very quiet. Perhaps no great genius, but likeable. However, the young did not like him. Because he had been minister of security in that April of 1976, and it was he who had arrested many of the demonstrators mourning for Zhou Enlai in Tiananmen Square. Would Hua Guofeng and Deng Xiaoping be able to work together?

More lecturing. The auditorium in West China Union University in Chengdu is crammed. Eight hundred, perhaps a thousand young faces, expectant. And what can I say to them? 'You must talk of education in the West, the young in

the West, that is what they want to know about . . . ' I speak
of the West, of the slow, painful march to democracy in the
West, of the erratic course of history, of the constant need for
watchfulness, for reappraisal. I speak of colonization, and the
harm it has done to many countries, but now this is behind
us, and we must learn to gain from bitter experience. I avoid
direct criticism of the Cultural Revolution – allusions are clear
enough. 'No man is an all knowing God. The greatest of
men have also committed crimes . . . in the past few years,
many people have suffered injustice, persecution . . . ' It is
early 1978, and though there is expectancy, and hope, policies for reform are still being elaborated. 'Tell us about life
. . . what is the meaning of life?' says a student. Life . . . I
expatiate a little . . . life, its gifts, its responsibilities. I do
not tell them about my own life, but speak of my wanting,
very early on, to be a doctor, having no rest until I became
one . . . accomplishing something helpful for others. 'There
are, however, always new beginnings . . . ' Afterwards, the
Party secretary is not too happy about the term 'new beginnings' and 'striving for oneself' and 'always trying to think
for oneself'. But things are in such a flux, that there is no
challenge. I am myself only an explorer, delineating that
strange and unknown land, the minds, the emotions, of
this next generation. The inheritors of whatever has been
done for good or ill until now.

A girl stands up. 'I have so many doubts that I even
doubt that I exist. Tell me, how can I be sure that I am?'
Laughter, subdued, but she is dead serious. From another
girl who stops me as I go away, 'I studied at home, my
father tutored me, now I want to learn foreign languages,
to see the world . . . but first I want a new philosophy to
live by.'

New fashions among the young burst into view. Flared
nautical-looking trousers for the boys, wearing of dark sun-
glasses, the label still stuck in the corner of the lens to prove
that they are imported from Hongkong.

Four or five of these smartly dressed youths come to me.

'You say: Think for yourself. But here we are *told* what to think.'

And later, from another group: 'We are told to seek truth from facts . . . but first we must know the facts . . . sometimes we do not know the facts . . . '

What can I do?

There is another issue, almost unspoken, until I drag it out. 'You say: no anarchy. But here some of the people I know feel betrayed. For the old ones have again taken power, and once again they will reign with the authority of the father.' The young man who talks to me thus is tall, quiet. I shake his hand, silently. I cannot say anything.

When the economic reforms begin inevitably new values will be created. With the opening to the West there will be new orientations. This will deepen the crisis of faith. My generation is calling it The Generation Gap. I hear it everywhere. From the intellectuals, my friends, who are baffled by their children, and their grandchildren. But this phrase is a solace; plaster to hide the proliferating ulcer, it accepts the incomprehension, the confusion, the crisis of belief, as if nothing need be done. Generation Gap. These young people I talk with are still influenced by the Cultural Revolution. In 1966, only twelve years ago, their elder brothers and sisters were told the world was theirs to transform, to reshape. They were given heady freedom; the freedom to accuse, to condemn their elders. They dragged their elders through the streets, they insulted them in wall posters. But now the generation they mistreated and accused is back, is back to man the state. Back to wield power. Power *over* the young.

In November 1977, Democracy Wall was born.

Two

DEMOCRACY WALL extends its solid brick, plastered with wall posters, 200 metres along the main avenue of Beijing's western district. Pamphlets, declamations, demands, complaints, poems, make it a vivid commentary on China today. Many of the writers are ex-Red Guards, now in their thirties, and young by Chinese standards. They are freed from the garotting silence imposed on them after the appalling brutality they exhibited, which led to their being sent down to the countryside villages. Now they have returned, returned to the cities, all 12 million of them, but they have not forgotten the slogans of the Cultural Revolution. GREAT DEMOCRACY. FREEDOM TO COMPLAIN; TO CRITICIZE; TO TRAVEL; TO AFFIX WALL POSTERS.

Democracy Wall is a great attraction. At all hours people stand in front of it, reading. Especially after work, at night. Some copy the wall posters. Others with flashlights, read aloud the contents they like best to the crowd. Wall posters are an old tradition in China. In my province of Sichuan, way back in imperial days, intellectuals wrote posters steeped in their blood. A cut on the small finger of the left hand supplied the needed fluid.

Some of my friends now call the young 'the lost generation'.

'Why the lost?'

'Because they have had no chance to study properly,' say my friends, scholars, now so happily back with their books. 'These young are full of grievances. But we must also remember what they did to us.'

'Twelve million of them,' says one famous writer. 'Twelve million Red Guards . . . they were sent to the countryside, but they are now streaming back into the cities . . . and again they write wall posters.'

'There are not only twelve million . . . there are the others, perhaps fifty million, from the age of twelve onwards, now in their early twenties, who have been influenced by a new sense of power. *Youth Power.*'

My friends are apprehensive, and who can blame them? I do not think they are entirely right. True, many of this Third Generation missed a traditional, academic education, but they travelled up and down the land, they went to remote provinces, to Tibet and Sinkiang and Inner Mongolia, and they are politicized . . . even if they don't know it themselves.

'They not only brutalized us, they fought each other. Some of them murdered, grouped into gangs . . . assaulted arsenals, stole machine-guns and rifles from army factories . . . battled each other . . . it took the army two, three years to suppress these youth gangs.'

'Now we must make sure that none of those who murdered, destroyed monuments, raped, vandalized, ever get into official positions,' said a poet, one of the secretaries of the Writers Association. He contemplates Democracy Wall with an amused eye. 'Wall posters . . . we are pretty tired of wall posters . . . so many were written against us.'

'But it is different now,' I say, weakly. Weakly, because he may be right.

'Is it really different?' says this poet, who has spent eight years in jail and whose wife killed herself. 'Is it really?'

I did not suffer what so many thousands, tens of thousands, of my contemporaries, Chinese intellectuals, went through during that decade of the Cultural Revolution. So how can I make assumptions, when I know how treacherous the slogans of democracy have been, and can become again, in China. In China, where the word democracy was only invented so recently?

I cannot ask them to forgive, to forget. The young tore up their books or burnt them, trampled into their houses, held kangaroo courts, ill-treated and tortured them . . . and yet, and yet, they have come through, my generation, sustained by that extraordinary strength which comes from knowing that, in history, it has often been so, and yet, always, in the end, they have been the keepers of China's culture, the bearers of her civilization. Oh surpassing all love is this total absorption, and it has made China what she is.

But the young, the young, are a different equation. Never in history has there been a generation with this formidable education in the realities of their multilayered country, but it was an education unbolstered by comparison with the past, unfeatured by rigorous analysis. And these millions of youths had never been taught history, for history was such a wayward affair, the Party altering history books, contradicting itself every five or ten years, that history had quietly become an unknown subject in many schools.

Now they are politicized, but in a totally different way from their progenitors. They resent catechismal Party classes in which fumous abstractions quite irrelevant to their own experience are being tenaciously spouted. Yes they are confused, but there is a fundamental tenacious base of hunger for truth in them, and this should be prized. They can only express it with one word, democracy. But democracy is also a nebulous term: translated in Chinese The People Are Master, it purports total release from any constraints.

The Cultural Revolution was for them a revelation of how China was still embedded in medieval arbitrariness. They realized then, not only that Party members disguised their fundamental Confucianism under Marxist phraseology, but that they themselves were infected with Confucianism.

When Democracy Wall began in 1977, the communist Party was at its lowest ebb. Not only had it lost credibility, but it was lacerated by inner conflict. Half of its near 38

23

million members had joined the Party between 1966 and 1973, during the first years of the Cultural Revolution. In 1973 another third had been admitted, when the Gang of Four strove desperately to capture power. Only one sixth of the Party members were seasoned veterans of the Revolution, truly faithful to their ideals, reliable and dedicated. These were the ones that Deng Xiaoping had on his side.

Deng had to avoid once again the launching of a 'class struggle', both within the Party and without. He had to fight for economic reforms and opening to the West, but certainly no political reforms could be envisaged until he was strong enough, pinioned by economic structural change. Otherwise there would be chaos. And perhaps what has happened in other parts of the world, in the USSR and some countries of Eastern Europe, vindicates Deng Xiaoping's manner of proceeding. 'First feed the people . . . for the people to eat enough is Heaven itself' wrote a Chinese poet. Without assured basic necessities, freedom in China becomes almost criminal, driving millions to hunger, to lawlessness. It becomes merely an élitist, intellectual exercise for the few ensconced in the cities. 'How can starving people discuss freedom when they are looking for food everywhere? All concepts of liberty must be subordinated to the imperative of first producing a modicum of well-being for the people.' Thus the poet-secretary of the Writers Association, as we discussed the Wall. I was not entirely convinced. 'Surely one can have both . . . one should have both.' 'Yes, but let us first assure abundance for the people,' he replied.

'Our young people today are probably the most politically inquisitive in China,' says Junjian. Junjian is back, back from partial oblivion, back in his old and beautiful house. He is as staunchly patriotic as ever. 'We are the knowledge bearers. It is upon us that the tyranny of emperors has always fallen, but we must forever forget ourselves, and work to assure the well-being of the people,' says he. Xia Yen, now eighty, was a young revolutionary in May 1919, when China's students rose against the military regime of those years, against colonialism which was rampant in China. He is now ardently for democratization. 'Let the people speak, we should not be afraid of words.'

And thus I also become imbued with a sense of responsibility. For I too, in a way, am a Chinese intellectual, and I am concerned.

Junjian, his wife Yanyun, a Manchu noblewoman, and I, sit under the withered peach tree in the garden of his house. In bygone years we sat many evenings under that peach tree blessed by the watchful maternal moon in the autumn sky, and talked, and talked. It is now dying. Junjian will plant another one, and in time we shall eat its peaches. Junjian avoids formulating any drastic opinion about Democracy Wall. Well has he experienced the danger of catchy libertarian phrases, which can turn into another tyranny. 'I would like to know how these young people, now frenzied for democracy, truly behaved during the Cultural Revolution,' he says.

I see many returnees, such as Junjian. Painters, writers, poets, essayists, journalists. They are ebullient. 'Now we can write freely . . . now we can paint . . . ' Some of them have a reaction against the wall posters of Democracy Wall. 'These young people . . . they are against bureaucracy and corruption, and that is right. But who knows when all this righteousness turns into malice, libel, fabrication, as happened during the Cultural Revolution?' An old writer tells me why he is against Democracy Wall. 'These young people . . . they are denouncing bureaucracy and corruption . . . ha, all they want is power for themselves. These wall posters calling for democracy will later turn into personal attacks, malice, libel, fabrication.' The old writer has greatly suffered, hence his resentment. A wall poster during the Cultural Revolution accused him of having an affair with a woman friend of his wife, simply because they happened to meet outside a cinema hall, and to greet each other. 'We did not even sit together in the cinema, but a few days later

25

the walls of my institute were plastered with wall posters against me, accusing me of immorality, of having slept with this woman, even giving the name of the hotel where I was supposed to have met her . . . ' The woman, unable to clear herself of the crime of adultery, committed suicide to prove her honourableness.

Confucius, Confucius . . . In medieval–modern–socialist China, so much of Confucius remains. Political deviation is so frequently coupled with sexual depravity, which means having an affair. A 'counter-revolutionary' is also often accused of rape, or of being a lascivious womanizer. No proof is given. It is Confucius, that terrible old man, still beloved by some Sinologists in France. He lived 2,500 years ago, 500 years before Christ, but in today's China he is much alive, in our minds, in our social behaviour, and also in the Party.

Zheng, the novelist, has just completed a novel about love. Love among the Red Guards. He says that in 1968, 1969, the Red Guards held communal love sessions. He is, of course, both titillated and shocked as he reads out extracts of his book. 'The Red Guards were the sons and daughters of high cadres. They felt that it was true communism . . . did not Lenin say that sex should be like drinking a glass of water? Free love,' says Zheng. 'The Red Guards appeared very puritan, but they indulged in free love sessions . . .' He licks his lips, continues. 'Then when they were sent to the villages the girl Red Guards were often raped . . .'

Bespectacled, stammering Li, once a Red Guard, wants to be a writer. 'I never hit or injured anyone,' he tells me. 'When the brutality started, I said I was ill, and stayed at home.' He tells me that the group to which he belonged distinguished itself by coming out with a poster against the man that Mao wanted to destroy through the Cultural Revolution, Liu Shaoqi. Liu was President of the People's Republic, vice-chairman of the Party, a powerful man, but Mao succeeded in bringing him down. The Red Guards launched campaigns of wall posters, vilifying Liu,

26

and the group to which Li belonged found a new angle to attack him. 'We accused him of sexual depravity. He was seen one afternoon in his office, holding his wife in his lap.'

'But it was his wife,' I said. 'And that is not a crime . . . '

Li pursed his lips. 'But it indicated that he was lascivious. The time, the place, were inappropriate. It was in the afternoon. These . . . er . . . things should only take place at night . . . it showed that Liu could not master his baser instincts . . . so we put up posters accusing him of gross turpitude.' I think young Li will become a proper official. The prurient mind still inhabits him. But when Junjian hears the tale, he laughs.

'There is a big change now. The young have changed . . . few are like Li . . . they no longer believe in chastity, and boys and girls now do live together before getting married. They want to understand what love means, so now there is . . . exploration . . . ' Junjian is right, for love is back, no longer taboo, it is finding a place in published books, and in poetry.

Many intellectuals cannot forget that during the Cultural Revolution, accusations of sexual deviation, of illicit affairs, were extremely frequent, and that those who indulged most in such accusations were fellow-intellectuals. 'Some people thought that they would save themselves by accusing others,' says Junjian. Writer Su, a charming and popular person, happily married, was denounced as a homosexual because, way back in the late 1930s, he had been in England as a student, and had admired and later translated the poems of Auden. That appeared to be 'evidence' enough, and Su was hauled before a court. Guilt by accusation was common then, as the wall posters and their effectiveness proved. But Su was so well liked that the denunciation did not stick. 'Can you believe that a scholar of repute would do this to another scholar?' Su asked, indignantly. 'It was fear,' explains Junjian. 'Many were afraid.' Now that the intellectuals are back, more than ever self-control, a sense of humour, and a capacity for forgiveness are required. For in their offices,

27

at their jobs, they work next to the very people who accused them, but who cannot be fired. 'In my office is the man who carried my manuscripts into the courtyard and burnt them in front of me,' says Hung, an excellent essayist and translator, a devotee of André Gide. 'What do you say to him? What do you do? Nothing. We simply do not exist for each other. I pretend the space he occupies is empty.'

Junjian tells me an amusing tale. 'I was invited to lecture at a certain university in England. I did not know that X had also been invited. Only when I met my hosts did they tell me, "We have tonight at the high table Mr X. He arrived two days ago, and he has been telling us of the ill-treatment he endured during the Cultural Revolution."' Junjian claps his hands upon his thighs and throws his head back, and laughs, laughs. 'I could not tell the eminent professors that X had been leading that band of Red Guards who ransacked my house. He was very clever at finding hidden manuscripts, letters, buried in the garden, or under the floor bricks.' It was X who had sealed the glass doors of Junjian's bookcases – 'for six years I could only stare at my books through the glass . . .' 'Did your hosts notice anything?' Junjian laughs again. 'Perhaps they realized that we did not speak very much to each other . . . but of course, we could not let them know . . . they would have lost face.'

Abundant Courage is a short likeable man of thirty, who often lingers by Democracy Wall. He tells me that he enrolled in the Red Guards at sixteen, but protested when the leader of his group began to torture an old Party man, making him carry 40 pounds of coal upon his head. 'This boy kept on hitting the man with his thick leather belt . . . his father was a high Party cadre. I noticed that some of the high officials' sons were particularly violent, perhaps they wanted to prove themselves.' Abundant Courage was jailed because he protested. He spent three years in labour camp, then another five planting rice when he was sent down to the countryside. But he took his books with him, and he became the village scribe, ran the school, and kept the accounts. 'When I left the peasants sent me gifts, and beat drums, and walked with me many miles . . . "You will not forget us, now that you go back to the city," they said to me.' Abundant Courage plans to marry, to learn English. He does not write wall posters but he reads them, and sometimes copies down a sentence. I shall meet him again ten years later, a rising star in the diplomatic service, who speaks good English, also German. 'I try to learn something new every day . . . ' he says.

Shining Agate is nearing fifty, but looks girlish, frail. 'But I am very strong, I can lift 40 *jin* of rice,' says she. That is 20 kilos. Denounced as a rightist when she was twenty, at the university, she spent twenty years in the countryside, and is now a well known writer of children's fiction. 'I learnt to write by listening to the peasants telling their stories to each other.'

She, and others like her, such as Dr Xiu, an epidemiologist whom I meet going to Geneva to attend a seminar on infective hepatitis, insist that their years in the villages were not lost years, but rewarding. 'We are not a lost generation, as some people call us. It is not true that one cannot make up for lost time. I think these were the best years of my life.'

Autumn Chrysanthemum is a well-known violinist. She greets me effusively. She is plump and myopic. I used to bring music sheets in secret to her. During the Cultural Revolution, afraid someone would hear her practising, her grandmother put blankets against the door and window of her room. 'That made me realize how wonderful, how important music was. That is when I learnt to pour my heart in every note . . . '

Cloud In The Wilderness, seven years in the countryside, looks like a young and pretty child, though she is near forty. She is determined to study library computerization, to rationalize the major libraries in China. I am able to help her to study in America, and she says: 'You are my dearest mother now.'

There are others, many others, so many, who waste

no pity on themselves, know the value of time, and want nothing but that China should be a better China for their children. They read the posters on Democracy Wall, the pamphlets hand distributed by the thousand. They say, 'Of course we want more democracy.' But they are wary of any massive political upheaval. Too often, starry-eyed, they have believed the slogans . . . now they want to work, to work. And they believe, they believe, in Deng Xiaoping.

One million two hundred thousand educated youths were sent, as paramedical personnel (called 'barefoot doctors') to the countryside during the Cultural Revolution. However one can loathe the Cultural Revolution, this was the first time that a public health service, rudimentary, but effective, covered China's 80 per cent of rural inhabitants. A network of accessibility to vaccination, first aid care, and family planning was created. Peasant families were trained by these barefoot doctors in basic hygiene. Epidemics were promptly reported. Immunization of the children was effectively attended to.

But now the barefoot doctors have left the villages, and swarm back to the cities. The village clinics are abandoned. The next decade will see a deterioration of public health care, renewed efforts from an efficient, but city-based ministry of health service, to cope with rural health demands. And because of the dearth of doctors, there will also be a return of sorcerers, wizards, charlatans, claiming curative powers . . .

Education also suffers when many primary school teachers drift out of the rural schools into the cities. The Chinese government will have to raise the salaries of rural school teachers to attract them back, but more than 50,000 primary schools will be reported in a bad state of disrepair. A news item that in one school the roof fell upon the children, and killed a few, arouses much comment . . . but it will continue to be difficult to find money for rural schools, until, almost ten years later, prosperous villages begin to fund their own schools.

That great ebb tide of the young, ebbing back into the

cities, twelve million, perhaps more, has to be cared for. They have to be found jobs. For many of them, Democracy Wall is a symbol. A symbol of defiance. Other democracy walls proliferate in other cities. The wall posters reflect the confusion, the doubt. Smashed idolatry, and anger . . . There is a problem of credibility. It is a big problem for whoever governs China. 'It is a problem for all of us,' say my friends. How will this situation be handled?

Gluepot in one hand, brush in the other, earnest-faced young men stick their latest effusions on Democracy Wall. I suddenly remember the wall poster I saw in the summer of 1974, all of four years ago.

A member of the local Friendship Association was with me. We strolled through the streets of Guangzhou, the southern city once known as Canton. He took me to a quiet and narrow lane tunnelling between grey walls, and there, along one of the walls, the wall poster spread, page after page. My guide looked away, he seemed rapt in contemplation of his own shoes. Obviously, I was meant to read that wall poster.

It was well written, reasoned condemnation of the special privileges enjoyed by Party members, the corruption among them. It argued for democracy and the rule of law. Socialism needed true democracy, needed mass representation. It was signed LI YI ZHE. I learnt that this was the composite name of three men. All three were to be arrested soon after. Now, in 1978, they were released, and on Democracy Wall many of the wall posters follow much the same line of argument as that of Li Yi Zhe.

'Deng Xiaoping approves of Democracy Wall,' said an earnest young man to me. He was putting up his own wall poster. His friend bounced up and down with excitement. 'Comrade Xiaoping was in France when he was young, and he spent his nights mimeographing a revolutionary paper . . . we are following his example . . . '

In November 1978 Deng Xiaoping had said in an open interview granted to an American and a Canadian, both journalists, 'I see nothing wrong with the wall posters . . . it is good to let the masses express themselves.'

A number of new, unofficial magazines appear. *Enlightenment, Exploration, April 5 Forum, Democracy and Law* . . . A crop of young poets burst into the limelight. Totally absent from their verses is the rhetoric of political commitment. In that autumn Beauty is back, and Love, freed from the Ice Age, burns bright on many pages.

1978 also sees the advent of a new literature, called 'literature of the wounded'. The recital of the sufferings and humiliations endured by so many Party and non-Party intellectuals during the Cultural Revolution. Harrowing stories, which, after a while, stale because of a certain sameness. There is no attempt to correlate the human agony to a wider social and historical background. 'But how can they relate to a historical framework?' I ask myself. For historical events are still not to be commented upon. 'We have endured history, we have the sensation that we have not made it,' explains Junjian.

One book I think extraordinarily good is by a woman, Dai Houying. She lives in Shanghai. It will be translated in English later, titled *Stones in the Wall*. But when I mention my delight in this book there is a strange reticence among some of my writer friends.

Despite a certain monotony, the new literature breaks all taboos. The characters are no longer imposingly upright Party members crushing depraved, devious (and of course sexually lascivious) counter-revolutionaries. And the new poetry makes waves. Some of the young writers discovered themselves when they penned defiant poems, praising Zhou Enlai, defying the Gang of Four, and read them in Tiananmen Square, in memory of the dead Premier, way back in April 1976.

Not all my colleagues are excited by the 'literature of the wounded'. Some of the older writers say this unpadlocked outpouring of emotion is distasteful, and lacks the dignified restraint of a true scholarly mind. Some call the minute description of one's personal woes 'narcissism' and 'obsessive navel cult'. But it had to be written, it had to come out, catharsis, a needed breakdown of reticence.

Junjian paces his old house, savouring proprietorship, planning to repair the leaking roof, repaint the walls, buy new bookcases for the many new books he has acquired. He plans to go to France, to England, to Scandinavian countries. He has received a medal from Denmark for his translation of Hans Andersen. Now he wants the Chinese Writers Association to join International PEN. 'It's a very good idea,' I say. I think there will be problems, but I do not wish to dampen his enthusiasm, and anyway Chinese writers must meet writers from the West, must have many encounters on PEN platforms. Feng Yidai, another very good friend of mine, starts a monthly magazine, *To Read*, which introduces modern American and European literature. It is an excellent magazine, and it has survived the vicissitudes which were to plague the cultural world of China in the next ten years.

Friends. So many, and when the soothing scent of tea beguiles the air around us, we rearrange our perpetually tremulous world, always on the brink of the unexpected, with words which caress it soothingly, stroke it back into order. One of the topics of our unrestrained talk is love. For love is contagious, it has spread, seized the middle aged, the staid men and women whose smooth faces so ably conceal their emotions. We laugh, a little bashfully, and they tell me that it has become fashionable to speak of The Third One.

'The third one'. This means the out of wedlock lover. The lover begins to creep into the new literature. Boldly, some women writers challenge ancient morality, sending a shock of pleasant indignation among male writers. Articles, books, are written, in every province, for and against romance, romantic love . . . and the third one.

Liu Xinwu, charming and able, who has written a breakthrough novel, *The Form Master*, has also written a beautiful story of love, *Juyi*. I became a fan of his because of *Juyi*.

33

I think it is his finest work. Our friendship will grow, to outlast the years. 'I am going to the countryside . . . what shall I bring you?' Liu Xinwu asks me one day. 'Bring me a small cloth tiger.' Village women make toy tigers out of bits of cotton, they stitch tiger heads on the bonnets of their babies, and on their shoes. In my childhood I too wore a tiger bonnet . . . and I collect small tigers, for they are beautiful.

I meet Gu Hua from Hunan province, large round eyes, a round face, an infectious laugh. He has a book: *A Small Town Called Hibiscus*. A very wonderful book. It will be made into a film, but the ending is deemed controversial . . . I find in my notes of that time a jotting: 'Talk to the culture minister about Hibiscus? It *must* be shown.' Gu Hua comes to Switzerland for a few days, and enjoys learning how to make a salad. He dials long-distance on my telephone and is happy because he masters the code, though he knows no English.

Life is good in the autumn of 1978, not least because the scientists, writers, and artists whose salaries were unjustly reduced are receiving the full amount due to them for the last ten years. 'I feel as wealthy as a Hongkong millionaire,' says Wenjing, who writes charming short stories. He was going bald, but now can afford an expensive lotion, guaranteed to make hair spring back upon any head. He tells me that there are four grades of writers. 'Like hotels. Four star, three star . . . ' A top writer gets many perks, a fine house, a car, a servant and trips abroad. 'What does one do to become a top writer?' I ask. The answer is tortuous and complex. Much depends, it seems, on seniority, but also on becoming an official in the Writers' Association. I remain baffled.

The time for summing up is upon us. We live with the manifold contradictions of the land, the culture. Such an old land, such an old culture, replete with recorded history incessantly recalled. The knowledge-bearers, the intellectuals, juggle with the millennia, jump easily from a poem of the third century BC to a quotation of the recent past. And it is this accumulation, this hoard embedded in the soul, which has made so many endure, which has sustained them. 'I never lost hope, for I thought of history . . . through agony and distress, disillusion and betrayal, through injustice and cruelty, I remained cheerful, knowing it was all a part of something larger than myself.' So says eighty-year-old Xia Yen, one of China's most respected writers. 'We are getting old, we are getting old,' continues youthful Xia Yen. 'We need to manufacture for ourselves some protective perimeter, for even in the gauzy air of spring we now breathe in this joyous reacquaintance among ourselves, in the reassuring prospect of reform, reform, some of us hear quiet thunder.'

'We have not yet fully digested or understood all that has happened,' says Yidai, 'for events have moved faster than our minds, and with crushing brutality. We have been carried like helpless flotsam by the flood . . . but perhaps the young will have mastery over events, more than we have had.'

'History is always too neat, because it is written by those who follow, time-removed from the immediate urgency of the event,' says Junjian. 'Well then, your grandson will explain you to yourself,' laughs Wenjing. Wenjing tells me, 'I truly *believed* at one time that I had indeed committed many crimes . . . I do not know how I utterly convinced myself of my own guilt . . . ' 'The Cultural Revolution . . . ' says someone . . . 'There may be another cultural revolution if all these young people coming back by the million have their way,' says another writer grumpily. 'Look at the wall posters on Democracy Wall. In China, chaos, rebellion, trouble, has always started with the pen . . . ' I do not agree. 'It is good that there should be some airing, for words in the belly are more dangerous than words that come out of the mouth.' But I am in a minority, though they nod politely. Many have suffered through speaking a little too freely . . . One can still go on *thinking*, even if one does not speak.

I propose an explanation of the Cultural Revolution which has inhabited my mind for a while. I say that a western psychoanalyst would probably consider the behaviour of the young Red Guards as the eruption of a long repressed Oedipus complex. 'The father authority is very strong, not only in families, even more so in the government and the Party,' I say. 'The whole system is in fact patriarchal . . . ' And so perhaps the need to kill the father, to make brutality a release, not only from political pressure but from the inhibitory character of the culture.

This shocks everyone. My fellow writers, despite the seamless courtesy which is second nature to them, are letting unease seep upon their faces. They do not look at each other, they do not look at me. My hostess repeatedly offers me tea and rushes to heap more nuts and dried fruit in front of me. But soon reassurance comes. Doubtless it is that western streak in me which has made me utter such blasphemy. Wenjing says: 'It is quite unthinkable for a Chinese son to want to kill his father . . . it is not in our tradition.'

But the young generation is changing, has changed. I hear them mutter 'patriarchal government'. One writer, a young girl, travels throughout China on her bicycle, interviewing ordinary housewives, waiters, salesgirls, bus drivers, teachers. Her mind roams as freely as her body as she pedals in the streets. She has the courage to confront her peers. 'Why did we act with such brutality? Why did we do what we did?' And soon, within the next two years, Mao and Marx will no longer be quoted, but Freud, and Sartre, and Nietsche . . . and it becomes very fashionable to talk of complexes, including the Oedipus complex.

A book will become a tremendous success with the young. It has been written in Taiwan, and it is called *The Ugly Chinese*. It declares that the Chinese are riddled with complexes of superiority and inferiority . . .

In 1989 I am in Canada, confronting three hundred Chinese students. Some of them are hostile. Their idea of democracy is to shout, to roar, not to let the lecturer speak. However, after two and a half hours, only ten continue to utter hoarse threats. One of the grey-haired Chinese professors who sits at the lecturer's table with me later tells me, 'When I tried to reason with them they shouted, "Go and die. All you people with white hairs should be put to death." '

The unthinkable has happened. Destruction of filial piety, of respect for old age. I tell the story to the ambassador of Sri Lanka whom I meet in Geneva, and he smiles. 'We also have such young people in my country. There is a group which proclaims that anyone over forty should be killed, so that the world can be made anew by the young.'

By the autumn of 1978 Democracy Wall is a year old. The posters have become more virulent. Daring denunciations capture the mood of the restless crowds which mill about at night. Not only are there millions of displaced youths, but also millions of other persons, ordinary people, who have come into Beijing to voice their grievances to the government. They sit in small crowds on the steps of official buildings, of the white-tiled communist Party headquarters. They protest against the injustices which have been done to them . . .

Cult figures emerge among the young men who write wall posters, edit magazines . . . Wang Juntao, of *Beijing Spring*, Ren Wanding, who has set up an association for human rights . . . Wei Jingsheng who runs a magazine, *Exploration.*

Wei Jingsheng is thin, forceful, articulate. On 5 December he publishes a major article 'The Fifth Modernization'. 'What is true democracy? It is the right of the people to choose their own representatives . . . the power to replace these at any time . . . without this fifth modernization the other four will not succeed.' He is referring to the four modernizations; in agriculture, in industry, in science and technology, and in defence, proclaimed by Zhou Enlai in January 1975, and taken up by Deng Xiaoping in his programme of economic reforms, and of 'opening the country'.

Wei Jingsheng is an ex-Red Guard, sixteen in 1966, when the Cultural Revolution began. He travelled far and wide in China, as did so many millions of youths. In one of the

37

poorest regions, he saw a horde of beggars, and among them a girl of seventeen or eighteen, stark naked, daubed in mud in lieu of clothing. This profoundly affected him. How could such poverty still exist in a socialist country? It spurred his search for a fulfilling system of thought and action. He had seen much good in the ideals of the Cultural Revolution, whose aim was to get rid of bureaucratic tyranny and give voice and strength to the people, but like all his generation, he had been bitterly disillusioned. Now, in 1978, he saw the return of the Party bureaucrats. 'Without democracy society stagnates . . . economic growth will be impeded . . . we must not be enslaved again.' At the time, a great many people were saying the same thing. Without democracy, there can be no true socialism, an official journal stated in January 1979. Without democracy, there can be no socialist art . . . wrote a Shanghai magazine.

In that autumn there were riots, attacks against Party offices by the crowds milling in the city streets, the jobless, the displaced . . . Precisely in December 1978, on Christmas Day, Vietnam started her offensive into Cambodia, and occupied the country.

Until that December, Deng Xiaoping appeared much in favour of appeals for democracy, for political as well as economic reforms. The Party chairman, Hua Guofeng, was against the wall posters, because many of them denounced the people that Hua employed. 'There are secret places in every department, in every government unit, where the followers of the Gang of Four still hide', wrote one poster. This was absolutely true, and it is still true today. In 1989, in 1990, and in 1991, I discover newspapers where, on the editorial boards, members of the writing teams recruited and employed by the Gang of Four are still in prominent place, still wielding censorship power on articles submitted.

Deng Xiaoping defends the wall posters, when Hua Guofeng condemns them. 'Everyone says we must dismantle these organizations, forbid the masses to criticize the government, the Party, the army . . . but initiative will disappear if we repress different opinions . . . I feel we must allow the masses to stick wall posters, and only arrest *bad elements*, traitors who sell their soul and state secrets for money . . . '

This is a hint to the fact that some of the ex-Red Guards affixing posters on Democracy Wall are constantly visited by western journalists and even minor diplomats . . .

The Third Plenum of the 11th Party Congress is held in that winter. Deng Xiaoping launches the slogan ECONOMICS IN COMMAND. No longer any class struggle. Party members, he says, must encourage and support 'people both inside and outside the Party . . . who dare to explore new paths, put forward new ideas . . . use their heads, emancipate their minds . . . ' He sounds almost like some of the posters on Democracy Wall.

Deng wins at the Congress, with the support and the solidarity of the First Generation, his fellow Long Marchers, and also the support of those who want reforms.

Hua Guofeng has to accept defeat, but he does so gracefully. He will continue to function, in a dwindling manner, till 1981.

A Party shake-up followed. It was quite impossible to rid it of all Gang of Four supporters, though an attempt was made to expel and punish those who had murdered or tortured other Party members or non-Party intellectuals, and inflicted losses upon the country, such as raiding army arsenals and machine-gunning each other when they formed Red Guard gangs. These must not be given the opportunity to return to power or cause turmoil 'under the cover of democracy', stated Deng Xiaoping.

Deng knew only too well that his major problem would continue to be his own Party, that protean, heterogenous mass of near 40 million, many of its members devoid of any real aspiration to service, but intent on their own self-preservation, in keeping their power and their authority. For the rest of his life he would have to tread the exiguous path between the craters of factional disputes, the all too easily aroused formation of cliques against him. Meanwhile he had

39

to push through economic reforms, opening to the outside world. Only through these reforms and the opening could the superstructure of authority, and also the mentality of the Chinese people, be changed.

It was precisely when Deng wrested victory against Hua at the Plenum, the very month that Vietnam invaded Cambodia, that Wei Jingsheng wrote a scathing article against Deng Xiaoping. Even if one has sympathy for Wei Jingsheng – and his plight deserves sympathy – it is difficult to understand why he chose that moment to launch such an attack: 'The social system in China is not democratic . . . we now have the choice between social reform which will lead to swift increase in productivity and living standards, or the continuation of a dictatorship like Mao Dzedong . . . Does Deng Xiaoping deserve the people's confidence? No leader deserves unconditional trust . . . Is Deng afraid of investigations in the past that might affect him? . . . We must choose between democracy and despotism . . . '

Flamboyant phrases, benefiting Deng's opponents. Especially the threat of reference to his past. For Deng Xiaoping had been the man in charge of the anti-rightist purge of 1957, which had put an end to the experiment known as the Hundred Flowers. This was an attempt, chiefly due to Zhou Enlai, with Mao's approval, to give more freedom of discussion to the intellectuals. Zhou realised that inertia, passivity, and fear, were widespread among the intelligentsia. However, the experiment had failed, and had been followed by a purge of 'rightists', carried out by Deng Xiaoping.

On 29 January Deng Xiaoping was in Washington, as guest of President Jimmy Carter. He toured the United States, wore a large Texan hat, said and did all the right things, including excoriating the USSR. He was an immediate success, a popularity maintained through the next decade. He successfully persuaded American businessmen into an investment surge in China. He became Man Of The Year on America's most prestigious magazine covers. For was he not in favour of free enterprise, of market economies? Had

40

he not said 'Black cat, white cat, what matters the cat's colour so long as he catches mice?' The notion that Deng was a capitalist in disguise permeated America's China-watchers and analysts. He was a man to be praised.

Wei Jingsheng wrote more explosive pieces, his last, on 27 March, accused Deng Xiaoping of having thrown off the mask of democracy. Repression, indeed, had begun, and there had been arrests. That Deng agreed to these arrests – even if reluctantly at first – is clear, although he did not initiate them. But his own position was endangered by the tolerance he had tried to show, and therefore also his plans for reform.

There were more arrests, such as that of Wang Juntao, founder of *Beijing Spring*. On 29 March Wei Jingsheng was arrested. The trials that took place had that recognizable flavour of accusations based on somewhat flimsy grounds, but admixed with doses of morality. In Wei's case, he was charged with having passed secret military information to a foreign newsman for a bribe of 535 dollars, and was condemned to 15 years' jail and 3 years' deprivation of political rights.

Amnesty International took up the case of Wei Jingsheng. A Frenchwoman approached me and asked me whether I could do something? I tried. I wrote a carefully phrased letter, talked to a vice-minister, to a vice-premier, to my friend Wang Bingnan, the president of the Friendship Association . . . 'Wei might have done something reprehensible but the sentence seems very heavy . . . fifteen years is a very long time . . . ' At intervals, during the next six years, I repeated my plea. 'No one can interfere with the law,' I am told by a somewhat haughty official, who explains to me the crimes committed by Wei. I point out that at the time of Wei's condemnation the rule of law, the legal system, had not yet been instituted, that it only began in 1980 . . . perhaps it could be possible to alleviate his sentence? I am totally unsuccessful.

Democracy Wall came to an end. First the wall posters

were to be affixed to a smaller wall, within a park, proximal to a local police station. Later a resolution in the National People's Congress banned *all* wall posters. Only one member of the NPC abstained from voting.

To say the arrests produced no effect would be a lie. In the following April of 1979, few were the wreaths offered in Tiananmen Square. But there was little overt comment. Some writers and social scientists were distressed. A few adopted a surprising stance. The poet Ai Qing, for instance, regarded as a liberal, commented that 'Young people spout slogans they do not understand.'

Perhaps I was naive, unaware of the very real danger because of the non-cohesion with the Party itself, but the necessity of creating dialogue with the younger generations became an obsession with me, and I constantly returned to it.

There continued to be, for a while, more freedom of expression in the press, in the official literary magazines, than there had been for many years.

Three

'STABILITY MUST BE our first concern,' declares Deng Xiaoping. And to ensure stability the Party must be taken in hand. Never has the communist Party prestige been so low, never cynicism among the cadres so blatant. The First Generation, and even some of the Second and Third Generations, the latter now in their forties, are haunted by the spectre of a return to chaos. 'Do not think that there cannot be chaos again in China,' warns Little Bottle. The fear of chaos, of 'turmoil', becomes an obsession for these older men, an obsession but also, for some, a convenient pretext.

A crackdown on corruption takes place. A major case of corruption in the Party makes the front page of the newspapers in September 1979. For the first time a Party member of fairly high standing is publicly exposed by the press. The man who has done this is Liu Bingyan, one of China's ablest journalists, a man of courage, unyielding to flattery, to material gain. His aquiline features become known to millions. Crowds gather to listen to him. Thousands of letters reach him from all over China. 'Men or Monsters', the title of his investigative report, is a runaway bestseller. Never, never has this been done before.

Deng Xiaoping is ruthless in his denunciation of his Party's authoritarianism, arbitrariness, corruption. He is so brutally frank and thorough, that China's worst critics could not have done better. The scorching diatribe is fully reported. Party members put personal benefit, perks, before service to the people. They pursue their own elevation, strive for position, pay and power, heedless of the country's good. They practise nepotism, bribery, oppress the people by exactions of all kinds. They build houses for themselves at public expense, require unpaid labour from the peasantry. At all times they exact special privileges, get their offspring into good jobs without the proper qualifications. They form cliques, factions and groups, and practise corruption on a large scale. 'Never before has a small Party official, running a county or a commune, or an institute, had as much power as we see today . . . a small Party cadre can decide everything . . . he makes the sun shine and the rain fall . . . all this must be changed . . . there are just so many petty tyrants . . . the very life of the Party, and the future of China, depend on our wiping out this state of affairs.'

Satirical pieces, poems, hit out at Party corruption . . . and yet, and yet, because Little Bottle does not entirely control the Party, there are also, at every echelon, in every unit and organization, Party cadres who ignore, or deviate from, any attempt at a clean-up. Officials who bear heavily on those who denounce them and exact revenge. And so corruption, fraud, still goes on . . .

A special disciplinary committee is created, and a supervisory committee. These scrutinize the actions, the life-style of Party cadres. Every Party member must account for what he did during the Cultural Revolution. Several hundred thousand Party cadres are expelled, or disciplined, or warned, but there are always groups, clans, factions, protecting their own members, pushing the crimes they committed upon helpless, innocent men who do not have protection. Many get away with the excuse that they were merely following the orders given at the time . . . how can they be accountable for their obedience, when obeying Party orders is an absolute requirement for membership?

Connections, connections . . . through that miasmatic web of relatives, relations, joint families, linked families by marriage, schoolmates, provincial and village associations. An affinity of linkages, a complex tangle of mutual interest, unbreakable as the cohesion that keeps stars revolving in a galaxy. What can be done about these connections?

Nothing.

It is quite impossible for a Chinese even to *think* of himself without thinking of his own niche within that intricate pattern of connections.

Deng Xiaoping pushes on. The rule of *Law* is proclaimed. No longer will there be rule by personal power. Bodies for drawing up legal codes are set up. Law studies are revived in all the universities. Lawyers in hibernation are recruited. 'The notion of law is rather vague in China, we must first teach the people what *Law* means,' says one of the judges/lawyers I meet. He is reckoned to be a 'first class' lawyer (here too, as for writers, there are categories), and is pleased to be back and working after twenty years in the freezer. 'But the most important thing', he says, contemplating the vague unknown before him, 'will be to try to make Party members understand that they will not be above the law. This is going to be a rather long and difficult task.'

Economic reform is accompanied, in the slogan coined by Deng Xiaoping, with 'opening up'. Which means opening to the West. In July 1979 four special economic zones are created, chosen for their proximity to the sea, ease of access to foreign investors, to foreign capital. This sets up a mild stampede among the officials to organize 'delegations for study' to go West. Among my own generation 'returned students' (which means that they have returned from studying abroad) are eager to go back to Europe or to America, visit old friends they have not seen for many years, renew bonds with the universities where they spent some youthful years. 'We must launch the saying "Learn the techniques of the West, to grasp mastery of the future" . . . that is what the Japanese have done,' says to me ambassador Hsiung, a knowledgeable man who, in his young days, was a 'mole' in the secret service under Zhou Enlai.

Everyone wants books, books, books in English. I am kept busy buying and sending books. Translators are in great demand, and the Translators Association edits a journal of high calibre. Old translators lament that during the Cultural Revolution so few of the young have acquired a grasp of any western language, and now there is an enormous demand for the study of English . . . followed by German, Japanese and French. Russian is not favoured at the moment.

The Writers Association admits new writers. Some of my contemporaries bristle at the thought of this invasion by untried young people. 'Call *that* writing?' says Yao, engaged on a seven-volume saga, the story of a great peasant leader of the past. He points scornfully at a book by a young unknown (unknown until a few months ago), which has become a bestseller. Older poets are not happy with the new poetry that is being written. It is obscure, 'mist-wrapped'. But Junjian likes the new poetry. Many young writers and poets come to him. The resentment of older writers is understandable. The young no longer want to read books by older men and women. They want to read their own generation's writers, they want to recognize themselves.

I have not forgotten Dai Houying, nor her book *Stones in the Wall*. But I still meet with blank stares when I praise her. I discover another book of hers, *Death of a Poet*, and am even more gripped. 'I must meet her,' I repeat. The officials of the Writers Association shift uneasily on the sofa where they sit. 'She is not a member.' 'It may be a bit difficult,' says Intelligent Principle, my very good friend and companion, who accompanies me on my travels, arranges my itineraries, fixes appointments, and is my adviser. She is from Honan province, and from a poor family. She and her mother were driven by famine to wander, and then came the Revolution, and she was cared for, and sent to school. She has been in an American university for almost two years. She is the person who knows my temper, knows when rashness will not work, who gives me advice about the people I want to meet, but always lets me do in the end what I want to do. It may be a little difficult because Dai Houying was a Red Guard, one of a group in charge of a camp for intellectuals, and there fell in love with one of the detained scholars, a poet, who committed suicide. Hence *Death of a Poet*. Because it is about love, love, it is frowned upon, though it has been published. 'I think she is very courageous to have written such a book,' I say, and off we go to Shanghai to meet her.

There are eight people in the living-room of the hotel suite when Dai Houying arrives. I do not know who they are precisely, because I do not ask, but they are writers, ready to take notes in neat mental notebooks. Dai Houying is not pretty, but radiates fierce integrity. I say to her, 'Tell me, *Death of a Poet*, it's true, isn't it?' Her eyes fill with tears. She whispers, 'Yes.' 'You are a very brave person.' She acknowledges her own emotions, lives them, and that is rare, very rare, in our Confucian society. Some months later, I hear that she has become a member of the Writers Association.

In 1987, Dai Houying is part of a group of Chinese writers invited to France. There she quarrels with French Sinologists who act as interpreters. 'I resent their taking us in hand. They do not know much about China . . . some of them do not even know Chinese well, they interpret erroneously,' she says.

An article appears in a Hongkong magazine, by no means pro-communist. The article reports Dai Houying's remarks, and those of other Chinese writers, regarding the power that French Sinologists seem to have. The publishers are utterly dependent on them to translate books from the Chinese. They cull, choose, criticize, not always guided by sound judgment, but by their own preferences . . . or prejudices. 'Either you please them, or you never get translated,' says Dai Houying.

She is not the only woman writer who breaks the taboos, the inhibitions. There is Zhang Jie, who writes of love outside marriage, and although it is platonic love, a longing through the years, the rigid Confucianists frown. There are some others, like Shan Rong, who makes a mark by writing a satire on 'a Marxist lady', entitled *On Reaching Middle Age*.

The film world too has a resurrection. My friend Szeto Huimin, once a Shanghai film director, arranges for me to see the new films, including those which have 'problems', which means not yet released for public viewing, until some scenes are corrected.

Szeto was making movies in Shanghai in the 1930s. At the time, he refused to give a certain minor actress, known under the name of Blue Apple, the leading role in a film. Blue Apple became Madame Mao, Limpid Stream, and never forgave him. He therefore suffered grievously during the Cultural Revolution. Now he was back, promoting the 'new wave' in films. In the decade from 1979 to 1989, very beautiful films were created in China, including themes such as youth delinquency. I met, through him, film makers in Beijing and in Shanghai. Some of the films produced during those years will become classics, not only of Chinese movie making, but worthy of international fame.

Liu Shaoqi, the main target of the Cultural Revolution, the man Mao Dzedong looked upon as a traitor, is cleared, reinstated into the Party. But even so, it is difficult to drum up enthusiasm for him, though it is true that his fate was undeserved. 'When shall we begin to reappraise the Old Man himself?' flippantly asks Y, who has a wife from Hongkong, property in Hongkong, and though an official in the communist Party straddles two worlds.

The 'Old Man' is Mao himself. Sacrosanct no longer. By moving to rehabilitate so many of the victims of the Cultural Revolution, Deng Xiaoping has aroused another problem. He must push through a re-evaluation of the Cultural Revolution. Which is going to be difficult. But Deng is a bulldozing man. Perhaps he will succeed.

I call again upon Yingchao. 'Elder Sister, do you think that I

48

should apologize to the wife of Liu Shaoqi? I wrote critically about her husband, in a book about Mao Dzedong . . . '

'You?' Yingchao is surprised. 'Why, what have you done against him? Nothing. Nothing at all. You did no harm to him.' She pauses, takes a deep breath. 'It was my husband Enlai who headed the committee that condemned comrade Shaoqi. Enlai *had* to do it. We all did things, we all said things, against our own heart . . . so did Enlai . . . you have done nothing wrong.' It must hurt Yingchao very much to tell me this, to reveal a flaw in her dead husband. And it hurts me too, even if I already knew it. How much pain, how much pain, inevitable. Zhou Enlai could not afford the luxury of his own integrity. He had to survive, to survive, to save all those he could save. Had he refused to condemn Liu Shaoqi, he would have lost all influence with Mao, been labelled capitalist roader, and power would have passed into the hands of those who now sit in jail, awaiting judgment. One day, Zhou Enlai's grasp of the issues at stake, his commitment to saving the greatest number by sacrificing the unsaveable, will be viewed not as opportunism, but as a *tour de force*. 'If I do not enter Hell, who will save the souls in Hell? If I do not go into the tiger's lair, who will capture the tiger's cubs?' he said, when asked what he was going to do.

There are always new beginnings in China, born out of the incoherence of too many changes occurring too swiftly for the human mind to accommodate. This is illogical life, and I share in it, questioning the known, chipping at absolutes and arbitrary truths.

At a dinner where we wield chopsticks with habitual dexterity – and such occasions are of paramount importance for exchanging ideas of import with light hints – I listen to an official of the Writers Association who entertains us all with stories of old Beijing. I deliberately commit a *faux pas* (I know that it is a *faux pas*) saying that I do not believe the emergence of challenges in the cultural sphere can be a great danger to stability. Though I detect a sympathetic undercurrent among some of those present, the majority are against me. Nothing is more dangerous than the wild dissemination of untoward ideas. I am made to feel that I am perhaps a bit too foreign. 'There is a generation gap, we must be patient with the young people,' says Y, with that put-on gravity which he wears at awkward encounters. 'Such agreeable young men and pretty girls hung placards round our necks, put pointed caps upon our heads, paraded us through the streets to be jeered at.'

After the delicious dinner, I walk to Tiananmen Square. A soft autumn evening, softness unspoilt despite the growing pollution in Beijing. Beijing is growing, growing, its horizon scissored by the spear upthrusts of skyscrapers. I remember a poet of many centuries ago. 'Suddenly the night wind blows cold, and all the blossoms are brought down.' Perhaps another cold wind will blow, and the brash blossoms of released minds will fragment into stray, meaningless petals . . . I place a small dahlia on the steps of the Heroes' Monument, and silently call to the spirit of Zhou Enlai. Somehow, whatever the wind, something is growing, growing, that will not be blown away. I hear the laughter of young couples, their arms about each other. I know that I cannot do very much, except watch, see, and learn.

The Fourth Congress of Chinese writers, painters, musicians, film makers, opera and other actors, is held in the Great Hall of the People in October 1979.

The grand old men and women of literature are all present, Mao Dun and Ba Jin, Xia Yen and Ding Ling, and gifted Bingsin, Heart of Ice, whom I have known since 1940, when we were both in Chungking during the Sino–Japanese war. There too is Zhou Yang, former vice-minister of culture in the 1950s, once much hated and held responsible for sending many writers, labelled 'rightists', to isolated regions, among them Ding Ling, the famous woman who had won the Stalin prize for literature in the 1930s. However, Zhou

Yang had suffered ten years' imprisonment during the Cultural Revolution. He rose to apologize to all those he had wronged, and this public apology was considered an act of courage, meritorious; many former rightists in the crowd came to shake his hand. Feng Yidai, the brilliant essayist and translator, tells me that Zhou Yang did not initiate the condemnations. 'He had to carry them out. He was always kind to me. He kept me working in the office in Beijing.'

The truth is that many of those present suffered at the hands of their fellow writers, their colleagues. This is called 'burrow infighting', and it goes on all the time among the intellectuals. They seem unable to practise that solidarity which is found among the peasants, among the workers.

The wife of Lao She, the great Manchu writer, is also present at the Congress. Lao She was a victim of the Cultural Revolution. Present too is the very person who encouraged the Red Guards to manhandle Lao She, shouting at them 'beat him, beat him'. Lao She killed himself the next day. 'We must try to forget, not nurture bitterness, for how shall we live with ourselves if we keep the worms of hatred alive in our hearts?' says Junjian.

The names of the dead are read out. Mao Dun speaks. 'Liberate the mind. We must liberate our minds. We must encourage and push forward democracy in the arts.' He receives an ovation. Ba Jin is pointedly critical. 'There has been far too much meddling in literature by bureaucrats who know nothing.' He will later remark that a good ruler is one who governs by inaction, does not impede talent, obstruct creativity. Ba Jin has started to write prolifically, to make up for lost time. When I call on him in his Shanghai house his agile fingers continue to trace characters upon the cloth of his trouser leg as we talk, because he cannot stop writing.

Deng Xiaoping is at the opening, and at the Congress is supported by his protégé, Hu Yaobang. Small-boned, with a quiff of hair shooting up from his forehead, Hu Yaobang looks like a restless sparrow. He will soon become secretary-general of the Party. He insists that he is not well educated, because when he was a boy of fourteen, in 1927, he became a guerilla fighter. Hu Yaobang is very popular with the intelligentsia. He advocates more freedom of discussion, removing the crushing weight of conformism. 'We have not supported you when you were in distress. We have not helped you when you needed help. Some of us have treated you with disrespect, have grossly interfered with your work, have not valued your labour.' Deng Xiaoping stressed in his speech that intellectual labour is to be valued as highly as manual labour, and that the intellectuals are part of the 'working class', which in socialism is *the* leading class. I remember Zhou Enlai saying exactly the same thing in the early 1950s, and saying it again in the 1960s. I am glad that Deng Xiaoping insists on repeating it. Perhaps now the stiff-necked, intransigent Party cadres will change their ways? 'Party cadres must stop harassing and persecuting intellectuals,' says Hu Yaobang. 'Anyone who continues these erroneous policies must be severely dealt with.' The applause, deafening, goes on and on . . . Suddenly it is as if a new day, bright with promise, is here.

Liu Bingyan, the investigative journalist whose searching thoroughness led to the first open exposure of a major corruption case in the Party, is present at the Congress. Another man, who also makes a mark, is writer Bai Hua. He is in the army cultural department, and he stands up to say that the duty of a writer must be to tell the truth to the people. Bai Hua will publish a book entitled *Bitter Love*, later to be made into a film. It is the story of a Chinese intellectual who returns from abroad to serve his country, only to be treated with contumely . . . in the film, he dies, desperate, and his daughter asks, 'You love China, your ancestors' land, but does the ancestors' land love you?' Of course it is a true story, true for many, including some relatives of mine, who returned from abroad, through patriotism, and who have been ill-treated.

'The Party cadres are forever frightened that the intellectuals will wrest power from them, power and authority

. . . and so they cannot bear someone better educated than they . . . ' says Y.

But there is hope, there is hope. With Hu Yaobang battling for the intellectuals, there is hope. Everyone I meet is happy with the results of the Congress. But ever cautious. Junjian, without bitterness, but also without illusions, remarks: 'We speak of tomorrow, but we have not yet quite seen the colour of tomorrow's sky.'

Fong is sophisticated, witty, and has many friends abroad. Now that Deng Xiaoping is opening wide the doors, there is a scramble for invitations to go abroad, and Fong manages somehow to be selected for many such delectable outings. Everyone knows that former rightists, people with a reputation for having been at odds with the Party, get invitations abroad almost automatically, while plodding conformists are ignored . . . Fong has been a rightist.

Fong discusses with me the new system of admission to university. It is now strictly by examination. The sons and daughters of intellectuals, of the 'bourgeoisie', will be advantaged, and the children of workers and peasants at a disadvantage – a total reversal of what was done during the Cultural Revolution. This is again going to create a certain élitism, and therefore resentment. 'But we need the best . . . we need highly intelligent scientists, technocrats, to push forward modernization,' says Fong reasonably. I do see the point, but I am against turning universities once again into breeding ponds for an élite cut off from the realities and needs of their own land. We shall then be back to a stratified type of education, with palpably lower standards in schooling, with poorly trained teachers and inadequate facilities and textbooks – or even a total lack of teaching material – for the rural areas. We shall have a few super-prestigious universities in the coastal cities, and from them thousands of youths, will be recruited to pursue their studies abroad. Fong smiles disarmingly. 'But why should a peasant have to learn to read and to write? His job is to produce food . . . it is a waste of time and money teaching peasant children. Primary school, yes, but afterwards . . . '

We are back, back with Confucius, Confucius in the soul of benign, agreeable Fong. The categorization of human beings, with the *Scholar*, the *Intellectual*, up above . . . a new literati. 'It isn't because the Cultural Revolution went too far in one direction that one must rush backwards, in the opposite direction,' I say. Fong ignores my remark, wittily praises the new wine he has discovered in a little shop.

There is indeed a dilemma, for China is poor, there are many problems to attend to, and higher education will possibly have to be selective. Of course I think there should be more vocational schools, polytechnics, more adult education courses, and that each village *must* have its primary school and a middle school within reach for the better students. In a provincial university where I give a course on the English language some five years later, only two of the forty students attending my lecture come from rural China. They are hardworking, they are good students, but when they graduate they will probably be assigned to a rural area, to a lower middle school in a small town, there to stay, and grow stale, with no hope of change. Yet it is also true that we need a pool of high-grade scientists, of talented movers and performers, and this can only come with good background education, which means having scholar parents, books at home. It is almost impossible to avoid rebuilding an élite, but I pray that this new techno-literocracy will lead China forward to better days, to more fulfilment for her people.

I have frequent and joyful reunions with painters who were my friends, with others whose work I had admired. Wu Tsojen and his wife Shufan, also a painter, are happy now. We sit together in his living-room, in the apartment he has lived in for so many years. Wu Tsojen speaks of The Eagle. He had painted an eagle, claws gripped upon a rock, every stroke an intent to soar, every feather a quiver of leashed strength. 'I made him look *farouche*,' says Wu, who speaks excellent French (he spent many years studying painting in

France). He wears in the winter a dark blue *béret basque*, which was not taken from him because the Red Guards thought it was a worker's cap. But the eagle was stamped upon, and shredded, by the students of the Painting Academy. However, Wu painted another eagle, similar to the one destroyed. This eagle was 2,000 kilometres away, in my province of Sichuan, it hung in the pavilion where the Tang dynasty poet, Du Fu, had lived in Chengdu. 'This is a piece of bourgeois work,' said the young official in charge of the pavilion. 'I think it is meant to show the unyielding revolutionary spirit of the masses,' I replied with utter seriousness. The young official heaved a sigh of relief, for he liked the eagle. And now Wu Tsojen was restored to honour, his living-room crowded with friends, callers, sycophants and students. 'The Cultural Revolution did one good thing . . . it showed us what we are like inside. Now I know who my real friends are,' said he. Wu Tsojen comes for a few days to Switzerland on his way to exhibitions in Europe, and delights Swiss friends who know of him and his work. I had written a book (*Les Cent Fleurs, La peinture chinoise aujourd'hui*) about peasant painting during the Cultural Revolution, and he tells me that painters like himself went down to teach the peasants. 'What will happen to peasant painting now? Some of it was quite good.' But now there is reversal, and peasant painting is no longer extolled.

I call on Li Kejan, accused by Madame Mao of deliberately painting rocks and mountains in dark pessimistic colours to show that he had no faith in the Revolution. For some years galleries did not dare to stock or sell his paintings. But now all is well, and there will be major exhibitions of his work. Li Kejan is a quiet man who does not complain, does not expatiate on what he has endured. 'It did me good to rest for a while,' says he laconically. His sense of honour does not permit him to wallow in self-pity.

As we sit and sip tea, he tells me how, way back in 1972, right after President Nixon's descent upon Beijing, and the week that followed which changed the world, Zhou Enlai started to plan China's opening to the West.

'We must build hotels. There will be many visitors, and also tourists,' said Zhou Enlai. He wanted China's painters to contribute some of their works to hang in the reception rooms, the hotel lobbies, 'the best way to make our visitors understand Chinese art'. But he had not reckoned with Madame Mao, forever on the prowl for flaws and bourgeois thoughts in everyone including the prime minister, whom she looked upon as the main obstacle in her way to power. She demanded to see the paintings selected and since she was in charge of culture Zhou could not refuse. A pictorial massacre took place. The paintings were full of shadows, and each shadow meant an attack against the Party. People were corralled from every office in the city to come and to criticize. Thousands filed obediently, more to view than to criticize, and a small black market in the works of the painters thus pilloried sprang up. Li Kejan laughs at the story. 'We survived.'

I visit Kuan Shanyue, in Guangzhou, and Shen Rojian in Shanghai, and Kuan Liang and Tang Yun in Wusih, and insist on seeing Huang Yungyu. He is the great friend of Gladys Yang, that courageous English woman who has worked for many decades translating Chinese literature. Her husband Xianyi is a remarkable scholar. Huang Yungyu is of the Miao minority, he has a reckless vitality about him, and bubbles with humour. He got into trouble because he painted an owl with one eye open and one eye closed. 'It is an insult to the Party, it means the Party is half blind,' said Madame Mao. Huang had to be criticized. 'But those who criticized me used to come up afterwards and whisper: Stand fast, don't worry,' Huang Yungyu tells me. When I go to see him he still lives down a narrow *hutung*, in a two-roomed hovel, the floor of brick and beaten earth. There is no kitchen and his wife cooks on a small stove outside the front door. In the winter the wind blows dollops of sand into the food. The common privy is 200 metres away. In

56

this narrow place Huang has lived and painted and painted for two years. Everywhere his scrolls are piled. Now he will return to his previous large and comfortable house, but he is nostalgic for the hovel. 'I did my best work there.'

I go to see another painter, Huang Zhou, a cheerful man, who has travelled widely in China, and painted many scenes of Tibet, and of the Uighur women of Sinkiang on horseback. But he is most famous because of his donkeys. During the Cultural Revolution he was condemned to peddle on the streets, leading a donkey. Huang Zhou loves to drink wine, and one day, he left the donkey tethered outside a wine shop. When he came out, no donkey was to be seen. 'I ran down the *hutung*, and at the end of it I found this young policeman, looking very cross, holding my donkey's bridle. "It's not right to leave a masterless donkey on the public way – that's obstruction," said the policeman. "But I was having a drink, I couldn't take the donkey into the wine shop," I protested. "Well, don't do it again," said the young policeman.' Huang Zhou's prolonged acquaintance with donkeys inspired him to paint them, and so he painted donkeys, donkeys in profusion, small and large, eating and playing and running, their meek stubbornness and their spirit of fun. 'Donkeys are very nice, nicer than people.' Now Huang Zhou is famous, and people flock to him, and many ask for a donkey. Some years later, when a high-powered Chinese delegation goes to Japan, it takes as a gift a rare scroll by Huang Zhou, depicting a hundred donkeys. Only Huang Zhou and I seem to find this extremely amusing.

I write an article about my painter friends, it is printed in Hongkong and it draws the ire of some Party secretary. 'It is not true that Huang Yungyu lived in a hovel with no window in the bedroom.'

I meet again Chang Shuhong, for thirty-five years curator of the famous Dunhuang Buddhist caves; near a thousand caves whose walls are covered in frescoes dating back to the third century.

I spent a week in Dunhuang in 1973, at a time when

57

there were no tourists, and stayed with Chang and his wife. Entranced, ecstatic, he and I walked through the caves, and were transported back in time, to those centuries of faith and beauty, and the passion that led the artists to record the history of Buddhism when it entered China. Chang has retired, he lives in Beijing with his wife, and he is worried about the Dunhuang grottoes. 'I hope my successors understand that the frescoes are fragile, that they must be looked after . . . ' He is worried, not because of any possible destruction, but because of the new plans for making Dunhuang a tourist attraction. 'Premier Zhou Enlai protected Dunhuang. The Red Guards were forbidden to come near it, but the tourists . . . ' Plans to bring tourists by the hundreds of thousands are being drawn up, and a large hotel is being built. 'That will be the end of Dunhuang,' moans Chang Shuhong. 'What the Cultural Revolution could not do the tourists will surely achieve.' And certainly Chang is right. Tourism will surely ruin the irreplaceable frescoes, witness to a faith in which 70 per cent, at least, of China's one billion people still ardently believe.

Four

GREENNESS, VAPOROUS MIST, and black soil drenched with life. This is Sichuan province, my province, land blessed by Heaven, China's granary, nourishing at present 110 million people, 10 per cent of China's population. Because of my years in Sichuan I love the smell of soil tended by man's hand, fertilized by man and pig manure. But economic reforms are coming. Promises of doubling and trebling the crops with chemical fertilizers, promises of getting rid of all pests with chemical pesticides. I hope that the myriad living things that burrow, crawl, writhe in the rich mud that spawns them will not die, for I am wary long-term of pesticides and other chemicals.

Here in this enclosed green paradise my family settled three hundred years ago. Here are still many cousins, and aunts, nieces and nephews, many old friends. Among the friends who come to meet me is Pan, who is half-Burmese, whose nature clings to happiness, who smiled his way through the Cultural Revolution. 'What helped me was this,' says he, slapping the small bottle of fiery *maotai* liquor, the local brew, which he carries with him. 'The poet Li Bo used to dance with his shadow under the moon after some cups. In camp I dreamt that I too was properly inebriated, and that Li Bo came down from Heaven to talk with me.'

With Pan I go to Xindu, 50 kilometres away from the provincial capital, Chengdu. Floods have occurred there, and I must go to see what can be done. We stop at the famous Precious Light monastery, which dates back to the Tang dynasty. The chief abbot receives us in a hall decorated with hanging pictures of stormy oceans, dragons born of the surf, and lion-puppies playing with spheres of jade. Seated on high carved wooden chairs, we ask some questions, but the chief abbot is in a period of silence and his young acolyte answers. He mentions one of my aunts, abbess in a monastery where old Tibetan books are kept in boxes of sandalwood and camphor. 'The venerable lady was my teacher.' Another aunt of mine, a young seventy-three, does Taichi shadow boxing two hours a day and paints pictures of the Boddhidarma, the founder of Zen. He was an Indian monk who came to China in the sixth century. One summer, when my life substance needed a pilgrimage to renew its pliability, I retraced the travels of the founder of Zen in China. 'Indeed,' says the acolyte pouring the special pale green tea of the monastery, 'during the recent events (he means the Cultural Revolution) Premier Zhou Enlai remembered us, and ordered the army to guard our gates, so that we were safe throughout the years, and now we have many young novices who seek enlightenment.' The government has given money to all the monasteries and temples that were broken into, to repair the statues and repaint the halls.

We drive another 15 kilometres and reach the heart of the disaster. A short-haired girl with round cheeks and superb teeth welcomes us. She is the county Party secretary. This is a great occasion for the county. 'Come, I'll show you.' We walk to the fields. Water does not char, yet there is a burnt look to them. No longer green, but covered with friable brown crust. 'River slime,' says the Party secretary. The bamboo groves round the houses have been knocked askew by the onrush of water-carried mud.

The villagers assemble, clap dutifully, then become garrulous, and with interspersed laughter shriek their stories of fear, and danger, and rescue. They mimic the whoosh of the waters pouncing upon them like a hundred hungry tigers. There are tales of rescue, and some grinning men and reluctant boys are pushed forward to shake our hands, Pan and me. Heroes, who waded or swam in the mud to save women, children . . . 'Were there many misfortunes?' I ask, and they point to the graves, a dozen earthmounds in a row, crowned with stubs of incense sticks, yellow paper money heaped before each. 'We try to promote cremation as there is so little land, no land for burial,' says the Party secretary. 'But we have to take into account the people's feelings.' The dead-by-water are the undead, and have to be propitiated, hence the county authorities have allowed burial-in-ground.

I make a contribution. A lucky six figure one, enough to put the village back on its feet, rebuild houses. This is possible because some money which appeared impounded during the Cultural Revolution has just been returned to me.

In 1960, at the time of the Leap Forward, I had sent money to China. I was not alone doing so. Thousands of Overseas Chinese knew of the distress at the time, and sent money. A special bank department was created to receive all this money, and it was more valuable than many other things, for it was all in foreign exchange, chiefly American dollars. At the time China was under an embargo, no imports of any kind were allowed by the United States and other western countries. The USSR's Krushchev, perhaps to curry favour with the United States at the time, had cancelled all contracts with China, withdrawn all Soviet experts, paralyzing Chinese industry.

It was then felt by so many of us Overseas that we had to help. We never consulted each other. We gave, sent money to China. But when the Cultural Revolution came the money represented a danger. It would have given Madame Mao another crusade. 'Money from abroad? Surely this is to subvert us . . . undoubtedly a CIA plot to corrupt, to bribe . . . ' I had already been accused, in wall posters, of being an 'agent' of the West . . .

Fortunately the money was registered under another name of mine, and I stayed mute. In 1978 an official of the Bank of China came to see me. 'We have an account for you.' By then, with unclaimed accumulated interest, it had become a fairly considerable sum in *jenminbi*, China's currency. 'We promised to repay all those who then contributed within twelve years . . . we are doing so with some tardiness, please forgive us . . . ' It was thus possible for me to make a donation. And since then, I have been using this money in China, to pay for my travels, to help friends.

Bathed in late afternoon light we talked with the village headman, who told us the colour of the flood water was pure, bright yellow, gushing bile. He showed haphazard teeth in a wide grin as he gestured towards the hills mantling the horizon. 'It is the mountains, they now melt into the rivers, the mountains are coming down, all stone and mud.' The villagers had picked the stones to build walls. 'It is not the first time, but it has never been so bad,' continued the headman, insisting I smoke a crumpled cigarette he had stowed in his pocket. On the return journey I said to Pan, 'I think too many trees are being cut on the slopes.' Pan nodded eagerly. He had waited for this opportunity to speak about the underlying gravity of the problem. 'We had great forests of white cedar once, but few are left, and still the lorries drive up, and the timbermen cut what they can find.' 'That is why the rivers run wild, the water leaps with mud,' said the Party secretary. 'The beautiful azure river Chialing is no longer blue,' said Pan. 'The streams run yellow now,' they chorused.

Back in Chengdu the mayor picked up the theme that evening at dinner. Perhaps one day the mighty Yangtse, China's colossal artery of trade and transport, which irrigates all of the Central China plains, would become another Yellow River, another great sorrow for China. The Yellow River brought millions of tons of silt every day to the ocean, and its bed rose and rose, and every year the dykes had to be made higher, and cities on its course now lay 20, 30 metres below the river's bed . . .

Of course, Pan and the Party secretary felt that since I was concerned, I should write to The Leaders, the men in authority at The Centre in Beijing. 'The leaders have many problems,' said Pan. A small matter like floods in Sichuan may not have been brought to their attention . . . but . . . if someone drew attention to it . . .

From this small beginning, a flood in my province, I became totally involved. I took trips in the inland provinces to view the deforestation. I travelled to the deserts of the northwest. I became an ecologist, without labelling myself one. And this has gone on for eleven years. The Desert Institute experts in Kansu province and I not only met, but I was able later to send two British desert experts to them, and the meeting was a success. The Desert Institute does a great deal of work, but like many other useful institutions, there is a problem of funding.

I dropped in on teams in charge of forestry, and found one of them engaged in massive deforestation. The man in charge of the team, very satisfied with himself, told me of the money made the previous year by cutting trees, 'and we shall make twice as much this year'. This led to a fairly rough discussion, rather un-Chinese in its directness, where I asked how many trees he replanted for those he had cut. 'This is a state secret,' he replied.

To my joy, once again I found that many other concerned experts in China were similarly engaged, warning against desertification, deforestation. Within two years teams of scientists were travelling to inspect the terracing of arid uplands, to promote the planting of bushes and grasses to hold the soil together in the vast Loess region of North China. A special long-rooted grass, called *Ning*, was being tried, and I made a trip to watch the planting on terraced hills. The peasants were being paid to plant it. Campaigns of education in all the schools began, to promote the greening of China. Deng Xiaoping was photographed with a shovel, planting a tree. Special forest guards were appointed to patrol the remaining forests . . . but it was a constant battle, it required unending watchfulness. It was heartbreaking to go to the southern provinces, and discover whole hillsides covered with the bristle stumps of thousands of young trees, cut as soon as they grew three feet high.

The provincial governors shake their heads. 'The people need fuel, and there is no coal in our provinces . . . we are building ports to bring coal from the north, where there's plenty of it. But we shall also have to change the habits of the village people, teach them to use coal. They prefer wood. They send their children to cut down the trees.'

One thing leads to another, from deforestation to soil degradation, to industrial pollution. All the time one has to teach, to change wasteful, wrong ways of handling the land. And industrialization, haphazard, everywhere seen as a promise of progress and prosperity to come, but creating massive pollution, eats up fertile soil. In one of my peregrinations I find a new paper factory, the pride of a small county trying to lift itself up by its own efforts . . . but the waste pours into the fields; a couple of cows are standing hoof deep in the waste water which submerges the grass they eat.

China has to feed 22 per cent of the world population on 7 per cent of the world's arable land. The population keeps on growing, and the arable land keeps on lessening, swallowed up, by industry, by the building of many new houses, of new towns and cities, by the very prosperity that economic reforms bring.

It is in Sichuan province that I meet Zhao Zeyang, eighteen months before he becomes prime minister of China. Since he is today shunned, demoted, perhaps I must tell both of my deep affection for him, and also of my disagreement with his policies.

It is magnolia weather; blissfully the almond blossoms in the spring, when Sixth Brother and his wife take me proudly to their new three-bedroom apartment in Chengdu. Sixth Brother is chief engineer for Post and Telecoms, also a representative of the People's Political Consultative Council at national level. 'Old Sixth, your two brothers, Third and

Fourth, have both been abroad. It's your turn now. You must go to see the new technology. We need many, many telephones in Sichuan.' Sixth Brother laughs. 'I'm too old now, I'm over fifty.' 'You're younger than I am, and we should all learn something new every day.'

I think that scientists, experienced men, who have worked in responsible positions, should be the target of training for new technology as much as the younger people. They know the problems of China better than the students who go abroad in large numbers. I speak to the Party secretary in charge at Post and Telecoms and he beams. 'What an excellent idea . . . we must discuss the matter.' But I have a feeling that he cannot do very much, though he ushers me out repeating that 'we shall certainly consider the matter'. To console me Sixth Brother cooks a wonderful meal, all the savours and odours of spicy Sichuan food, stirring those memories lying in wait. We talk of Third Uncle, my father's younger brother, Sixth Brother's father, who died during the Cultural Revolution. Third Uncle cared for me when, during the Sino–Japanese war, I was in Sichuan province, doing midwifery at a hospital just outside Chengdu. He spent many hours talking to me, of the family, of the customs of Sichuan. He rooted me into this land, this province, more than my father had ever done.

Now Sixth Brother tells me what really happened to Third Uncle during the Cultural Revolution, how he died. The story comes in fragments over a leisurely after dinner evening, every piece filling in the main canvas. A story goes on forever, unfolds new panoramas of perception. The family stories live on in all of us, and now our children and grandchildren are also listening to them.

Third Uncle died in 1968, uncared for by the doctors, fearful of attending to a 'capitalist'. And yet Third Uncle had been honoured as a 'patriotic capitalist' in the time of Zhou Enlai, for he had not fled the country, but elected to remain. However, this was forgotten when the Red Guards started their rampage. In his last illness none of his sons or daughters-in-law were near him, only his wife, Third Aunt, and she was not allowed to leave the house. Meanwhile Sixth Brother was being grilled about me. I was then an 'illicit connection abroad'. He was repeatedly asked: 'But how can Han Suyin be your relative? She is a spy . . . all those with relatives abroad become spies . . . how much money did she give you to spy for her?' Sixth Brother had replied: "She is not a spy. Premier Zhou Enlai receives her." But they sneered. These Red Guards who questioned me were members of the May 16 group. That was a group led by a student named Liu Linkai, and it was special, its task was to gather material against Premier Zhou Enlai, in order to destroy him.'

Third Uncle's body was buried in a common grave, and though Sixth Brother searched, he could not identify the bones. In 1979 a posthumous ceremony was held for Third Uncle, also for other members of the 'capitalist' family to which he and I belong. Apologies to the spirits of the dead. But Sixth Brother would like to have a proper grave, a fine stone with excellent calligraphy to commemorate the virtues of the dead man. All he has from Third Uncle are a pair of worn cloth shoes, a cane, the cup in which he drank tea, his writing brush and inkstone. He asks me if I have anything, and yes, I say, I have kept some of his letters, I shall bring them and we shall find a good site and bury all these, in memory of the dead man.

I am more determined than ever that Sixth Brother should go abroad. I believe that China's hinterland is important. I think that China's future lies in Asia, and that the inland provinces should be developed. Not all investments should go to the coastline provinces. At the time, I seem to be very much in a minority. But five years later, it is not so, vice-ministers as well as economists and scholars point out that it would be a great mistake, leading to dangerous inequality, to neglect the heartland. 'To decorate the front door and leave the back door unattended, is a mistake.' More forcefully, local experts will say that it is 'a geopolitical error'.

Third Aunt has shrunk with age, but her skin remains ivory delicate. She pats my hand. She is extremely deaf. 'Do not get excited,' she says to me. 'I think Sixth Brother should go abroad,' I shout. 'Eh?' Sixth Brother's wife who knows the right pitch says into her ear: 'Elder Sister says your son must go abroad.' 'It will cost a lot of money,' replies Third Aunt, again patting my hand.

I want to talk with some officials on the need for new technology, better telephones, telecommunications . . . perhaps I should have brought beautifully coloured pamphlets from AT & T, or Bell . . . but this proves unnecessary. In an apparently casual but carefully prepared way, an official tells me that Party secretary Zhao Zeyang, in charge of Sichuan province, is inviting me to dinner. Would tomorrow evening do?

Zhao Zeyang is a name to conjure with then, enormously popular in Sichuan. 'If You Want To Eat Rice; Ask Zhao Zeyang' runs a popular ditty, and in China where 'food is Heaven' it means that 100 million people like what he has done to stop the Red Guards, to restore order and some prosperity to the province. Yet Zhao is not from Sichuan, but from Honan province, that stubborn, drought swept, locust infested northern province where I was born, and spent part of my childhood, because my father was building a railway there. He came as Party secretary to Sichuan in 1975, and immediately took matters in hand. 'Secretary Zhao came to our office in an open shirt, his jacket on his arm,' an accountant in one of the armament factories which I visit tells me. 'We had nothing to do and we played cards all day in the office. He walked in. "You're going to stop this," said he. His voice was mild. "Who are you to give orders here?" shouted our department head. "My name is Zhao. From now on those cards are going to take a long rest, and you are going to work again." '

There are many such stories about Zhao Zeyang. I remember him well, despite my own reservations about some of his policies. His lack of lordliness, his mildness, his competence in Sichuan, are still remembered. 'Father and Mother to the people' they called him in the alleyways of Chengdu. No greater compliment for an official in China.

Zhao Zeyang stood relaxed, at ease, behind the white screen which concealed our table from the main dining-room. He looked not only approachable, but there was a great sweetness in him. His hands, the backs unveined, were very young, though he was sixty. Here's our future premier, I thought, as we sat and made talk about the harvests, good ones expected, and this allowed my friend Pan to put in a word about the flood-stricken villages. Which opened up the topic of deforestation, of land use. For all conversation is a well-prepared ballet, building up a situation, a story. I talked of the mud and stone avalanches precipitating the hills into the rivers and Zhao looked grave. 'It is a problem all over the country . . . it has been ignored for a decade.' We then talked of transport, energy, developing electric power . . . ' 'We are at the beginning of long-term planning, on a large scale, for energy development,' said he, 'but we must also reform our minds. We can no longer think in the old ways.' I brought up then the subject of science, the dire need for knowledge, and thus naturally to Sixth Brother. 'I think he should be sent abroad for six months, to see what is being done about telecommunications in Europe and in the United States . . . I can arrange some visits with companies . . . 'Of course,' said Zhao. 'I am only now learning a lit-tle about telecommunications . . . I see no reason why your relative should not go abroad to bring back new knowledge . . . your family is patriotic . . . '

Sixth Brother was to be issued a passport. I arranged for him a six-month tour. Belgium, France, Switzerland, and the United States. I paid gladly for his travel, and hospitality was greatly helped by the companies involved. But there was at first a hitch. The passport had to be approved by seven dif-ferent local departments, and of course it was to be expected that what was approved by one department head would be obstructed by another. Somehow, in that tangle of levels, someone brought up the matter of Sixth Brother's father being a 'capitalist'. The son could not be politically reliable. 'This is Cultural Revolution thinking,' I blurted. For three weeks it looked as if permission would not be granted, on the grounds of political unreliability. Local Party echelons are redoubtably skilled in obstructiveness, in demanding further investigation, in delaying tactics, until the project is either given up or the demanding party commits a mistake. Zhao dealt swiftly with the impedimentors. 'Patriotic capitalists are one of our great assets.' Sixth Brother flew to Europe, and on to the United States. Everywhere he was treated most kindly, and on American planes the air-hostesses placed a board round his neck with his name, to identify him to his sponsors, because at first he knew very little English. Sixth Brother returned six months and a day after his departure. 'The cadre who tried to stop me lost face. He warmly recommended two other engineers, and those fellows never returned to China.'

In September 1980 Zhao was confirmed as premier, and the popular Hu Yaobang, who had talked so vigorously for freedom of discussion, became secretary-general of the Party in 1981. This was all Deng Xiaoping's work. Little Bottle from Sichuan bulldozed his way towards economic reforms. 'To carry them out,' he said, 'Rejuvenation of the Party and of the government was indispensable.'

This was to become one of the main pillars of his policy. Younger people must come into positions of responsibility. The old leaders and officials must yield, gracefully, and retire.

It was to prove the most difficult thing of all to accomplish. For the 'old ones', the First Generation, were fabulous men, legendary warriors of the Long March. They had created an epic and in their minds still lived heroic years of guerilla war. The First Generation was not prepared to stand down. 'No life tenure for anyone from now on,' repeated Deng Xiaoping. He gave the example, relinquishing all the positions he held, except that of chairman of the Military Commission. He was at the time busy reshuffling the army

commands, cutting down on all too powerful regional commanders, attempting to pare the army budget, to reduce the
army from 3 million to 2 million men.

I was to see and talk to the Prime Minister Zhao Zeyang
several times during the next ten years. He remained most
likeable, informal always. I met him once at a reception in
Geneva during a trip he made to Europe and he showed me
his wrist watch. 'I am in Switzerland the country of watches
but I continue to wear my Chinese watch,' said he.

We were to disagree on the way economic reforms were
carried out. He became prone to listen to a certain group of
young economists and advisers, in a think-tank he had set
up. Some of their initiatives were certainly inappropriate for
China. What finally brought Zhao Zeyang down were the
student demonstrations of 1989 in Tiananmen Square.

We hold a family consultation. Fourth Sister and her hus-
band, First Sister and Fifth Sister, Third Brother, Fourth
Brother and his wife, and Sixth Brother. We discuss what
I should do with the four houses that my father left me.

In China every peasant owns his house. In the cities
many former bourgeois, like my father, also own their
house or houses. But during the Cultural Revolution sixteen
families of workers occupied the four houses. They threw
out the original tenants, all bourgeois, to whom my father
had rented the houses.

Now I could claim them back. Technically, said Fourth
Sister's husband, who is someone important in aeronautics,
there should be no problem. My friend Intelligent Principle
also says there is no problem.

We go together, she and I and Fourth Brother, to the
Housing Bureau of the eastern sector. We sit in the office
of the housing director, drink tea and smoke cigarettes. 'The
Chinese government recognizes the right of inheritance, the
right of ownership of bank accounts, houses . . . these
houses are yours,' says the director. 'Well then . . . ' says
Fourth Brother, hopefully. 'There are problems,' says the

director. 'We must think of a way.' 'Yes we must think of a way,' says Intelligent Principle. Docile, I repeat: 'We must certainly think of a way.' What is the obstacle, obstruction, impediment? I do not ask. I have never collected rent from the sixteen families inhabiting the four houses . . . We all sip more tea, and think, and agree that thinking requires time, and that we must meet again after a good think. Fourth Brother is impatient, but I say, 'Look, how are we going to rehouse sixteen families?' 'They should be thrown out,' says Fourth Sister-in-law, who is rash, and does not understand the situation. 'Next year we may find a way,' I say. 'I am not in a hurry.' 'You must fight for your rights,' insists Fourth Sister-in-law. 'We *suffered* during the Cultural Revolution . . . this is owed to us . . . ' But what is owing? She and her husband are well housed, a new apartment, and I don't really need a house in Beijing right now. However, I go through all the motions. I try to buy a house, quite enormous, twenty-nine rooms, a large garden, but Fourth Sister-in-law notices that right in the middle of the garden there is a trap-door leading down a staircase into the underground shelters built during the Cultural Revolution, when it was expected that the USSR might throw bombs on China . . .

During the next seven years, twice a year, I visit the Housing Bureau, smoke a cigarette, drink tea, chat with the director who assures me every time that I have all rights to the houses. I learn, during those seven years, an enormous amount about rehousing in Beijing. The city is being rebuilt. It is now five times as large as it was in 1949. Its population grows. Six million, eight million, nine million. Vast apartment houses mushroom everywhere. I learn that Overseas Chinese have returned to claim their houses, and they are asked to find alternative accommodation for the unwanted tenants. 'Everyone now wants flush toilets and bathrooms . . . it is modernization,' says the housing director.

By 1987 I look forward to these pleasant bi-annual visits to the Housing Bureau director. The problem of getting the

71

houses back becomes quite secondary. What is fun is the talk, the tea, learning how Beijing works where housing is concerned.

'When the foot of a wall is reached, one finds a way round the wall,' quotes Intelligent Principle. Suddenly, an empty house is found. An empty house, in over-crammed Beijing. That engorged city where living space is something like 3 square metres per person according to some pessimistic statistics? It is a miracle. Suddenly I regret that the visits to the Housing Bureau will now end, and the great and prodigious stories of rehousing.

Since 1985 the Housing Bureau has set up housing exchange units. People can swap rooms, accommodation, and this has proved very useful and popular. The empty house I want is in the western part of Beijing, my father's houses in the eastern. 'There is no problem, we have good relations with the comrades in the western sector,' says the eastern district Housing Bureau director. He sends men to measure the ground on which stand my father's houses, and that of the new house, and I am given back a good deal of money, so much per square metre, since the area of the new house is smaller. Documents are signed. Seals are stamped. Everyone is pleased. The only present the director takes is a stone from Lake Leman in Switzerland. 'I collect stones . . . many people bring me stones. I have stones from Brazil, from Egypt . . . this stone will make me dream of Switzerland, where I shall never go . . . but I shall be happy holding the stone in my hand.'

Five

THE PUBLIC TRIAL of the Gang of Four is held in 1981. It will be conducted according to Law, Law instituted in 1980. It is shown on television. Madame Mao, Limpid Stream, gives a dramatic performance. When the policewomen take her back to her commodious rooms in the jail reserved for important persons, she asks them: 'Did you see me on television?' She and her acolytes are condemned to death, and one excited journalist asks me whether she will be executed. 'No. The death sentence is often suspended, with a two years' grace period. Should the accused behave well during these two years, it will be commuted to a life sentence. This is what will happen to her.' This is what happens.

A formal reappraisal of Mao Dzedong's final years, and of the Cultural Revolution, is published. It is a document of importance, entitled *Resolutions on Certain Problems in the History of the Communist Party*. It is an extremely astute balancing act, and although I am not entirely in agreement with the analysis, I realize that it had to be done, both to keep 'Mao Thought' as part of China's guiding theoretical framework, and also to condemn the Cultural Revolution as an aberration of Mao Dzedong.

Deng Xiaoping speaks of 'socialism with Chinese characteristics'. 'Deng means sinicizing socialism by adopting some capitalist methods,' say two social scientists I know. The Social Science Academy is a monumental building. It is a huge hold-all, where one encounters hundreds of scholars with very different views. Everyone who has ever been

73

anyone, but cannot at the moment be inserted into a proper niche, is to be found at the Social Science Academy.

'A Chinese scholar who does not understand politics will find his knowledge inadequate,' warns a contemporary intellectual. The word should be politico-economics. Everything hangs on the economic reforms which Deng Xiaoping promotes with unrelenting vigour. The reforms are altering the context, the meaning, the application, of every accepted theory and former concept. And with the 'opening' which is taking place, there is an invasion of western films, television, books. New images, with an enormous impact, new sensations, creating new needs and new aspirations.

Deng Xiaoping declares that there must be free elections at area and district level; later they will be held at county level. In the cities, each district will elect its candidates. Everyone can vote, or become a candidate, except criminals deprived of political rights, and youths under eighteen. Every institute, university, factory, department, organization, (all of them called 'units' in Chinese) participate. Already in August 1979 Deng Xiaoping announced the intent to separate the role of the Party from the role of the government, 'to release initiative'. Local elections come under the heading of government, the Party must not interfere.

This makes Deng Xiaoping more popular than ever. Stories about Little Bottle circulate, about his bridge playing, for he is a bridge addict. Bridge clubs are now established in many 'units', and Chinese players want to compete on the international bridge level. Deng's style of work is also a subject for popular comment. Whereas Zhou Enlai worked eighteen hours a day, checked everything personally, reread every letter written by his secretaries, or ministers, Deng works only three to four hours (some say two) a day, giving a broad outline of what he means, letting subordinates get on with the work. 'We must train many young people to take responsibility,' says he. And this, coupled with his determined effort to 'rejuvenate' Party and government, are approved by the population.

The elections are greeted with enthusiasm. There is feverish excitement in many universities. In Peking University, students congregate to listen to speeches by candidates. Candidates need only three sponsors. Wall posters appear, for the interdiction on wall posters does not apply inside campuses. One student, who gets a great many votes, boasts that he is not a Party member. In Changsha Teachers College, non-Party students contest the elections.

Obstruction begins.

Despite the orders from 'the Centre' that there must be no interference, the lower Party echelons do not see it that way. They fear loss of power; they do what they have always been good at doing, bypass, ignore, deviate, distort, allege 'anti-Party' machinations. They organize 'teams to keep order' during the elections. They cannot openly defy the new law on the electioneering process, but they pretend that the elections are rigged by factions against socialism. In Peking University, in Changsha, the Party teams refuse to recognize the candidates freely elected.

The provincial authorities, however, which represent the government, take the side of the students in Changsha, and back the elections. A major dispute occurs between Party and government officials. Tao Seng, a student prominent in the electoral dispute, is briefly arrested, but released after three days. He travels to Beijing, to petition 'the Centre', and to demand punishment for the local cadres who abused their authority. 'No one ever stated that the elections were illegal. But the Party cadres tried to frighten the students,' a member of the Changsha Writers Association tells me.

The National People's Congress is, according to the constitution, the highest authority in the land. Until now it has merely been a compliant body, agreeing with already determined Party policies. However, the Standing Committee of the NPC appoints an investigation group, which reports that the Party cadres have acted illegally, exceeding their authority. 'No reprisals against the students are allowed,' states the group. But the local Party cadres refuse to recognize the group findings. 'Wait and see . . . sooner or later, we'll settle accounts,' they threaten.

Of course, what happens is that a small group of students now act irresponsibly, indulge in needless provocation. They demand the dissolution of the communist Party. Inflammatory posters appear. 'The Communist Party must go . . . Party organizations in the university must be abolished . . . '

This plays right into the hands of the Party cadres, who now gloat. 'We told you so. We always knew that these were anti-Party, counter-revolutionary elements . . . ' The ultras among the students, now imperil Deng Xiaoping's authority. He had promoted free elections, and if he is to maintain the drive for economic reforms, he must now condemn the students . . .

The local Party cadres have won. Not only do they ignore the students' choice in the universities, but also the candidates elected by the population in several city districts.

'It is childish to want all Heaven in one nibble,' mournfully says to me a nuclear physicist, whom I have known for some years. 'Instead of helping to achieve step by step democratization, this small bunch of hotheads have done just the opposite.'

A student I talk to also realizes what precipitation, irresponsibility, have destroyed. 'We have *bangdaomang*,' he says. This means try to help, but achieves exactly the opposite. The best word in English for it is *boomerang*.

In Peking University a student named Hu Ping, who received many votes when he called for democracy, freedom of speech, and of the press, is identified with 'turmoil'. For in the wake of his speeches come wall posters calling for the restoration of the four freedoms of the Cultural Revolution, the restoration of Democracy Wall. This appears once again as a deliberate provocation. 'There is danger from the Right, but also from the Left,' says Deng Xiaoping. By the Left, he means the ex-Red Guards and Party cadres who would like another Cultural Revolution. 'We must proceed as if walking on thin ice.' In the alleyways and *hutungs* of the cities appears a ditty which finds its way into the official newspapers.

ABOVE (in the Party centre) THERE IS A POLICY.

BELOW (among the Party cadres) THERE IS A COUNTER-POLICY.

'Outward compliance, actual obstruction', the newspapers write. Deng Xiaoping is caught in a quandary. His only support can come from the more orthodox, older leaders, erroneously regarded by western experts as against economic reforms. They are not against reforms, but they know how dangerous it is to hasten change. They want to go very prudently. They cannot abandon the socialist system, even if they know that there must be modifications. There cannot be chaos in China.

And perhaps today, seeing what has happened in the USSR, the Chinese way of proceeding appears sound, and wise.

The well respected economist, Chen Yun, who stood up against Mao in the past, who fought for private plots for the peasantry, is not against reforms and opening up. But it must be done in a well-paced, planned way. He and many of his colleagues look askance upon the sudden 'opening up', which brings in a flood of vulgarity, which brings in pornography, sex films, prostitution, unneeded luxury goods . . . this is the way to havoc, disaster.

Deng Xiaoping has to act against those who want to 'eat all Heaven in one nibble'. He too is haunted by the spectre of chaos. He cannot allow, in the name of free elections, the abolition of the Party, or a renewal of the Cultural Revolution in the name of democracy.

Hu Ping will later leave China, go abroad. Tao Seng remains in China, and becomes a prosperous trader in antiques.

Conversation in Beijing is challenging, exciting. Tumescent rhetoric, but also sober exploration of the validity or not of

Marxist theses, of the practice of socialism in China.

It is in the citadels of orthodoxy, the institutes dedicated to research in Marxism-Leninism-Mao Dzedong Thought (such is the formula for theoretical guidance in China), in the Social Science Academy, in the Young Communist League, that vivid discussions take place. Gallons of tea are drunk at meetings, endlessly the arguments go on. Deng Xiaoping's slogan SEEK TRUTH FROM FACTS has compelled this search for doctrinal accuracy, but of course it also implies heretic deviation, from previous doctrinal interpretations. The aim is to adapt theory to the elastic reality of today, to what is really happening, the economic reforms. The Party must change, must rejuvenate, not only its members, but also its ideas. It must abandon fossilized thinking, be educated into new concepts. It can never never relinquish power or 'leadership'. But what is leadership?

In this effervescent atmosphere, a slogan is launched by secretary-general of the Party Hu Yaobang. TO BECOME RICH IS PRAISEWORTHY. There is no contradiction between being a socialist and achieving material prosperity through hard, honest work. One of the tenets of socialism in China is 'to each according to the work he does'. Mao Dzedong had pronounced himself against total egality. Hu Yaobang wanted to make this clear, but alas, he has not hedged his slogan with legal reservations. Thus it is interpreted by many as meaning: 'Anything goes, provided one becomes rich'. It seems to condone black marketing, corruption, bribery, speculation, fraud . . . it will take some years to modify it into TO BECOME RICH BY LEGAL MEANS IS PRAISEWORTHY. 'The notion of law is very vague, very vague, law is an abstract concept to most of the Chinese,' lawyers repeat.

It will take more years to teach, to apply the law. Meanwhile the lawyers and jurists are busy, drawing up a civil code, a criminal code, drawing up regulations to govern commerce and trade, and the joint ventures with western companies.

1982, and a cold wind blows. It blows down our necks, insinuates frost fingers into our body crevices. A movement against 'bourgeois liberalization (b.l.) has been launched. All political campaigns start in the field of culture. With condemnation of a book, a play, a newspaper article. 'Bourgeois liberalization' is ferreted out of the written word, criticizing socialism, insidiously spreading capitalism. This time, one of the targets is Bai Hua, the author of *Bitter Love*. His book was published in 1979 and obtained wide readership. A film based on it is now shown, and Deng Xiaoping is reported to have seen it (he has not read the book). He professes himself 'astounded'. The film-book thus becomes a target, and Bai Hua writes a self-criticism. Plays and poems by young writers are also attacked, though accepted a year, two years ago.

But the real target of b.l. was to be the gross corruption among Party cadres. Party men act as go-betweens for foreign companies investing in China. They suggest, in return for services rendered, that their sons and daughters receive scholarships to go abroad. Or that a Swiss bank account should be opened for them. The newspapers write of a 'very small, very small, infinitesimal minority' of Party cadres who indulge in these practices . . . Even if Deng's original aim was to condemn such activities, it is easy to divert the target, to crush expendable, defenceless writers, ascribing all nefarious influence to them. 'We must not lose our self-esteem, not worship all foreign things,' says Deng. But Party members go into business, and smuggle videotapes and films from Hongkong, and Japanese TV sets.

In middle schools teachers are abused, even beaten by their students. There is a wave of youth delinquency. The newspapers do more than hint at it. Even though they use the acceptable formula. 'A very very small number of youths . . . corrupted by bourgeois liberalization . . . ' Many young people, possibly a few million, are jobless because they do not want to leave the big cities. They stay idle, with their families to feed and house them. 'I am now having to feed my grandson, he is twenty-four,' says an old cadre to me. I meet some of these future delinquents in one of Shanghai's narrow *lilong*, or lanes. Outside a Taoist temple where I listened to ancient music, some twenty of them stand, or saunter. Languid, arrogant, ready to pick a quarrel, smoking, playing cards, squatting on their heels in the middle of the lane and moving for no one. They are dangerous because they act in packs. Older people are frightened of them.

Special re-education camps for delinquents are set up. I visit a model one in Shanghai. It is well run, it even has classes in violin and piano. It tries to reinsert into society those who leave. Two other camps, in Kansu and Sichuan, are not so well equipped, the dormitories are small and crowded. In Kansu one camp operates a factory making buses. 'Our buses are sold all over China,' says the director, proudly. There is a workshop, turning out precision instruments, and the workers are young murderers. The average age of the camp population is eighteen to twenty-four. Ten per cent are girls, mostly here for pilfering, or prostitution. There are stories told me of parental neglect, but further investigation reveals a more disquieting pattern.

After the Cultural Revolution, a number of ex-Red Guards jailed for brutality, assault, robbing arsenals, were released from prison or labour camps. Thrown back into society, they find it difficult to adapt. They form gangs. They have made friendships in prison, in camps, and now they have their own networks, a brotherhood, secret societies, all over China. They recruit younger boys, teach them to steal. They have their own passwords, secret code language, and they prosper on the black market which the liberation of control has allowed. And they run prostitution rings in the big cities.

The movement against 'bourgeois liberalization' limps along. A few arrests take place. One of the three men who wrote the famous Li Yi Zhe poster of 1964, and who was released in 1978, is rearrested for 'attacking Marxism and preaching bourgeois humanism'.

Humanism. A debate on humanism has begun in 1981, and it will go on for a while. A famous editor writes that humanism is absolutely essential for socialism. On the occasion of the centenary celebration of Marx's death, Zhou Yang, now fiercely pro-democracy, speaks up for humanism. He also mentions alienation, a topic of discussion. Alienation exists, he says, in society at large, and among the young. This does not please the fierce keepers of orthodoxy, who contend that there is no alienation in socialism. Zhou Yang argues that a writer, a journalist, may write erroneously, but this should not automatically make him a counter-revolutionary.

Hu Yaobang, who has called for a free forum of discussion for the intelligentsia some months ago, is now compelled to hedge his remarks. It is clear that he has been pressured to do so. He asks the newspapers to stop writing only critical articles on what goes wrong. Eighty per cent of newspaper articles should be on achievements, on what is well done.

Deng Xiaoping must reassure the orthodox, curb the anarchic few. He is irritated by the discourse of the intellectuals. There are so many things he has to do . . . and it is all the more important to him to create a climate of amiable agreement, not of controversy, because in 1981 talks for reunification with Hongkong have begun. Deng Xiaoping is elaborating his thesis of *One Country, Two Systems*, which means that Hongkong will remain capitalist and co-exist with socialist China. This formula, he says, will also apply to Taiwan. For it is already noticeable in 1981 that Taiwan, despite its material success, foresees the day when it will reunite with the Motherland. In Deng's mind, therefore, the intellectuals should shut up . . . stability must come first, not the stirring of uncontrolled ideas . . . 'First must come food for our billion people, stability in the countryside. Stability before anything else.'

The disbanding of the communes started in 1980. A new system, the contract system, replaces it. At the same time, Deng Xiaoping introduces the separation of powers between

Party and government authorities in rural areas. No longer will Party cadres meddle in production, tell the peasant what crops he should plant.

The contract system works as follows: land is leased to the farmer for 15 years (later extended to 30 years). The farmer is allowed to hire labour, to sell and buy his own produce, and save for a fixed quota of grain (or cotton, or oil) to be supplied to the state, he can do what he likes. By 1983, 95 per cent of the contracts are between local authorities and individual peasant households, and 5 per cent with collectives, or villages. Only a very few communes refuse to disband. They prosper, they continue to prosper right up until today – 1991.

By 1985, farmers are allowed to subcontract their land to other households. This is because some farmers have found other gainful occupations, and do not till their own land. The rise of the individual farm-entrepreneur, the *Geti*, now begins. Geti is a term later applied to anyone who operates a business on an individual, private basis. Very swiftly there are Geti tailoring shops, repair shops, shoemakers, hairdressers, dry goods shops, restaurants . . . A considerable private sector, which thrives swiftly. There are major articles, crowing triumph, about the Geti, how much they earn, how this proves the policies correct. One enterprising Geti farmer and his wife are invited to France. He receives a medal. The Geti bask in official approval. And of course it is true and yet not quite true. For there is resentment. The Geti's life is not always easy. Egalitarianism runs very strong in China. It is now called 'the red-eye disease' meaning envy, jealousy. The Geti is deluged with demands. Demands for money. He suffers these exactions from local Party cadres, but also from his neighbours, inhabitants of the same village. He has to 'share', to show himself generous, to give presents on any and every occasion, to reconstruct the schools . . . otherwise he finds his fruit trees cut, his fields ravaged . . .

Yet the new system undoubtedly has its outstanding successes. 'It has revitalized the countryside,' says Prime

Minister Zhao Zeyang to me. He derides the communes 'where every member wanted not to work a minute more than anyone else. In the morning the members walked in step, careful not to walk too fast, not to get to the fields before anyone else . . . ' The contract system has also monetarized rural China, something which has not happened in other Third World countries. The peasant income triples, quadruples, with freedom to sell produce, although one third of the increase is due to a rise in state purchase price of grain and oil. The state continues to subsidize grain and oil, selling it to the city population at a rate far below what the peasant receives.

Party cadres in rural areas are enjoined not to meddle with production. Their role is to give 'guidance', in health, in education and welfare . . . but Party cadres are also astute peasants. They want a share of the money. The peasants with increased income build new houses, many of them two-storeyed. They buy furniture, TV sets . . . millions of houses will be built in the next decade. Party cadres, who have connections, begin to monopolize such enterprises as transport and building materials . . .

The next step is the development of agro-industrial enterprises called Village-township enterprises (VTE). New towns grow up, centre of several villages, or erstwhile communes. Free markets and fairs are held there, and shops mushroom.

The VTE operate small factories and workshops, to process the many consumer goods required. Their equipment is by no means modern, but very soon they will compete with state enterprises for raw material such as cotton, coal, silk, and even steel. With bewildering rapidity these changes are taking place. Somehow, the intellectual debates in the cities – which are also part of this great change – seem a little unreal, compared to what is happening in rural China.

Change brings problems. By 1985 there is definite polarization between the successful and the not-successful in each agglomeration, as there is growing inequality between prospering areas near the coast, and the hinterland, which does not benefit from any foreign investment.

Zhao Zeyang tells me that one third of the labour force in rural areas is redundant. 'The communes concealed the problem. Basic sustenance was provided for all, productivity was low, everyone was cared for. But it destroyed all initiative, it kept peasants tied to their fields.' Now, the peasant from individual households starts going to the cities during the slack seasons, hires himself out to work there, to make more money. And thus begins a massive peasant exodus, which in 1988–89 reached around 40 million. Extra, redundant labour from the villages to the cities. For the cities need them. The cities are changing, building, building, skyscrapers and hotels and habitations for their millions. They need carpenters and bricklayers and masons and painters. Early in the morning one sees them walk into town, these long files of peasants, men and women. They walk with that supple unhurried walk of theirs, which covers 20, 30 miles a day. They carry their bedding, clothes wrapped in cloth, sometimes a kettle or a wok . . . they are healthy, and they work hard.

Not everyone is enthused by the dissolution of the communes. 'The individual farm in China will prove far too small, no mechanization of agriculture will be possible with the individual households. They are making money now, but it is a step backward . . . many millions will now leave the soil to rush to the cities, as happened in Europe, during the Industrial Revolution . . . '

There is validity to these criticisms. Throughout the countryside lie great piles of rusting farm machines. The communes had started mechanization, now the individual peasant dismantles the machines, sells the pieces for scrap. It is true that, in China's most productive, but also most populous provinces, Central and South, individual farms are extremely small. In the slack seasons, the man of the house goes away, goes to the city to hire himself, for odd labour jobs, leaving his wife to care for the fields.

Village schools, and the universal primary education which was the main aim of the Chinese Communist Party (and which did work well for two decades), is a casualty of the new system. Schools do not have teachers. And in those which still function the number of female children shows a remarkable decline.

'Educating girls is a waste of time and money.' Girl-children, both in India and in China, are considered an expense, since they marry into other families. With the return of the individual farm, old customs, feudal traditions, return with a vengeance. Patriarchal authority is supreme again. Women are only there to serve the men, the family. Marriages once again are arranged by parents, and this provokes conflict, for some of the young do not accept this imposition, they commit suicide rather than be married against their will.

There is a return of bride barter, selling girls to be married . . . One memorable case is that of a university graduate, engaged on a study in the villages, who was kidnapped, gagged, forcibly married to a peasant. It took three months before she was discovered, and freed.

There is a return of female infanticide. Female infanticide existed in Old China, as it exists also in India. The communist Party, when it came to power in 1949, put a stop to the practice. But now it is again fairly frequent, in rural areas, and that is because of the new one-child family rule enforced by the government.

A major casualty of land privatization, of the contract system, is family planning. How can it operate when the peasant is on his own, and wants sons, many sons, cheap labour from his own male offspring? Should the peasant be successful and diversify his activities, he will want all the more a number of sons to work for him.

I hold long talks with Prime Minister Zhao Zeyang on family planning. For the greatest threat to China's longterm plans for prosperity, for modernization, for raising the living standard, is demography, the ever threatening population

85

increase, which despite attempted controls, still runs ahead of all planning. Since 1980 the one-child family has been proclaimed as the duty of every citizen. Fines are to be paid if there is more than one child, and in the cities, the second child will not benefit from free schooling, or medical care.

The one-child policy is enforceable in the cities, among the intelligentsia, the office employees and the factory workers. But 75 per cent of the population live in rural areas, and are very difficult to control, especially since the return of individual farm households. The Party cadres are told not to interfere in production, and so they do not interfere . . . in anything at all. It is their way of exacting revenge for their diminished power. There is a great dearth of doctors or nurses to carry out family planning education and implementation in the villages. In Sichuan province, middle-aged women, retired primary school teachers and nurses, and also midwives, are recruited to educate and persuade the women. Some villages institute reports on pregnancies, a 'quota' on the number of children allowed to be born. But the peasant finds ways of beating the quota. He simply sends his wife away to an area where she has relatives. There she gives birth, and leaves the baby. Later the child will be brought back as a 'nephew' . . .

'You know it is going to be difficult,' I say to Premier Zhao. I have had arguments with an American expert, who affirmed that the scheme of the one-child family would work. He had been all of three weeks in China. I disagreed, but experts take disagreement with almost the same fury as Party doctrinal pundits . . . Zhao agrees that it is going to be very difficult. 'But if we say one child, the likelihood is two. If we say two, it will be three . . . even with strict measures we shall reach 1.3 billion by 1995. We hope to stabilize round that figure but the likelihood of 1.5 billion by the year 2000 must be envisaged.'

Fifty per cent of China's population is under thirty-eight years old in 1982. In another census, 60 per cent are found under thirty-five by 1990, with round 300 million youths under eighteen. The sheer number, pressure, weight of so many young people, all needing education, feeding and clothing and jobs later, all now hallucinated by visions of the West, of a good life, which is still not within reach for them, is mind-boggling.

Therefore the reforms, which do go in the sense of greater freedom, and are staggering in their boldness, must be accompanied by a wide movement of education in responsibility, in thrift, hard work, self-sacrifice. Far more difficult to accomplish this than anything else. 'We must teach civic responsibility, patriotism, self-restraint,' says Zhao Zeyang. The Party is resurrecting from the past the soldier Lei Feng, a hero dating from before the Cultural Revolution. Lei Feng was incomparably virtuous, helpful, thrifty, and all he wanted to do was to help his fellowmen and obey the Party. 'We want to inculcate the spirit of Lei Feng among our young people,' says Zhao. I am dubious. I do not think the young will be attracted by this role model. For them, Lei Feng was a dumb guy, a stupid fellow who did not enjoy life, did not try to make *money*, was 'too obedient'. I venture to tell Zhao that a better model might be the Great Monkey, who thought of himself as equal to Heaven, but in the end served his master, the Buddhist monk who went to India to bring back to China the Buddhist scriptures.

All of us, in our childhood, have read the tale of the Great Monkey, and his deeds. But I am not sure the Fourth Generation, the young today, have read the Western Pilgrimage. They appear cut off from their own cultural sources, rejecting them in favour of this new invasion from the West, models from a fascinating otherness.

'So long as the countryside is stable, China will be all right, we do not fear problems and troubles in the cities,' say some economists to me. They know the seething within the millions of youths in the cities. They know that turbulence can start. But it is, in the end, the villages, the rural areas, which are important. This may have been true in the early 1980s, but China is rapidly getting urbanized, and I am not sure this will always be so.

I visit some successful Geti. One of them has acquired a piece of rocky wasteland in Sichuan. There is a small stream nearby, and he builds fishponds, and rears chickens. Chicken manure is good for fish, and fish bones ground in meal is excellent for chickens. He makes 12–15,000 yuan a year, a fortune. He employs the children of poor peasant families in the nearby village. Two of these families own a patch of land, but have five to six children each. He will build a school, a hospital . . . Another Geti runs a fleet of trucks, employing his two brothers, two brothers-in-law, and four sons. He has a monopoly on transport in the area, the villagers depend on him to get their produce to market. An enterprising man . . . who also happens to be the ex-Party secretary. 'To get rich is praiseworthy,' he says unctuously, quoting secretary-general of the Party Hu Yaobang.

It is true the countryside is prospering, even in hitherto poor areas. Despite the return of feudal customs, the influx of charlatans and magicians, the loss of schooling, the downgrading of women . . . perhaps, if prosperity continues, there will be once again what the Chinese call 'readjustment'. This return of the past is not peculiar to China. In 1991, one sees it happen, in the USSR, in Eastern Europe . . .

'We shall now have to institute taxation,' says an economist to me. If the notion of Law is weak and vague, the notion of tax-paying is totally non-existent, and of course there will be obstruction, resistance. Collecting taxes proves a difficult and dangerous career. In some areas taxmen are ambushed and murdered.

Deng Xiaoping presses on, presses on . . .

I return to the city and am rather wroth, for the university young do not seem interested in learning what impact the reforms have in rural areas. Perhaps they will, once they get out of those cloistered hives which are university campuses.

They look outward for role models, they look towards the glittering television stars, they envy rock singers. Their notion of worth is money. 'Worth is how much money one makes,' say the students. They resemble in this estimate of worth many young people in the West. When they talk of their parents they say: 'What have my parents earned after all their sacrifices?' They feel that their parents have been, like Lei Feng, 'too obedient'.

Six

In mid-1983 another campaign begins. Against spiritual pollution. Once again Deng Xiaoping makes a speech directed against corruption within the Party, but he also blames 'bad influences' which must be resisted. This gives the opportunity to those hankering for renewed importance, for a return of Cultural Revolution days. The campaign starts with methods akin to what took place during the Cultural Revolution. Meetings are called, writers and artists are harangued on their duty to eradicate 'spiritual pollution', whatever the term may mean. Xia Yen and Ba Jin are obliquely criticized. Xia Yen because he has not opposed 'mist-wrapped poetry', Ba Jin because he is against official meddling in literature.

But times have changed. The writers, the artists, are singularly non-cooperative. It is impossible to find anyone to denounce a colleague now. The writers fall ill, or have pressing engagements out of town, or relatives afflicted with woes needing their urgent presence; or sit in stony passivity, at the end of the harangue leave, wrapped in total silence.

The campaign officials try another Cultural Revolution recipe. For a brief four to six weeks officials start cutting off the long hair of the girls, refusing entrance into organizations to prettily dressed women, or to those who wear lipstick. Policemen walk up and down in watchful twos in the dance-halls which have mushroomed everywhere, to make sure that there is no illicit activity . . . The campaign peters out. It is so obviously unpopular that the officials give up. However, there is still one theme they can pursue. Criticism concentrates against those intellectuals who have carried out an open, major discussion on the theme of Alienation.

At a dinner party that autumn, given by the Writers Association, I am asked what I think of alienation. I had not followed the discussion, being busy, with my friend Feng Yidai, trying to set up prizes for efficient translators. I felt translators should be encouraged in excellence, and since they are badly paid, monetary rewards would be welcome.

'What do *you* think of alienation?' asks one of the writers.

Everyone seems to wait for an answer. What can I say? 'Alienation is a well recognized medical, psychological condition . . . it is often found, especially among frustrated adolescents . . . '

Someone clears his throat. 'Han Suyin is foremost a doctor, a *medical* doctor,' says my friend Junjian.

When we are alone he explains. Certain editors and writers of eminence have been discussing alienation, and insist that it exists in a socialist system. Now wrath has descended upon them. There is no alienation in a socialist system. 'But of course there is,' I protest. Junjian sighs. 'Zhou Yang, also others, are being criticized for their views on alienation.' The strange thing is that the woman writer Ding Ling, who has been to France, and received a medal, is a strong supporter of those who condemn spiritual pollution. She is against Zhou Yang and those who maintain that there is alienation among the young in China. 'How odd of Ding Ling . . . I think I'll call on Zhou Yang.'

Zhou Yang is happy. He has asked a photographer to be there, and he and I are photographed together. I think it strange that a man once reckoned a Stalinist should now stick his neck out to defend a 'bourgeois' notion. We chat. Of the weather, his health, my health, the campaign to promote politeness and civility which is going on, not a word on alienation.

I also call on Ding Ling. I have no quarrel with her, and she has an admirable husband, who deliberately chose exile with her, through love, for almost a quarter of a century.

Perhaps Ding Ling is against alienation because she has never forgiven Zhou Yang with whom she quarrelled, way back in 1955–56. She earnestly assures me that we must not fall for the lures of the West. In a way she expresses the disquiet we all feel at the increasing corruption, the deliquescence among the power-holders . . . But I fail to see how youth alienation, which is so obvious, should not be openly discussed.

I lecture on the computer revolution. I have done this since 1980, and it always interests the university students. I have brought with me Alvin Toffler's books, and I hand them out. *Third Wave* is pounced upon. It proves extremely popular. Each student is given twenty-four hours, no more, to read the book.

And now I get into trouble, because of *Third Wave*.

A covert political attack is launched against me. An article in the *Worker's Daily*, without mentioning names, accuses those 'who disseminate such books as the *Third Wave*' of promoting 'capitalist ideology and spiritual pollution . . . '

'Pay no attention, no attention,' says my friend Feng Yidai.

'Ignore it,' says Junjian.

I decide, however, to pay a little attention, which means that I do a quiet investigation. I find out who is behind the article. It is an eminent, well-known scientist . . .

Suddenly, all is well. Premier Zhao Zeyang has read the book, and stated that every person in China should read it. The book is translated and circulates in all universities.

Two years later, in the course of a renewed campaign against spiritual pollution, an article appears in *Red Flag*, the official Party newspaper. It takes the shape of an interview with a European left-wing personality, who declares with great indignation that *Third Wave* is an evil book, which should not be allowed to circulate. 'It is sheer poison' states this European communist . . .

'Pay no attention, pay no attention.' The consoling chorus of my friends. 'Premier Zhao endorsed the book,' I say, wondering what is happening. 'Some people have different opinions,' says Feng Yidai.

Fate is kind to me. I receive a letter from a benevolent American lady, who belongs to one of those ultra-generous American foundations, and is keen on helping Chinese students come to America. She sends me a letter she has received asking the foundation to sponsor a certain student. This student turns out to be the child of the aforesaid eminent scientist who thinks *Third Wave* is 'spiritual pollution'. I therefore take great pleasure in recommending his child, saying I know the family is a scientist's family. Then I write a pleasant letter to the scientist, saying that I am happy he does not fear his daughter's political rectitude will be endangered in Toffler country, America.

Another small battle is waged, on behalf of science fiction. Science fiction is attacked as spiritual pollution, damaging to the soul. I write an open letter of protest and receive a courteous reply. It is not science fiction itself, but writing about ghosts, encouraging superstition, belief in non-existent, supernatural phenomena.

My critics, I think, should go to the countryside of China and meet the magicians and wizards who invoke spirits to cure the peasants, now that the doctors have all gone . . . Science fiction continues to limp, although a few writers become successful at it, and I preserve links with them. Meanwhile, Batman and Superman make their appearance on television screens, and delight a new generation of Chinese children . . .

The students of teachers' colleges specialize in questions which are lethal traps for the lecturer. They come from diverse social levels, among them many workers' children. They seem more well read than university students.

'How would you mentally handle a situation where you are told to believe precisely the opposite of what you were previously asked to believe?'

'What do you think has fuelled the success of the four small tigers, Hongkong, South Korea, Taiwan, Singapore?'

'How do you explain that we are still so poor?'

'Do you think one's standpoint also influences what one calls *facts*?'

'Why is Chinese TV not like western TV?'

'Do you think it is right for government or Party leaders to tell lies?'

'What is truth?'

I detect a hunger for an infallible and perfect faith to live by. A hunger also for cult figures, heroes to revere. This is something alien to me. I do not feel haunted by a need for absolute truth, neither am I tormented by belief in any heroic figure. Even Zhou Enlai, for whom I have a very deep, enduring love, was not a man I endowed with every perfection. But these youths lust for belief, for perfection . . .

I find a dismaying ignorance of history. Not only of western history, but also of Chinese history. This again is not their fault. They were simply not taught history. 'How can history affect me? I do not need to know the past,' says a student who is the class 'joker'. There is always one, who tries to make the others laugh at the lecturer.

I tell them of Barbara Tuchman, the American historian, who in an essay 'When Does History Happen?' (*New York Times*, 8 March 1967) quoted the Cambridge University Professor Carr as saying: 'The belief in a hard core of historical facts, existing independently of the interpretation of the historian . . . is a preposterous fallacy.' 'I declare myself a firm believer in historical facts existing independently of the historian,' said Barbara Tuchman, and I agree. I tell them my own writing has been fuelled in great part by historical episodes, by 'facts' lived, endured, witnessed . . . 'The marriage of my father, Chinese, and my mother, a European, was due to historical facts,' I say, and everyone laughs. 'You too are products of history . . . whether you know it or not, like it or not . . . for my part, I prefer

94

to situate myself knowledgeably, and that means learning history.'

Literature is a fascinating medley. The students ask about Balzac and Bellow, Charlotte Brontë and Doris Lessing and Judith Kranz. Most students are astonished that so little poetry is written in the West. In the cities of Shanghai and Beijing youth theatres play Shakespeare, Arthur Miller, and Molière. Shakespeare (*Romeo and Juliet*) will also be played in Lhassa, in Tibetan, by the students of a newly opened university there.

Knowledge comes to this generation of young Chinese in disorderly heaps, although they still get old-fashioned courses in Dickens, and Jack London. Perhaps it is a good thing, though it is distorting, that they do not distinguish between the decades, and for them Hemingway is brand new.

Because of this passion for all things from the West, Chinese opera suffers. The young prefer TV, prefer western films. I meet the son and the daughter of the great Mei Lan Fang, the Beijing opera's most famous female impersonator. Many of the young do not know of him. But they will queue for hours for tickets to see *Rambo*. This generation does not know the old guerilla songs, but they love jazz and rock, and the songs from Taiwan and Hongkong. Discos are opening in all the cities. Discos are not only for young people, the middle-aged also love them, they say it is good exercise for the body.

'Tell us about America,' the students ask me. America is great spires of crystal reaching for the sky, gorgeous, well-fed people, who hop in and out of cars, of bed, never get grimy, have nice houses, draw guns, shoot people they don't like, and walk out in the sunset their arms round a gorgeous female . . .

New societies crop up, dedicated to painting, sculpture, and poetry . . . and the result is that China's new painters and sculptors will, within a short time, produce work of considerable merit and beauty.

'Tell us about Freud . . . do you believe in Freud's theories?

Can you explain Freud to me?' Freud is fabulously popular, and there are youth clubs to discuss him.

'I believe in Sartre . . . I believe in existentialism. I think this is the only reasonable attitude for a human being.'

Time and again, I discuss Sartre. I acquire a little reflected glory when I admit that I met Sartre, and also Simone de Beauvoir, in Paris. They talk of Sartre with awe, with fervour . . . ask me whether I can get them a signed photo of Sartre . . . There are also the film stars. In those years (1983–84) it was Alain Delon. 'Alain Delon, Delon,' sighs in swooning tones a girl student wearing the latest fashion in leather skirt. 'Have you had the good luck to meet him?' I have to confess that I had no such good luck, and she loses interest. Before The Great Change, started by Deng Xiaoping, the students wanted to become Marie Curie, or Einstein. But now it is the film stars, from Taiwan, from Hongkong, from France and the USA: and a little later it will be Madonna and Michael Jackson and Johnny Halliday.

I cannot refuse to become involved. Not only in the problems of education, but in other projects and problems. I continue to follow the efforts against desertification, against the continuing mud avalanches due to deforestation. This brings me to the subject of the projected high dam on the Yangtse River, called the Three Gorges project. My concern about this project will bring me to a meeting with the Party secretary-general, Hu Yaobang.

The Three Gorges project is controversial. 'It's *not* a good idea,' says Rewi Alley, who is an engineer and has followed the plans drawn up. 'In fact, it is a bloody bad idea.' Somehow, and because it concerns my province of Sichuan, I am approached by several people, and asked – asked rather intensely – to see whether this project can be reassessed. The proposed dam will be 185 metres high, the highest in the world. It will be the largest in the world. It will destroy one of China's most beautiful landscapes, the Yangtse gorges. But above all, it may bring about ecological catastrophe, and place China in debt for at least two decades.

'Those who want it do not know that river. They will not be able to control it. All the claims made about controlling floods below the dam are spurious . . . only 30 per cent of the flood waters, perhaps . . . and as for what will happen above the dam, especially to Sichuan province, the granary of China, it is frightening even to think of the potential for disaster which will be created.'

'Sichuan has major rivers, tributaries of the Yangtse River, all rushing down from the uplands of Tibet. We could build ten small dams instead of that huge one, right in the middle of the Yangtse River . . . '

'If anything happens, a hundred million people will be affected.'

'Just to build the dam, ten million people will have to be displaced . . . '

These are the arguments against the dam. There are, of course, people for the dam. I shall also meet them.

Way back in the 1950s Zhou Enlai had studied the Big Dam project, sent teams to investigate, finally turned it down, and instead launched the building of a dam lower down the river, the Gezouba, which today functions well.

'We have already had the misfortune of building a dam on the Yellow River,' says an engineer bitterly. 'The Russian engineers helped us . . . but they didn't take into account the huge amount of silt the Yellow River carried . . . within six years of its completion the dam was silted up, and Zhou Enlai went to see what could be done. "Perhaps we'll have to blow it up," he said, grimly, surveying the area, for the dam had cost a great deal. Fortunately this was avoided, but the dam never fulfilled expectations. Now we build smaller dams on the upper reaches of the Yellow River, at much less cost, and they are doing well . . . '

'You better tell *them* it's a bad idea,' says Rewi.

'Why me?'

Rewi grins. 'For the time being, at least, some of your suggestions seem to get through . . . for the time being.'

So I investigate, pore over material, consult engineers, read . . . I find that people against the dam dare not speak . . . 'There's a lot of pressure . . . from some of the higher-ups . . . Someone wants to go down in history as a great dam-builder . . . ' 'But who am I to talk? No one will listen to me . . . ' This is what so many say. I go to Sichuan, go down the river, investigate. I see the city which will have to be drowned when the dam is built. All the electric power generated by the dam will go to the coastal cities. Thus the gap between the neglected inland provinces and the coastal provinces will become even bigger . . . the future cost in disequilibrium, social unrest, not to mention strategic problems, will be immense. I therefore begin to write a memorandum, to write letters to 'the leaders', discussing the dam, and one of those I write to is the Party secretary-general Hu Yaobang.

Within the next two months, on my next trip to China, I meet Hu Yaobang.

There is another twist to my meeting the secretary-general. I had been attacked by certain Sinologists, who, disregarding Chinese realities, disregarding scrupulous scholarship, had made against me what can only be called *procès d'intention* ascribing to me all sorts of motives which I never had.

In a fine flurry of delicious, self-serving indignation, a certain member of the French PEN club had written to his counterpart in China, to say that I should not become a member of the projected Chinese branch of PEN. His counterpart was, of course, my friend Junjian. Junjian was indignant. 'How dare this Frenchman tell us what to do? And what do they know of what you did to help . . . they do not know the facts . . . ' 'They like to work themselves up, condemn someone like me because I do not care for them,' I tell Junjian. But Junjian is not happy until other friends also take up the matter, and suddenly I receive a very nice letter from Hu Yaobang himself: 'We all know the fine contributions you made, and how you tried to help during the Cultural Revolution' is the gist of it.

Shameful to say, one Chinese intellectual sought to damage me by warning publishers in China not to translate my books. But this attempt came to nothing. He was the same man who had, once upon a time, accused his colleague Su of being a homosexual . . . 'Ignore him, it's not worth thinking about,' Junjian says.

Hu Yaobang comes up to me to shake me by the hand, and really he looks like a sparrow, alert, small-boned, so entirely himself, immune to pomp or protocol. There is an innocent forthrightness about him. He talks swiftly, says what he thinks, and sometimes does not think before he utters. We have an hour of informal, happy converse. 'I have not only come to thank you for your letter, but also to speak about the Three Gorges dam,' I say, and hand him my letter against the dam. 'I know nothing about the dam,' says Hu. But he promises to read the letter. We discuss literature. Hu is for wider discussion, airing different viewpoints, but he is also 'against slavish, colonial mentality, entirely turned to the West, ignorant of China's realities . . . '

He agrees there are problems with the young generation. 'The Fourth Generation . . . but I have confidence in them, they will learn.' They have no anchoring references, no comparative knowledge, and the flux of change is confusingly swift. 'The reforms even confuse many of us,' says Hu.

There is another problem that we discuss. Scientists feel their knowledge is not being used adequately. 'Now that more trained scientific personnel will return from abroad, they will be discontented if they find themselves suffocated with all sorts of silly rules, unable to deploy the skills they have acquired, and if the equipment, the laboratories, are hopelessly antiquated. There is too much bureaucracy, too many rules. We should not be afraid of being criticized for our defects . . . we must reassure writers, not call them counter-revolutionary the moment they write something we don't like . . . '

Thus says Hu Yaobang.

In the evening physicists from the Academy of Sciences come to dinner with me. Among them is an eminent man with whom I had discussed the problems of fundamental research during the Cultural Revolution. It was Zhou Enlai who had asked me to see him then, and I see him again. He bemoans the fact that because of the Cultural Revolution many scientific institutions lack younger scientists . . . there will be a problem when the professors in natural sciences retire in a few years' time. There is a gap in continuity. But he, and the others, are full of praise for Hu Yaobang. They tell stories about him, and these stories make up a man's personality. When Hu Yaobang was in charge of the Academy of Sciences, he insisted that researchers should have leisure time, time on their own, without being harassed to produce results. 'The Academy of Sciences is not a production unit . . . it does not grow cabbage, or plant potatoes,' said he. A brilliant scientist was to be demoted because he invariably reached his office late, and he was divorcing his wife. 'That man does more in an hour than some of you do in a lifetime,' Hu had stormed at his detractors. 'He needs quiet, he needs time to think . . . and he needs a happy family life.'

But Hu Yaobang's spontaneity, his alacrity in immediate response, is a problem in a country where every word uttered by 'the leaders' is diktat, sacrosanct, compels implementation. One day, Hu Yaobang announces that he thinks chopsticks unhygienic, because they are made of wood, not metal, whereas forks and knives can be sterilized. At the next banquet I attend at a Chinese embassy abroad, there are forks and knives on the table, fortunately also new chopsticks, hygienically wrapped up in tissue paper. Mine host raised his fork, but soon gave up. Within a week we were all back to our unhealthy chopsticks.

The major issue the scientists discuss is the big Three Gorges dam. Many, such as Zhou Peiyuan, the president of the Academy of Sciences, have qualms about the project. By winter, a number of articles appear against the Big Dam. The issue is now widely debated. Although the minister in charge of hydro-electric power invites me to lunch and tries to convince me, I am not convinced. The debate grows, and by 1986 the National People's Congress also starts to discuss the project. Major projects such as this should not be decided by just a few people at the top, boldly declare some members of the NPC. 'We do not want to go the way of Africa, of Latin America,' I say, and I am not alone in saying this (I hope). Overseas Chinese, scholars, engineers, join the debate on the dam. They write letters against the project. A movement against the dam begins among Canadian ecologists, for the dam is to be built by a big Canadian company, and the feasibility study is done by the very company which is to build the dam. China has its own dam experts, they feel that they have not been consulted . . .

The dam project is finally shelved for five years, although I am told work quietly continues on it. By 1990, there are more discussions about the dam. In May 1991 I meet two provincial governors. One of them, the governor of Hubei province, is very much for the dam. He tells me that it is not true that 10 million people will have to be moved. Only less than a million. He tells me that the dam will produce an immense lake, and its waters will be syphoned by a canal, to provide water for arid North China. He says that of course inland provinces will get the electricity from the dam. One of the major points of dispute is the fact that electric power from the dam will all go east, and although the dam is built in Sichuan province, Sichuan will get none of the electricity from the dam . . . But each province has its own interests at heart. I meet the vice-governor of Sichuan province, and learn that what the governor of Hubei has told me is not quite correct. Sichuan will *not* get electricity from the dam. The people of Sichuan are opposed to the project. They would prefer ten small dams, whose aggregated cost will be less than the big one. It is also not correct that less than a million people will have to be moved. 'This is true for Hubei province, but what about Sichuan? We shall have to move many more people.'

Sardonically, an acquaintance says that the dam is a syndrome. 'It is part of our national inferiority-superiority complex. Like all people who have been humiliated in the past, there is a tendency to show off, to want the spectacular. The dam has been written up as the world's largest, highest, should it be built. And some of the leaders don't seem able to think any further. We are still slapping our cheeks to make them swell, to prove how fat we are. We should learn humility.'

Haste, impatience, an urge to want immediate successes . . . therein lies the greatest danger to the enterprise of economic reform. The temptation to make a show appears irresistible to some of the 'leaders', and they ignore corrective protests. 'Everything is decided by a small clutch of people . . . not necessarily well educated. And too often those who do know do not dare to object, to oppose.'

Seven

I OCTOBER 1984, the 35th anniversary day of the People's Republic. It is a bright sunny day, the air balmy. Atop the meridian gate of the Forbidden City, facing Tiananmen Square, the leaders stand. Deng Xiaoping, flanked by Hu Yaobang and Zhao Zeyang. There are the Long Marchers, that tough hardy group of survivors, The First Generation. Television crews from many countries sweep the stands with their lenses, sweeping us into taped memory. Four plaster busts lead the two-hour long procession filing past: Mao Dzedong, Liu Shaoqi, Zhu De, Zhou Enlai . . . all enmity erased by death, the busts all the same size. 'Look, missiles,' says a military attaché from a western country, standing next to me. The missiles roll by, followed by carnival floats – factories, and skyscrapers, and sports and Chinese opera – and workers and peasants and national minorities, all fifty-six of them. Then come the religions, Buddhist monks in red or saffron, Taoist priests in black, Islamic imams white-capped, and Christians of several denominations. A large contingent of intellectuals draws laughter, for they are the only marchers who do not keep in step with each other. University students in serried rows carry banners: XIAOPING WISH YOU WELL. The use of his personal name denotes affection. That night firecrackers explode a myriad blossoms of light, laser beams dance athwart the sky. Half a million people congregate. To the sound of music they dance on Tiananmen Square.

Hu Yaobang has invited 3,000 Japanese as guests of the Chinese government. Many are young, for it is to promote youth contacts that they are here. However, a joke circulates among the people. Some of the 'young Japanese' are in their sixties. 'Ah, but now everyone is young, up to the day he or she dies in his chair of office' the joke continues. It is a dig at the high cadres, who despite all attempts at 'rejuvenation' cling to their positions.

The show costs 35 million yuan. Some say it is expensive, but it is indeed an occasion for rejoicing. Four days before 1 October, a text of 33 pages was signed between the British and Chinese governments, ratifying the reunification of Hongkong by 1997. The document states that Hongkong will remain capitalist for fifty years. One Country Two Systems. Deng Xiaoping says it will take certainly half a century for China to catch up, meanwhile Hongkong *must* remain capitalist. 'It is good for all of us.' There is another reason for content. Since 1981 committees have been formed to promote trade and person-to-person relations with people in Taiwan. Anyone with relatives in Taiwan is sought out, asked to contact 'brothers across the straits'. Despite a few truculent noises from the island, everyone knows that this coming together is inevitable. The economic reforms in China are proving that the myth of the division of the world in two irreconcilable blocs is a myth. China must evolve her own system, whatever name it goes by, accommodating the opposites, proving that contraries work together. One Country Two Systems will also apply to Taiwan.

The harvests of 1984 are amazing. 407 million tons of grain, the largest amount ever reaped in China's history. There are 43,000 free agricultural markets, 25 million Geti specialized households, 13.8 per cent of all rural households.

I meet students from an English language class, and ask them whether they have been to the countryside. Some seem to consider the question incongruous. They ask me the size of a farm in the USA? When I tell them how large the farms are they sigh. 'Then why are ours so small?' I have to explain history, tell them that China's population is five times that of the USA, that we have 800 million peasants (almost), that

China is only at the beginning of the first industrial revolution, even if the second, the computer revolution, is already upon her.

A programme for the scientific education of peasants is set up, but the experts I meet tell me that the agricultural colleges implementing the scheme must themselves find the money to teach improved methods of agriculture to the peasantry. Why so little money for projects of paramount importance, when big sums go into far less vital plans? Only 5 per cent of the total budget goes to education, and I feel there is something wrong with the education ministry. In this year 1984 transformation of industry begins. Premier Zhao and his economists say that market forces must operate. But, retorts aged economist Chen Yun, market forces must integrate with socialist central planning. Otherwise there will be problems, disarray, uncontrollable inflation, scarcity in basic items, profiteering on a large scale . . . The debate goes on and on . . . it will continue until now. The idea of Deng Xiaoping is to make every industrial 'unit', plant, factory, responsible for its own profit and loss. The responsibility for production must be in the hands of a manager, not of the Party, which must refrain from interfering in production. Competition must be introduced. 'But this is going to be an extremely complicated task, with more obstacles and difficulties than any other,' warns Deng Xiaoping. No one really knows the way in which this industrial restructuring should be handled. And there is no trained competent managerial personnel. Nor are there market surveys. All this must be learnt. 'We can but try,' says obstinate Little Bottle.

By year's end, Deng's attempts to extirpate some of the First Generation from their power-holding positions are more or less successful, since quite a few tender their resignations.

A new batch of officials come into power in the ministry of Culture, and in the Writers Association. Wang Meng, a rightist, rehabilitated after twenty years, is the new culture minister. 'I don't really want the job,' he tells me at dinner. 'I want to write. Now I have no time.' The Fourth Congress of the Writers Association convenes at the end of December 1984. Some of the entrenched older members do not like what is happening. A small flood of energetic young writers push their way in. There is free election of officials, and the congress is remarkable in the number of ex-'rightists' who are candidates to official posts. Aggrieved older writers hold a meeting of their own, and again agitate the spectre of 'bourgeois liberalization'. However, they fail to sway the congress. At a meeting of the Central Committee, Hu Yaobang has fought hard for freedom of writing, and for democratic elections of officials in charge of culture and the arts. 'This is the first time that unconditional support for the freedom of creative writing was publicly proclaimed,' notes investigative newsman Liu Bingyan.

The meetings of the congress are stormy. Conflict arises between the writers, and in the end, the young, and the 'rightists', win by an overwhelming margin. Many of the older writers are 'first class' writers, and they feel very angry. They have top salaries, houses, transport and travel conveniences. But now their books, articles, essays, may no longer be printed. They know that the younger writers will squeeze them out from magazines, and that publishers will now perhaps refuse their books. The younger writers who accede to official positions go on delegations abroad, to the United States, France, England. They are interviewed, some are translated.

My friend Junjian craves no official position, and his heart is at peace. He writes, writes, and does not worry about being published or not. 'The issue is not only that of literary freedom. It is that now a new lot of people have come into power. And despite all the talk of freedom, they are behaving exactly like the ones they have replaced.' He is amused by the high-handedness of the young reformists. 'They have also caught the virus of officialdom. Some of them are as bureaucratic as their elders.' Junjian who counts as 'old', is now set aside. He is refused the amenity of a car to take him to the airport, although it is his due, and he is going to catch a plane to England where he has to attend a symposium. 'It is like musical chairs,' says he, laughing that splendid laugh of his which has sustained him through the decades. 'Everyone gets a turn.'

Publishing houses are setting up as private, individual companies. A good many of them make far more money reprinting lurid, pornographic material from Taiwan and from Hongkong, or bad translations of foreign books, than in printing the novels of Chinese writers in China. It is no longer 'literature for the sake of the revolution', or 'literature for the peasants and the workers', not even 'literature for the sake of literature'. It is now all a matter of making money. 'To get rich is praiseworthy.' What is wrong with making as much money as possible? 'You call it trash. But what if the people like this kind of trash?' says one publisher when he refuses to publish a book by Junjian, a good book, which will soon be translated in English and do well in England. 'Your book is too old-fashioned . . . young people do not want to read this kind of thing any more.'

Not only the virus of officialdom is about. Venereal diseases, syphilis, gonorrhoea, which had disappeared for two decades, are back.

Prostitution now exists in all the large cities of the coast open to the outside. It thrives with the tourists, the big companies, the traders and the entrepreneurs of all kinds who swamp the hotels and dance halls, and have money to fling around. It is seeping into the inland towns as well. In Beijing and Shanghai, one meets beautiful young girls, in expensive clothes. They sip orange juice, giggle a lot, they are never alone, they come in twos or threes, adopt nonchalant attitudes, and often the pimps with them are smart young men, who claim to come 'from Hongkong' and speak a few words of English. English is essential to approach the foreigners. One meets the girls, going up in the lifts.

Doctor Ma Haide, whose American name is George Hatem (for he was an American before he joined the Chinese revolution, and adopted a Chinese name) worked for years, in the Fifties, eliminating syphilis and gonorrhoea. He will get the Lasker prize for his success. 'Some of our young doctors have never seen a primary chancre. For two decades we did not have more than a few cases a year, and chiefly in out of the way places. But now we see cases every week.' What does he feel, he who has devoted his life to eradicate VD, seeing it return? He smiles gently. 'I can only say: we did our best.'

A nationwide sweep takes place against crime, against prostitution. A few privileged sons of high cadres are arrested, and one of them is shot. 'At last, at last, the government is not swatting flies, but tackling the tigers,' say the people. The sweep is popular. In Changsha the inhabitants of a city district actively help to round up the criminals. 'We knew them by sight . . . they terrorized us.' Forty thousand attend public executions, and clap and clap. An American with me is indignant. He is against the death sentence for crime, any crime. But a Chinese young man with us, one who was a Red Guard, but has worked his way out of his past, and devotes himself to his job as a teacher of mathematics, is surprised. 'If there is no justice, how can one distinguish good people from bad people?' 'He is quoting traditional wisdom,' I tell the American.

The editor of a popular magazine calls on me. She wants an article on the young women of China today. What do I think of the way they dress, their attitude to life? I do not propose to write such an article, which will infuriate too many Chinese mothers. 'I'll write you an article on Aids.' The editor is surprised. 'Aids? But there is no Aids in China . . . ' 'But you'll soon be having it here too.' 'But there are no homosexuals in China,' she replies, a little indignant. I do not tell the well-meaning lady that of course there are homosexuals in China, 'A very very small number' to use the phraseology of officialdom. They are discreet, for here, as in Hongkong, homosexuality is punishable. 'I think your public should be informed about Aids.' The article is printed, and soon after the jubilant editor calls. 'Two months after your article appeared a case of Aids was found,' says she. 'It was a foreigner.' But a month later a Chinese is found dying of Aids. 'He got it abroad, he went abroad,' says the lady, defensively.

'With prostitution, and also free love, which does exist, I think you'll find Aids spreading in China . . . and soon you will find there is also a drug problem,' I reply. I am grieved to sound Cassandra-ish, but the evidence is already there.

In 1989 I meet a physician engaged in the nationwide search for Aids cases. There are a number in Yunnan province, 'a few hundred'. The figures are published. 'The largest number is among drug addicts . . . they use the same syringes,' says the physician.

The government announces measures. Any foreigner staying over a year in China will have to submit to a test for Aids. Notwithstanding the test, a young foreigner dies of Aids in 1990, after having infected five Chinese women. The government will announce the death penalty for bringing in drugs, a measure which Malaysia and Singapore have already put into effect for some years.

'We have to revise all our sterilization methods . . . the danger is a spread to rural areas, where sterilization of equipment is very inadequate . . . '

The son of Deng Xiaoping, Deng Bufang, was pushed through a window during the Cultural Revolution, and his spine was broken. He remains a quadriplegic. He has started the first ever organization, nationwide, to help the handicapped in China.

Deng Bufang invites me to a meeting with his associates. One of them is married to a woman who is almost totally paralyzed. It is a very moving occasion, and since I have my own small group of handicapped, some eight of them, whom I try to help, we exchange views.

I was introduced to this group by Feng Yidai, whose niece is crippled with rheumatoid arthritis. The group is headed by Sun, a splendid woman, who seems to be dying of progressive muscular atrophy. The group wants to be self-sufficient, refuses charity. They have coined a slogan: 'We are as good as anyone else.' They want not pity, but to be considered as worthy as any normal person. Until now, handicapped are not allowed to go to university, because they do not fulfil the requirements: Sound mind, sound body, sound morality . . .

Deng Bufang will do an admirable job, but he is caught in a grand-scale organization, and though I sympathize, I feel there is little I can do to help him. He will collect a good deal of money and a magnificent hospital-cum-rehabilitation unit will be built.

My small group, under Sun, go out on the streets on tree-planting day to plant trees. Sun has started a newspaper, and it is read by around 4,000 handicapped people throughout the country. Sun organizes picnics, outings. 'We are just as good as anyone else,' she repeats. Is not teaching self-help, self-respect, initiative, better than creating new clingers, barnacles on the ship of Bounty? But of course an organization is also essential, for there are very few women or men with the spirit of Sun.

Through a cousin of mine I become acquainted with Deng Xiaoping's daughter Deng Lin, who is a painter. My cousin is her secretary, and we all go to lunch together. I view some of Deng Lin's works. She is a good, forceful painter, with a strong brush, not languidly pretty, and I like her work. Her face is paralyzed on the right side. 'When I was a baby my parents could not take me with them when they left the guerilla base . . . some poor peasants cared for me . . . but there was no medicine, nothing . . . ' This is the laconic way she describes being left behind when the Long March began, way back in 1934. Mao Dzedong, too, left two of his children behind. And my Fourth Sister, who was also in the guerilla war, lost three of her children. She never found again the peasants she had left them with. In

1984, with everything going so well, with China seemingly on the verge of achievement, prosperity, success, brutally memories of the past return. 'You should tell this story to all the young people of today,' I say to my Fourth Sister.

I do not join the group that play bridge with Deng Xiaoping, but my friend, Katherine Wei, an American-Chinese, does so. Katherine Wei and her husband not only run a large shipping company, Falcon, doing business with China, but they are bridge champions on the international circuit. Katherine plays bridge with Deng whenever she is in Beijing. She tells me the Deng rule. The loser must crawl under the table. 'He crawls too, if he has lost . . . he has a wonderful wry humour . . . ' says Katherine. But not everyone likes Deng Xiaoping, because he is not suave enough. When he hears a remark he disagrees with he is prone to bark out: 'Stuff and nonsense.' Though not vindictive, he is extremely stubborn . . . or so say those who have tried to persuade him and met rebuff.

One of the men hostile to Deng Xiaoping, whom I shall call Hung, tells me that he is making an in-depth study of Little Bottle and his career. It is whispered about Hung that he is not a favourite because he made a flippant remark. 'We can now criticize Mao, Zhou Enlai, everyone . . . every event during the Chinese revolution can be reappraised, discussed, except the purge of the intellectuals in 1957, when so many were condemned as "rightists". Everyone knows that Deng Xiaoping conducted that purge.' Hung draws my attention to Deng's cleverness. 'One day his letters should be published, though this will not happen very soon. They are masterpieces of promises unkept.'

Hung gives me several examples of Deng writing fulsome letters of contrition, and then doing precisely the opposite of what he swore never to do again. 'Surely you cannot expect a man of considerable intelligence, a shrewd politician, to be frank when he manoeuvres for survival?' I think back to Zhou Enlai, who had to do so many things, say so many things, against his own convictions. Hung shrugs.

'If you oversharpen the knife blade, the edge will blunt . . . ' he says. In that early 1985, Deng's popularity seems assured. He is also lauded abroad. But there is a flaw. Deng Xiaoping, or at least those around him, seem dizzy with their own success. The sycophants gather, and the opportunists. Would-be-historians praise him by distorting all the facts of history. 'For centuries China was closed, until Deng Xiaoping came and opened wide the doors', writes one rather ignoble would-be scholar. Articles derogatory to Mao, to Zhou, are written, to prove that Deng was right, was always right . . . and this is a very bad sign. It means that less than ever will 'the top leadership' listen to a contrary opinion.

By 1985 I had decided to set up a small Fund for science scholars to go abroad. Only people who had worked for several years, and had achieved results, would be funded. I insisted that each one be interviewed personally, to judge of his or her proficiency. Too often students and scholars went abroad with insufficient knowledge of the language.

The Fund began to operate a year later. There were both English and Chinese trustees. The English trustees were Graham C. Greene, director of the Great Britain-China Centre in London, and Geoffrey Oldham, director of the Science Policy Research Unit at Sussex University. The Chinese trustees were the President of the Friendship Association, Wang Bingnan, the president of the Social Science Academy, Huan Xiang, and a director in one of the State Council's think-tanks, Wu Mingyu. The Fund has now become a small institution on its own, well regarded, and totally independent of any political change.

I also encouraged an adult education college in Tianjin, a city extremely well run by its able mayor. Retired professors got together to operate adult education classes, and this college was to be recognized on a national level. It has graduated more than 8,000 men and women, who have followed courses without leaving their jobs.

Feng Yidai and I also instituted the Rainbow Prize for translators, and Vincent and I set up a prize to be given to scholars specializing in Indian studies. This prize is run by the internationally well-known scholar of Sanskrit, Professor Zhi Xianlin.

All these projects, which do well, made me more aware of the problems and difficulties encountered by educators and scientists, they also show their courage, dedication, and knowledge. It was, it continues to be, for me a priceless experience. 'We shall not cease from striving to educate until the day of our death,' a seventy-four-year-old professor told me. He had been a student in 1935, when Japan invaded North China. Together with other students, he walked out of the university in Tianjin, carrying books, microscopes, equipment, and walked 4,000 miles inland, to reach my province of Sichuan. There, during the Second World War, while Japan conquered more and more of China, the universities went on teaching. And when in 1945 victory was won, he, and so many others, returned to Tianjin, and elected to stay and to serve the country, even though they were not communist, even when the communists triumphantly drove out Chiang Kaishek and assumed power in 1949.

'We want the young today to have the same spirit. There is in front of them another kind of war, a war to conquer difficulties, to build up their country. It is another Long March,' say these men and women. Many are my contemporaries, but some are younger, the Third Generation. However, they too have this fervour. And because of them, because they give their lives, every second of their lives, to China, to the Chinese people, I am grateful to be with them, and perhaps to strive, as they do, until the day I die.

Eight

1984 WAS A YEAR of grace and apparent success, but 1985 was to show the contradictions, the conflicting situations, the growing discontent and profound malaise which accompanied the reforms. It was in 1985 that the first nationwide explosion of students on university campuses took place.

The trigger factor was the shocking Hainan car scandal, which broke out in that summer. It was the biggest case of economic corruption in the history of China since 1949. All the culprits were Party officials.

Hainan, that large and largely undeveloped island hugging South China's Guangdong province, had been listed as another special economic zone, open to joint ventures with foreign corporations. Already Club Méditerranée, searching for unspoilt beaches, had planned a holiday camp there, apparently for nudists. It failed to get permission. But something far more deleterious occurred when Hainan Party officials used bank loans earmarked for 'development of industry and technology' to purchase 300,000 Toyota cars, 2.5 million colour TV sets, 250,000 video recorders, 130,000 motorcycles (Honda and Yamaha), and sold these imported goods at high prices within China itself. Twenty-seven out of twenty-nine Chinese provinces bought these goods, to resell in turn at a profit.

On 18 September, the students of Peking University held a demonstration against this 'new invasion' of China by Japanese goods. 'What could not be achieved by Japanese military conquest is now achieved by trade' proclaimed their posters.

114

And of course, they were right to protest against this misuse of funds. Twenty billion dollars of credit were earmarked for 'development in technology'. Was this development? Was this technology?

18 September was the day fifty years ago when Japan invaded China. A memorable date.

'We are patriotic. We are against corruption.' Writer Yameng, aged thirty, comes to see me. He has published a book revealing smuggling rings in the areas bordering Vietnam. 'We love our country,' he says.

The sudden explosion on the campuses is not only due to the Hainan scandal, later known as the Toyota affair. It is also the result of accumulated grievances, which were not obvious until now. The most unpopular factor is inflation. Inflation has come to China, where for thirty years prices had remained fixed. The people are not accustomed to inflation. Their salaries are low, they can make ends meet if costs do not increase. But now, due to cuts in food subsidies, and the price rise of consumer goods due to a liberated market, their purchasing power is diminished. This hits many of the urban families, and above all the intelligentsia, the scholars and the professors and the scientists.

There have also been cuts in education allowances. It will now cost a good deal to send a son or daughter to university, whereas in what some people wistfully recall as 'the good old days' education was practically free. On the university campuses, due to lack of money, and slack administration, the dormitories are dirty and overcrowded. Canteen food for students has deteriorated. Yet the cost of meals goes up.

'There is a big problem with the people in charge of caring for cleaning, for allotment of apartments to professors, for plumbing . . . ' says my cousin, who has in vain requested another apartment for himself.

Why is this? The administration of several universities, including Peking University, cannot cope with the increase in prices of what is needed to run the University, just as the hospitals can no longer cope with the increase in prices of Petri dishes, glassware, sheets, coal, food.

The students are told how much better off they are than their fathers or their grandfathers. They are lectured and told to *tinghua*, which means 'listen and obey'. They resent this peremptoriness. There is no system of adequate consultation, despite the students union, which is run by Party bureaucrats. Everything is decided 'above our heads', say the students. 'We want to be consulted, to share in decision-making. Not always to be told that what is decided is best for us.' The weekly political courses are for them a farce, the vocabulary corresponds in no way to the living reality. Material success has not solved the faith crisis, not provided inspiration, quite the contrary, since the living conditions of intellectuals, the parents of many of these students, have eroded. The intelligentsia has suffered more than any other sector of society. 'It's no use studying . . . there is no money in it,' say the young, who contemplate a life in academic posts as a long-term sentence to poverty. Their parents are also losing hope. 'We are getting poorer, not richer.' Their dwindling resources are also a great loss of face. 'I am still earning what I earned twenty years ago, but a school dropout, who opens a bicycle repair shop, earns now twice, three times, what I earn as a professor for thirty years.'

The entrepreneurs, youthful, but some not so young, fill the best restaurants. They boast, at times, of their years in jail and labour camps. 'We learnt a lot there. How to smuggle . . . how to get by. We learnt how to get free passes on the railways for our goods and for ourselves.' The university student from an average family cannot afford to take his girl-friend to an expensive restaurant. Perhaps a discotheque, no more. He sees ex-delinquents drive new cars, their arms round pretty girls with rosebud mouths, dressed in the latest fashions copied from Paris. These carpet-baggers have an unlimited trove of imported cameras, video-cassettes, Marlboro cigarettes, and Lancôme, Chanel and L'Oreal cosmetics.

1985 is also the year in which reforms in industry are being attempted. 'Eating out of the big communal pot must stop.' This means that no longer will there be the cushioning of industrial factories, with the state providing for everything, from birth to death, irrespective of whether the factory works or not, earns or not. Industrial units must become responsible for their own profit and loss. The old system of funding by the state will be abolished. Managers will now run enterprises, develop initiative, the Party must not interfere. Initiative and competition must be introduced . . . All this is happening all at once. An avalanche of change.

Student demonstrations take place not only in Beijing but in other cities as well. In December, to commemorate the rising of the students against the Japanese on 9 December, 1935, a few hundred youths make their way to Tiananmen Square. They deposit a wreath at the foot of the Monument for Heroes. A few students are detained but released within the next few days. Four of them are expelled from the University. Officials of the municipal Beijing government and the National People's Congress go to the University to talk with the students. 'You may come into the campus, but not your Japanese car,' the students manning the gates tell them.

A government-backed company has established a needed taxi service. The cars are Japanese. The Chinese car industry is floundering. Production has almost stopped of the antiquated Red Flag limousine. No one wants Chinese cars in China, certainly not the high Party cadres. A fever for all things foreign possesses the Chinese consumer, and the example is set by the young sons and daughters of high cadres, known as the 'crown princes'. Cameras, TV sets, refrigerators, dishwashers, air-conditioners, cigarettes, cosmetics. And beer. Chinese beer is excellent, but it is a question of status, of face. To serve 'foreign' beer indicates superiority, and 'connections'.

Corruption in high places is a permanent topic of talk. Everyone has his or her own story, apocryphal or not. It is true that now meat and fish, prawns and poultry are expensive, many families cannot afford them, but there are special shops for top Party cadres, charging especially low prices. About one third to one tenth of what the man in the street pays.

'How could this batch of officials in Hainan swing such a deal in the name of developing technology?' we ask. My husband Vincent is sharply critical. China had the use of 20 billion US dollars in foreign credits to import technology to renovate her industry. 'Buying cars and TV sets is *not* importing technology,' we both tell angry officials. Some of these billions have disappeared in the pockets of Party high cadres.

The policy of decentralization has made it possible for each province, each region, to handle its own foreign exchange, to make its own contracts. Even small counties can do so now. Bloomingdales of New York has a contract for handcrafted furniture with a county. The hardworking county people are getting rich, but this is money well earned, a straightforward contract. Many of the contracts which are made with joint ventures have no legal infrastructure, no system of supervision, to determine exactly how the bank loans are being used or misused.

'Do you really have to import all this stuff when you should be using the money to remodel your out-of-date industrial plants, build new industrial plants, purchase new machinery?' my husband asks. 'Do you realize that within four years you will have to spend the same amount of money for spare parts for your Toyotas as for buying new ones?' Vincent is unsparing in his forthright criticism. Every unit, every organization, wants a piece of the cake. Everyone wants to buy computers, though few know how to use them. Never mind. This is 'modernization', and a computer can be resold at a profit. It is the same with some imported machinery, which lies around for months, rusting away, unused. 'Everyone behaves now as if money will keep flowing in, endlessly. In this way, you will be following the same pattern as Africa, as Latin America . . . you will not be able to carry out industrial reform.' This is my husband. And far from being unwelcome, he and I find that we are voicing what many people think, but do not say.

The grain harvest that year declines. From 407 million tons in 1984 it drops to 378 million tons in 1985. It is not the weather. It is the peasant.

Nothing begets alarm more than a poor harvest in a land always dangerously close to famine. A provincial governor tells me that an American has today a potential reserve of grain equivalent to a ton per person, but a Chinese only has 50 kilograms.

Why has the grain harvest fallen? Because the peasant is astute. He is also hit by inflation, though less than a city dweller. He realizes that growing grain is not going to make him wealthy, for he gets very little money out of it. The government subsidy does not cover the price increase of other goods. And chemical fertilizers, pesticides, have gone up in price as well. 'Growing wheat and rice is earning holes in your pants,' says the peasant. Therefore he turns to cash crops. He hires himself out for most of the year in the cities, where a vast amount of building goes on. Blocks and blocks of apartment houses, luxury hotels, tall semi-skyscrapers . . . hence the grain harvest falls, and China has to buy wheat abroad.

The student demonstrations of 1985 are the outward expression of the contradictions, the upheaval which economic reforms have incepted. Or rather, the way in which they are carried out. No one is against reform, but a continuing debate goes on within the Party, the government, on the way reforms are handled. At the beginning of 1986 the debate grows fiercer. Hu Yaobang, the Party secretary-general, is taken to task for too much laissez-faire in political matters. He has opened his mouth without due caution (but then Hu is like that, he talks without restraint). In December 1984 he has said: 'We cannot expect the writings of Marx and Lenin . . . to provide solutions to our current problems.' There is a correction the following day. The last sentence should have been – 'to provide solutions for *all* our current problems.' Somehow the crucial word *all* was lost on the way to the newspapers. The Party journal *Red Flag* in its no 3 issue of 1985 seeks to redress the situation. 'We must study Marxism in close connection with realities . . . make a clear distinction between what is applicable and what is not . . . ' But the intellectual debate in all institutions, philosophy departments, in the academies, continues with renewed vigour.

In early 1986, the old economist Chen Yun manifests his disagreement with the way the reforms are conducted. He belongs to the First Generation. He is not a Mao follower, for he resisted Mao's great leap, advised private plots for the peasantry. He is perturbed by the waste, the profligacy, the ill-conceived, short-sighted plans which threaten to ruin China's balance of payments, plunge China into debt. He has no real power, having retired in 1984, but he has been appointed head of the committee in charge of Party discipline. And he has done his job well. His integrity is undoubted, his words are heard. Chen Yun issues a statement. It criticizes both Hu Yaobang and Zhao Zeyang. Due to lack of vigilance, both have allowed Party cadres to do business, and the high cadres and especially their sons and daughters, the 'crown princes', are involved in money trafficking, in setting up bogus companies in Hongkong . . . and also in the Hainan scandal. One of the sons of the prime minister Zhao Zeyang is allegedly involved in the Hainan affair.

Behind closed doors the issue is debated. It is of first rate importance, for it is also a struggle involving the conduct of the highest in the land. A directive is issued. No offspring of any high Party official will engage in business deals. The death penalty will be meted out in cases of massive corruption. 'Some tiger cubs will now lose their pelts' predict my social scientist acquaintances. At last some 'crown princes' are being stopped from their limitless profiteering . . . But will this directive be enough to stop the ever-growing deliquescence, corruption? Even Deng Bufang, the crippled son of Deng Xiaoping, is allegedly involved in a major company making money in Hongkong. It seems he did not personally dabble in business, but his name, and that of the Handicapped Organization he has set up, have certainly been used by some of his associates.

A golf course is erected near Beijing, for the solace of foreign businessmen, diplomats, and the Japanese. The latter find it cheaper to fly from Tokyo to play golf in Beijing than to pay the enormous fees of Japanese golf courses. A golf course does not seem an important affair. But it has taken land, land fit for cultivation. Arable land is scarce in China. India has twice as much arable land per inhabitant as China. A golf course needs water. Much water. And North China is arid. Beijing suffers from an ominous scarcity of water. The capital now contains 9 million people, and the underground water level has fallen precipitously. The reservoirs built in the Fifties are badly silted. The rivers run dry part of the year. 'We shall probably buy water from Japan to keep the golf lawns green for the businessmen,' says George Hatem, alias Ma Haide, grinning at me to take the sting out of his words.

In the universities the toilets drip, drip continuously, twenty-four hours a day. Not one of the students seems to notice. Nor do the university administration send a plumber round. The students leave the wash basin taps wide open. Precious water runs, runs out. I have sometimes closed the taps for them, for I am hyper-sensitive to the sound of running water, dripping water . . . 'I would refuse a diploma to any student unless he can fix a washer, repair a toilet,' I tell an amiable university professor. 'How delightful, what a great sense of humour you have,' he replies. He thinks it is a joke.

And then a campaign for saving water begins in Beijing.

'We must all be conscious of the necessity of saving water' the newspapers pontificate. I tell my students, in a lecture, that in New York, one summer, we were all enjoined to place a brick in the water tank of the toilets, to save water. They think this is odd. 'Why should a rich country want to save water?' they ask.

I become acquainted with the new rudeness syndrome. It is high fashion for the young to wear a permanent scowl upon their faces, to answer monosyllabically, to ignore older people or brush them off with 'Meyou' which means, 'No such goods' even if the goods are on the showcases. Surliness is de rigueur for them. Waitresses in restaurants, hotel staff in hotels, comb their hair, inspect their faces, totally ignoring the requests of clients. In the bank where I try to cash money the girls are so busy trying on new sweaters that they pay no heed to the herd behind the counters. I buy a pair of Chinese slippers in a big store, they are flung at me across the showcases which stand between clients and shopgirls. Most of the clients meekly catch the footwear on the wing, but I fling mine back. Once again, it is the foreigner in me. The shopgirl, round-eyed, disappears behind a curtain to report. A glowering man emerges, and I smile sweetly at him. 'I thought we were playing a ball game . . . the young miss threw the shoes at me, so I threw them back.'

The next time I go, I am agreeably surprised to note that there is no more shoe-flinging.

Campaigns to teach 'spiritual civilization' take place. It means teaching courtesy, integrity . . . enterprising provinces even launch smile campaigns. In Kansu province, I discover a store tucked away in a side street where a prize has been given to the best smiler, an attractive girl, whose picture is displayed.

The manager of a hotel in Chengdu asks me to talk to the staff. 'They are young, inexperienced (he means untrained). Many tourists are coming now, we must be spiritually prepared to receive them . . .'

With the late Premier Zhou Enlai, 1974. He was already ill with cancer.

Madame Deng Yingchao, widow of Zhou Enlai, 1987.

Deng Xiaoping, October 1977.

With Prime Minister Li Peng and his wife, 1991.

Lecturing at a Teachers' university, 1984.

Talking with students after the lecture.

My good friend, the great writer Xie Bingsin, at the age of ninety, 1991.

The grand old man of Chinese literature, Ba Jin.

Huang Yungyu, the eminent painter, when he was 'in disgrace', 1977.

below left: The painter, Wu Tsojen, in 1982. *right:* Li Kejan in 1977: he gave the picture to me.

The huge stone Buddha at Leshan in Sichuan province.

At the foot of the Buddha.

Some of my small group of handicapped.

At Third Aunt's Buddhist funeral, with Vincent and my Sixth Brother.

With general secretary of the Party, Jiang Zeming, 1991.

The author, 1992, in front of a poem by Zhou Enlai.

He must have had a little problem with the rudeness syndrome among his staff.

But when the young staff – all of them graduated from middle school, many of them just assigned to their jobs in the hotel – assemble in a big hall, I find them eager to listen. This is something out of the ordinary. I feel that they want to be valorized. Perhaps they had other ambitions, which now are beyond reach for them. 'Your work is important. It is as important as the work of an ambassador' (titter, gasp). 'When people from all over the world come to your hotel, what they will remember of China, what they will tell their friends, is the way you smiled, how you tried to please them, your courtesy, the way you keep the rooms clean, and especially the bathrooms' (laughter, delighted). I give some object lessons. 'Do not stick your fingers in the rice bowl you bring to a guest' (big laughter). I offer to demonstrate how to get spots out of carpets, and there is uproarious hilarity.

The hotel will do well, for the manager continues to 'train' his staff by asking guests to give them a talk . . . it gives these young people a sense of belonging. They become proud of their jobs, of work well done.

Change, change . . . everything is changing, the web of social relationships, concepts, attitudes, behaviour, expectations . . . I travel much, covering as many provinces as possible. To Tsinghai, and up to the upper stream of the Yellow River, to watch reforestation, to watch the building of small and important dams. 'We shall change this Yellow River into a blue stream one day,' the wonderful engineers and workers there tell me. They are unknown, they will remain a lifetime here, but it restores my faith to meet such people. I travel many mountain roads, new roads, in a jeep. My drivers are army-trained, entirely reliable, and that is essential, for the mountain roads are sometimes dangerous. 'Just watch . . . if you see a few stones, or some sand, come pelting down, tell me quickly . . . the mountain might come down on us,' the driver tells me comfortably. And adds: 'This happened to one of my comrades about three weeks ago.' There is the constant peril of lorries, trucks, buses, hurtling away at far too great speeds on these winding roads. But a worse danger are the motor-cycle madmen. Groups of young men on Honda or Yamaha motorcycles, roaring past, swerving blindly round bends. On one such excursion we meet fourteen of them . . . and when we catch up with them the next day they have stopped by the roadside. Four of them went over, into the ravine. I go into the foothills, the heartland, exploring, meeting the national minorities. The Yis, who know they are heaven-born, are being persuaded to stop slash and burn agriculture. The Miao are doing well. I meet sturdy Miao women, loaded with silver jewellery, and who carry their husbands on their backs, or pull a cart in which the man sprawls. 'Men are so frail, they can't walk too much,' these women tell me. But the women also want TV sets, and some have them. And they dream of washing machines.

The country is astir, astir with *doing*. Vitality. I feel bathed in life, life abundant, unceasing activity, an ocean of people working, stoically, unendingly, and determined to get on, determined to live, and live better. Truly Deng Xiaoping has started something, the outcome of which none of us can predict. . .

In September 1986 I accept a long-standing invitation to lecture at Fudan University in Shanghai.

Vassar-educated, the president of Fudan University is a woman, Xie Xide. She is erudite, charming, with many friends in Europe and the United States.

'What shall I lecture about?' I ask. 'Anything . . . talk about science, the need for science, perhaps about literature too, your books . . . '

I go to Fudan that afternoon and there is a feeling, indescribable, of restiveness in the air. It is the way the students frown, watching my car. It is the way they walk, or congregate in threes or fours, and do not greet Xie Xide who is with me.

The lecture is not successful. The small hall is full, but there is palpable sullenness, blanking out all of us, Xie Xide, myself, and the professors who sit behind the green baize-covered table with me. There is even hostility in the last three rows, at the back of the room. There sit the new intake, the freshmen. They talk to each other, do not interrupt themselves to listen to Xie Xide's introductory words. Faced with this pre-empting rejection, there is nothing I can do. It affects me. The audience is not with me. The room's acoustics are poor, my words reverberate, hit back at me from the window-panes. The freshmen drum fingers, shuffle feet, and at the end rise in a big clatter of desks and throng out.

Any questions?

A student rises. 'Which is the better system, capitalism or communism?'

I have been asked this question once before, at the Chinese People's University in Beijing. I give the same reply. 'The question is not which is the better system, but what must China, a Third World country, do to develop her own system, adapted to Chinese conditions, to Chinese reality. I personally have no belief in *any* isms. All systems change, evolve. They *must* change, must evolve. Capitalism in the West has evolved, and certainly it is no longer the capitalism of the days of Marx. It is now hedged with legality, it has rules, laws, trade unions . . . Socialism is a new system, its concepts difficult to put into performance, especially when capital accumulation is needed in order to build up an industrial base . . . and in socialism capital accumulation is not easy, for socialism, by giving everyone security, does not stimulate initiative. Productivity in China is low . . . therefore it is necessary to accomplish certain reforms. However if capitalism now came to China, simply overthrowing everything in the present system, it would not be the seasoned western type capitalism with its guaranteed freedoms, its legal framework. It would be savage, ruthless exploitation of the many by the very few . . . I don't think you people could stand it. I think many of you would find life very difficult . . . '

After the lecture Xie Xide says: 'The acoustics were bad.' 'Not only the acoustics, the whole ambiance . . . what is happening?' She smiles a motherly smile. And we drop the subject.

That evening we have dinner with members of the NPC in Shanghai. They exult, because 'now we speak up, we dissent, we file negative votes.' The NPC at each level must assert itself, question, demand, react. 'We hope for more open discussion . . . Deng Xiaoping has called on us to emancipate the mind . . . we must do so . . . ' 'Hope is a path, a path that is kept a path by being continuously trod on,' says Xie Xide. She is very wise.

We talk of the young. Someone thinks the young are 'not at all as we were'. He quotes the Big Three. According to him, every university student wants to be in a Big City (Beijing, Shanghai, Tianjin, in that order. Anything else is way out and unacceptable). He wants a Big salary, and a Big job. 'There is a fourth Big,' he adds. 'An opportunity to marry a beautiful girl – not too bright, which threatens the male ego – and become a Big Shot through Big connections.' I think the man is a little unfair. But then he spent his whole life working for the revolution, working . . . and his wife is very ill, and they have two rooms, one of them partitioned by a curtain so that his son and daughter-in-law can have a bedroom. 'We must let the young work out their frustrations,' says Xie Xide. 'It is our fault if they are disgruntled.'

Five weeks later, in December 1986, the students at Fudan University, as well as in 150 universities and institutes across China, begin the largest street demonstrations yet seen, waving banners and posters, demanding Democracy.

Nine

THE STUDENT DEMOS of December 1986 began in the University of Hefei, capital city of the poor province of Anhui. With economic reforms, there was some improvement in the peasant's condition, but an exodus from the countryside, notably of women, took place. Thousands of girls hired themselves as maids in the large cities, where they earned far more than at home.

In the science and technology University of Hefei two scientists were outspoken in urging democracy. One of them was the astro-physicist Fang Lizhe, now well known in the United States where he lives, giving testimony to the US Congress when required. Fang was neither harassed nor persecuted when he talked and wrote. He went on trips abroad. He was, it seems, backed by like-minded reformists in the state council think-tanks. Four such think-tanks now existed, and Zhao Zeyang relied on their advice. Fang Lizhe deplored the passivity of Chinese intellectuals. 'Intellectuals are regarded as useful tools to carry out Party policies, and no more . . . something like necessary hair to tuft naked skin.' Intellectuals should participate in all decision-making. The role of the scholars was to initiate and lead social change, not to follow Party directives. 'Modern China cannot be built without us, the intellectuals. But we have no say in the shaping of policies.'

Apt sentiments, which elicited much sympathy and support. Especially since the living standard of the intelligentsia had so rapidly declined due to inflation and the cuts in subsidies for house rents, medical care, and education.

In that year, elections to Hefei University were scheduled. In 1980, the elected candidates had not been allowed to take their seats by the local Party pundits. Students and professors were prepared for another obstructive display. On 5 December, 3,000 students held a rally against the manipulation of electoral process. On 9 December, they were 10,000.

9 December was a significant date. Fifty-one years previously, on that day, the students of major universities in China had marched to protest against Japanese invasion of China. Now again they marched, not against Japan, but against illegal Party interference. The banners they displayed were forceful, even if emotional. 'Oh my people, my people, when will you really be the masters?' 'Ten thousand years are too long . . . seize the day, the hour'. (This, incidentally, is a quote from Mao Dzedong's poem.) 'The policy of treating the Chinese people as dumb beasts is the cause of China's backwardness'.

Between 9 and 20 December, 150 institutions of learning in 17 cities held marches and demonstrations. Thirty thousand students from Shanghai colleges and universities, including Fudan, proceeded to march through the narrow encumbered streets of Shanghai. They walked to the Shanghai Municipality Party office, a porticoed edifice, an ex-colonial British building of grey stone. They were joined by a crowd of 50,000 Shanghai denizens, who also had their grievances. Inflation, unsatisfactory living conditions. Shanghai was overcrowded, with its 12 million people in an area which had housed only 3 million. Rehousing had been impressive in Beijing, in other cities, but in Shanghai there simply was no space to build or to rebuild. 'We cannot even pull down a house because we have no space for temporarily housing the residents while the house is rebuilt,' said the Shanghai housing officer to me.

Shanghai was a major foreign exchange earner, about one third of China's export revenue came from it. Yet it could only keep 25 per cent of the money, having to give the rest for help to less fortunate provinces, among them Tibet, which received a billion yuan a year from 1980 to 1987. The special economic zones in the south were allowed to keep up to 80 per cent of the foreign exchange they earned – why not Shanghai? Hence popular discontent.

In Tianjin, demonstrations were minimal. This was due to the mayor, Li Ruihuan, an ex-carpenter, one of the most volubly understandable, most practically-minded persons it was my good fortune to meet. Li had rebuilt the city, promoted personal initiative. He invited the students to talk with him. 'What is it that bothers you?' They complained of cramped dormitories, of bad canteen food. 'We'll do something about the food immediately, but it will take a little time to build more dormitories. Now what is it that really bothers you?' Silence. 'I know, it is difficult for you. Believe me, it is also difficult for us. We have a vast land, an enormous population. And so many problems . . . but any time you have anything to say, just come to me.'

Li Ruihuan has been promoted, he is now a major figure at 'the centre'. But his new job is one of the most difficult of all. It is to renovate China's news media, the propaganda ministry . . . where the die-hards are ensconced.

Tianjin handled the aftermath of the student demonstrations very well. This was due to the president and professorial staff of Nankai University, one of China's best. Nankai has a great tradition of scholarship, of science. Its fame also rests on the fact that, when it was only a college, way back in 1913, it had among its students a shy adolescent, whose name was Zhou Enlai. When the security police came to Nankai to demand the ringleaders of the demonstrations, they were told: 'We have no counter-revolutionaries in Nankai University.'

As January's icy wind bit into exposed faces, and ground fine grit into eyes, tempers rose. The student posters became aggressive. DOWN WITH MARXISM-LENINISM-MAO THOUGHT . . . WHAT IS FREEDOM? ASK WEI JINGSHENG.

Once again, the demonstrations have a counter-productive effect. They bolster the diehard sector in the Party who frown upon the laxness of recent years. Deng Xiaoping and his picked men, Hu Yaobang and Zhao Zeyang, are confronted by those who see in the student movement an anti-Party, counter-revolutionary conspiracy. But the 'conspiracy' is due to the western media, to the films, to Voice of America. It is illogical to think in terms of a neat conspiracy. It is the wind, the wind, the wind of change . . .

Hu Yaobang becomes the target of anger; it is because of his forbearance, his speeches, his way of handling the student demonstrations with a minimum of punishment (only some expulsions from the universities), that, it is said, socialism is in danger.

The man who breathes sulphurous condemnation of Hu Yaobang is Wang Zheng, a veteran Long Marcher, important because of the army units he controls. He is a member of the military commission, and also the head of the Party school. There is something fanatical, Savonarola-esque about him. Wang Zheng stresses ideological purity and openly attacks Hu Yaobang.

Hu resigns on 16 January, after making the usual self-criticism. He is said to have committed mistakes 'on issues of political importance'.

Premier Zhao now takes over Hu's duties temporarily. It is astounding that no one to replace Hu can be found, but this is due to Deng Xiaoping. Although having to give way on the Hu case, Deng Xiaoping stubbornly resists any attempt to elevate one of Wang Zheng's key men (a man just as disliked as Wang, if not more) to the post of secretary-general of the Party. That would be a disaster. Zhao now has two jobs to cope with.

The economy is not doing well, showing signs of strain, of anarchy. There are (unreported) workers' strikes. The possibility of young workers – now educated, literate – joining with the students in a putsch cannot be ignored. There are also the 'floaters', the half-employed, workers of all kinds, on a temporary basis. They have existed, though ignored, for two decades. But with the influx from the villages, there may be some millions of them around now, all claiming to be 'workers'. Hu Yaobang resigns, but remains a member of the central committee and the politburo. He will attend very few sessions. He stays at home, reads a great deal, practises calligraphy.

It is the entire spectrum of reform, the impact of reform upon the ideological sphere, which is under reappraisal. Hu's departure does not solve the dilemma.

I was in the United States in February and March 1987. There I met Chinese scientists and students. The students sympathize totally with the demonstrators in China. They too are concerned with inflation, rising prices. They have a very odd view that, if the Chinese government changed, all problems would be immediately solved . . . by democracy. Which to them is a very nebulous concept of 'free to do as you like'.

I write a memorandum about the students. 'The time has come to be truly concerned . . . it is absolutely necessary to institute serious dialogue . . . essential to involve the young in matters of importance.'

I am not the only one to say so, to write it. Many others urge dialogue. Two months later, dialogue is announced in the newspapers. At least a thousand scholars urged dialogue, but not one of them is mentioned. How will dialogue be conducted? 'To talk to the young in rigid political terms is like preaching virginity to American youths in their twenties,' says my social science friend, who has listened in to a dialogue session. 'No longer can we, the older ones, refugee ourselves behind such phrases as "generation gap", or "there is no common language between us". The barricades, which some young people call The Great Wall, between the generations, must come down. Dialogue must be the prelude to constructing participation structures.' The word 'transparency', *toumin*, is heard. It means *glasnost*.

I believe that it is wrong to say that the young are materialistic, selfish, yet even Liu Binyan, a man whose record is one of dissidence, of exposing corruption, will say: 'This is the most selfish generation . . . I have known.'

Physicist Ge, on the contrary, thinks that the Third and Fourth Generations 'are genuinely concerned about issues. But they are not given a chance to express themselves.' The problem is that, when students demonstrate, the leaders are often flamboyant, but shallow, self-centred individuals, who for a brief while enjoy a *prima donna* role in what is both a show, but also, an inching of history forward. These leaders take over, and push to excess, demand the Party resign power, imagine themselves immediately as ruling the land . . . it is the feudal in them, that undying feudalism. 'We have a lot of little emperors,' says Ge.

Dialogue . . . were Zhou Enlai alive, he would be pacing the campuses, shaking hands, walking into the dormitories, queuing at the canteen . . . dropping in on research students in the laboratories and asking them to tell him what they were doing. He would joke with the girls, compliment them on their hair, their dresses. He would bring with him an aura of purpose, dedication, but also authority, not peremptory, but always there. He spent hours and days talking with the Red Guards, far more unruly than the students of today. It was phenomenal to watch him then . . . Why is it that, today, no one really talks *with* the students? Why do they only use the patriarchal mode of communication? 'You've got to listen . . . and obey.'

Astro-physicist Fang Lizhe, investigative journalist Liu Binyan, and others, are expelled from the Party. Eight other Party members are asked to withdraw voluntarily. One of the volunteers describes a Party official puffing up five flights of stairs to his apartment, to ask him to withdraw . . . He has now organized a party of his own. A wine connoisseur party.

A book, entitled *The Ugly Chinese*, written by Bo Yang, a Taiwanese author, is now criticized. Yet it has circulated freely for some time. It has been avidly read. 'What makes the Chinese so cruel and so base? An unbalanced personality, constantly wavering between two extremes. A chronic feeling of inferiority and an extreme arrogance. The result of a split personality . . . ' And so on.

'Do you feel this is a correct analysis?' a pompadour haired, high-heeled male student asks me. (High heels for men are fashionable this year.) I would like to speak a little of masochistic tendencies, but it will not be apt. 'If you really think you are a little like this portrait drawn by Mr Bo, then perhaps it's time to do a little self-changing.' The girls laugh. Most of the girl students do not like the book. They say it's half-baked Freudism. After the lecture the pompadour student drives his bicycle up to me and taps the pillion. 'Would you like to come for a ride with me?' 'Not today,' I reply, knowing he simply wants to get his own back. But Intelligent Principle is incensed. 'How dare he insult you?' 'He is only trying to prove he is very modern, very western.'

Another student stops me. Belligerent. 'No one over forty can really understand us young people.' Round us a small crowd listen. 'Perhaps it is true . . . but in my case, I shall try till I'm eighty.' Laughter. Releasing laughter. 'You've got to tease them, but make them feel you are not treating them as inferiors, but joking with them on equal terms,' I tell Intelligent Principle.

Equality between the generations. A very very difficult concept in Confucianist China.

I spend ten days in Lanzhou University lecturing on the English language and its history, a topic which allows many asides, which allows all kinds of questions. The students are a very good lot. They ask many relevant questions, they probe. About sex, and Aids, and are there any poor people at all in the West? They take notes. Most of the students here do not come from high Party cadre families. Here in Kansu province, life is not easy. 'We are sure we shall have a voice in the country's future,' say the students, 'but we would not like to wait too long . . . ' I assure them that we 'must walk the road of democracy. It is a long and difficult road, but we shall get there one day.' There is the usual joker, a tall, willowy boy. 'I'd much rather saunter along the river bank, under the trees, and write poetry, than attend lectures,' says he. 'This is an excellent idea, you should do this right away,' I reply, gravely. The students like repartee, jokes, smiles. They like *to be treated on equal terms*. I try my best. Later a professor apologizes for the student. 'He does not listen-and-obey.' But perhaps he will be a good poet.

More rumours, as spring slides into summer. That Wang Zheng and his protégés would like to launch a massive purge of the intellectuals . . . But Deng Xiaoping is adamant. There will be no purge. However, there are Parkinsonian tremors in the Writers Association. One writer I met in Manchuria (I liked his book, and I went to see him, as well as another interesting young author) is now in trouble. It is not clear why. But he seems to get out of trouble easily, he will merely correct some 'erroneous views' in his new book.

My friend Liu Xinwu, who brought me cloth tigers from the villages, is also in trouble. But it is trouble of another kind. Xinwu is editor of *People's Literature*, a monthly magazine. He has let slip into it a provocative story about the sexual and other habits of Tibetans. The Tibetan students at the National Minorities Institute are angry. This is Great Han chauvinism . . . Tibetans are extremely touchy people. A small demo of Tibetan students takes place, which has Party support. The author flies – or withdraws – to Hongkong. This ends the affair, except that Xinwu is suspended, because though he says he never read the story, he is chief editor, therefore responsible. I telephone and ask him to dinner, but he says he is unwell. However, later, we meet for a cup of tea. We do not talk of the story, nor of the Tibetans. It would make him very unhappy.

There is discontent in the hospitals, where physicians' salaries are appallingly low. An appendicectomy only costs 4 yuan, less than one US dollar, but in private practice doctors charge far more. Prime Minister Zhao opines that hospital staff should be allowed private practice 'in their spare time'. This is unfortunate. The result is that it is sometimes difficult to find an experienced surgeon or physician at the hospital. Private clinics open, advertise expertise in plastic surgery. Personable girls all want to become models. They want their noses, eyes, figures, improved, and pay up to 2,000 yuan for a new nose, which is the yearly salary of a clinical practitioner in a hospital.

A fashion show is held in Peking Hotel. Eminent women, representing the Federation of Women of China, sit in the front row, while on the platform the models walk in and out, turn, glide, pirouette. Among the viewers is Kang Keching, one of the twenty-seven women who survived the Long March. She was a stalwart and beautiful girl, a guerilla, carrying wounded soldiers on her back, shouldering the guns and knapsacks of those too weak when they crossed the high Snow Mountains on their way North. She belongs to those days of epic fervour and hope, and now sits here watching the girls show their slit to mid-thigh long dresses, their hip-clinging skirts. She turns to me with a little smile. 'Times have changed, haven't they? The young have happy lives now . . . ' I do not know what to say, and she seems to guess my discomfort. 'Perhaps it is a different kind of happiness . . . for we were happy too, very happy.'

The United Front committee asks me to come and discuss certain matters concerning education. The Front is made up of intellectuals belonging to the eight non-communist parties. These eight parties have endured through the years, though their function is not to contest, but to 'advise'. Now it is clear that with the reforms, there is a stir among them. And also because of student unrest. Of course no one will discuss the unrest. We discuss education. Glowing statistics

135

have been published. 800,000 primary schools, 90,000 secondary schools, 1,200 universities, 1,000 fully recognized adult education institutes . . . these are the figures for 1987. But the educators in the United Front feel concerned. There is a paucity of young professors, assistants, lecturers, scientists, researchers . . . part of it, of course, is the brain drain. Of the many thousands sent abroad (35,000 by 1987) only something like half return. Old professors cannot retire, they must continue to teach, there is no one to take their place. But of course, it is not only the loss to the outside world, it is, perhaps more, the loss due to what Mr Wu, the president of the UF, calls delicately 'inappropriate handling of education problems', which includes the very low salaries, the impossibility for many intellectuals to have enough space to relax, to study, in their cramped rooms.

We talk of this, and of dialogue, dialogue with the young . . . Everyone warmly commends the idea. No one comments on the content and manner of dialogue. Mr Wu asks my husband and myself what we think of news coverage in China. This is a major cue to speak frankly, and Vincent is trenchant. 'Cocoon mentality still overwhelming . . . ostrich stance . . . rearranging facts to try to please . . . ' The audience nods, nods happily . . . now they can quote him, for they have been thinking the same thing. Vincent's no-holds-barred style is a great gulp of oxygen. We both speak of 'rather futile rules and regulations and restrictions'. I end up by speaking of Martin Luther. Why Martin Luther? 'Because he broke the authoritarian rule of the Catholic Church . . . enlightenment can only come through breaking set ideas . . . ' Perhaps the analogy will displease a few, but this is an academic debate. We toast each other politely in *maotai* wine. 'A most useful discussion,' says President Wu. We end up with some casual remarks. 'The young should be trained in the habit of discussing democratically . . . merely to condemn bourgeois liberalization does not provide an answer . . . '

There will be further hardening on what is called 'the

soft front'. This is what Tsing, the daughter of my very good old friend, Heart of Ice, the author Bingsin, tells me when I go to see her mother, who is now all of eighty-seven and still lively, clear-minded, writing essays. But Tsing is angry. She has a great capacity for passionate wrath. She says there are attempts to bully 'the soft ones', which means the vulnerable teachers in the English Language institute. 'They are never able to get their act together . . . they are far too easily split, turned against each other,' says Tsing.

I call again on the prime minister *cum* secretary-general. Zhao invites me to meet him in a beautiful pavilion in the Middle and Southern Sea, Zhong Nanhai. Zhao looks fit and calm, although there are rumours, rumours of a big argument in the Party. We talk of education, of course. Obviously what we talked about at the United Front, and at other meetings, has been transmitted. Also our remarks about the news media. Zhao gives a hint and I pick it up. 'There is a widespread demand for more information and better information, both in China and abroad,' I say, putting the matter in courteous, diplomatic language. Zhao laughs. 'Yes, we learn about ourselves by listening to Voice of America,' says he. 'Our Ministry of Propaganda is not always in touch with what the people want to know.'

This, of course, shows that there is a deep rift between those who run 'culture', and especially 'propaganda', and the premier.

Rumours, rumours. Rumour of high level corruption. It is said that an American Foundation is trying to reach the think-tank experts which the prime minister has set up to advise him. Through helpful donations, these experts go on trips abroad, and their offspring are most welcome in top American universities. Is this true or false? The summer is an uneasy one . . .

Sam Noumoff, a political economist resident in Canada, and Geoffrey Oldham, the director of the Science Policy Research Unit of Sussex University, are my very good friends and with them I talk at length of my findings, as they do of theirs. Both of them go very frequently to China, and are received by top institutes. Both are as worried as I am at the way China's economy is heading. Statistics give a glowing report of increased peasant income. There certainly is great improvement in living standards for a good many peasants. However, much of the income (about 25 to 30 per cent) comes from other occupations. 'The Chinese peasant finds a way of making money not only through cash crops but by working as bricklayer, carpenter, mason, in the slack season'. Beijing has a population of a million 'floaters', there are now reckoned to be some 40 million in the whole country. Rural unemployment in some northern provinces is 25 per cent of the total labour force.

There is disquieting news that in some areas the peasant is no longer paid in cash for the grain he sells to the state, but in I.O.Us. This is because of cash flow problems. Liquidity problems. These I.O.Us the peasants call 'blank paper', because they are *not* redeemed within the time limit as they should be by the local banks. (The latter plead a scarcity of funds.) Neither can they be exchanged for goods, or deposited as worth expected money. There is also no way of getting the peasant mobilized to repair dykes or roads, as used to be done when each member of the commune was required to do 30 days' labour a year on public projects. The abandonment of grain planting by many of the peasants forces the government to import rice and wheat. In 1987, for the first time since 1980, when it was abolished, rationing is reintroduced. Flour, oil and meat will be rationed to keep the prices down. Inflation is soaring.

Public security is not as good as it used to be, say the people. On certain lines, train gangs rob passengers. A smuggling network exists along the fretted coastline of South China. A thousand innocent junks sail in with forbidden cargo.

It is more difficult than ever to collect taxes. Twenty-seven taxmen are reported to have been murdered . . .

Drugs come in.

In October 1987 Zhao Zeyang as secretary-general makes a speech which is intended to be reassuring. The fundamental task is to expand the productive forces . . . the only criterion for success is economic development . . . in industry, both state control of large enterprises, and market forces, must learn to co-exist . . .

The debate behind closed doors on the economy rages on. A Party congress is held. It is decided, by common consent, that Deng Xiaoping, who has no official position in the Party or the government, will be the arbiter, the man consulted in moments of crisis, and that his verdict will be accepted as final. This is to ensure that confrontation between the two sides will not paralyze the Party. The arrangement is a state secret, not to be divulged.

Industrial reform.

It has been going on since 1985. It also affects arms factories. Through a relative of mine in the army, I visit some of these arms factories.

In the 1960s, around 1,000 arms production plants and related research institutes existed in the inner provinces, such as Sichuan. Now they are listed in the new five-year plan (1986–1990) as redundant. The plants must move, or turn to producing consumer goods. By 1988, 121 former arms factories and research institutes will move out of Sichuan province, move eastwards. I fear this will increase the economic gap between the favoured coastline provinces and the under-financed inland ones. Sichuan could become a power house for the hinterland, should the government spend some money to build hydro-electric plants on some of the ninety or more torrents that rush from the Tibetan plateau into Sichuan.

I see some arms factories, now turning out refrigerators and dishwashers instead of aeroplanes. I also visit other factories where the new system of 'control by the manager'

139

is being applied. The managers all seem to have the same scraggy build, the same overtired look. They look like people needing a good meal, some sleep . . . 'Yes, we are in control . . . ', the problem is the workers.

For over three decades the workers have had housing, schools, hospitals, sports grounds, transport – all provided by the factory. No worker is ever fired. 'Some of our young workers are Third, Fourth generation . . . their parents, grandparents, worked here.' In one factory there are 6,000 workers, but with parents, children, wives or husbands, there are 34,000 people to care for. 'Old people live longer, thanks to the socialist system,' says the gaunt manager. 'They live a *very* long time . . . ' The longevity revolution has hit China. In 1949 the average life expectation was 35 to 40. In 1988 it is 68 to 71. Retirement is at 55 for women, at 60 for men. Pensions, and benefits, weigh heavily upon the factory budget, 37 per cent of the budget in an industrial plant goes into these two items. Since each factory is now to be responsible for its own profit and loss, and state subsidies are cut . . . the manager swallows hard. His Adam's apple works up and down. 'It is very difficult to make a profit.'

In another factory I encounter the bonus problem. Bonuses are given to deserving workers, but because of egalitarianism, no worker can be singled out for excellence, every worker must get a bonus, whether he works or not. 'One worker to whom we gave a bonus came to beg me to take it back,' says the hollow-cheeked manager. 'He could not bear the cold-shouldering. "Please take the money back, I have no friends left." '

In another plant, the manager is having a nervous breakdown. The assistant manager receives us. He is slightly haggard. The manager tried to discipline a worker who was sabotaging the machine he worked on. After several warnings, the manager threatened to apply a new regulation, which permits a cut in wages if the worker is unsatisfactory. That evening his house was besieged by some thirty to forty relatives of the worker. 'Father, mother, uncles, aunts, seven cousins, their wives, the wives' relatives . . . ' they sat in his living-room, his bedroom, refusing to move until he had reinstated the wages. 'The manager is now resting in hospital . . . he is very tired.'

In another medium-sized factory, the manager had spent part of the night getting milk for the children's nursery. The milkman had not delivered the milk, the workers sent a delegation to the manager. 'It is your responsibility to get the milk.' He went off on his bicycle to plead with the milkman, and the milk was finally brought.

I think this manager breed is quite admirable. 'Of course, there are problems now, but we shall solve them,' they say, smiling, out of their tired faces, at me.

A new contract system is being worked out to apply to the workers. A contract signed between factory and worker. If the work is unsatisfactory, wages will be cut, there is even a hint of dismissal in the air. There is also the vexing problem of quality control. There are many other problems looming. Market surveys, to make sure the goods are in demand, and not simply filling warehouses . . .

Author Shan Rong undertakes a study of industrial plants and is pessimistic. *There Is No Way Out* is a small book she writes on the state of industry. 'There is truly no possible way in which we can modernize the industrial plants with the present system,' she tells me. 'And the workers are even more of a problem than renewing the machinery.'

However, I do not entirely lose hope. I visit a big steel plant. It has coped well. Any worker who does not improve his performance after three warnings is sent to re-education through labour camp (no salary) for a few months.

'This seems to work,' says the manager. Who is well fleshed. Perhaps he has solved the problem.

In other factories I see, in southern provinces, the Japanese system is applied. Singing the factory song, competition between the workers, prizes for the best worker every week.

But the major problem, which is whether the state will go on subsidizing large, costly, and unprofitable enterprises, remains unsolved.

Ten

1987 WAS DISILLUSIONING. 1988 was worse. There was a sense of catastrophe . . . only my friend Harrison Salisbury, touring certain prosperous provinces, seemed convinced that the economic reforms were doing well. In March Li Peng, whom western media described as Zhou Enlai's adopted son (which was not correct, for he was never adopted) became prime minister *de facto*, after having been acting premier since the previous November Party Congress. I had an informal one-hour talk with Li Peng the day before his appointment was confirmed. Deng Yingchao suggested the meeting. Though Li Peng was not adopted, he had been one of the orphan children that Zhou Enlai and his wife Yingchao had cared for.

Li Peng has no charisma at all. This was quite obvious the moment one set eyes on him. Nor did he try to charm. He was, he remains, what he was trained to be, a solid, hard-working engineer. He possesses a single-track obstinacy, so that in conversation he will pursue one subject until he has said everything that he knows about it. I think Li Peng would be very happy with a hard hat on, in coal mines, on derricks. He has an analytical mind. His manner is formal, but he is probably capable of intense emotion, which he tries very hard – and unsuccessfully – to conceal.

We talked about education, about the students abroad. Why not have western professors come to teach in China? Li Peng listened quietly, never interrupting, and then told me that he had talked with two Chinese physicists,

Nobel prize-winners. 'They tell me that mathematicians, physicists must be trained very young,' said he. Then he added: 'Though it is true that what is dignified by the name of "research" often amounts to our Chinese students working in American laboratories at cut rates . . . ' I told him that the United States did not allow foreign-trained medical men to do any work with patients, to attend to the sick at their bedside. It was, therefore, a waste to send medical graduates for 'research', when we needed practitioners in every hospital. 'Our hospitals are getting terribly understaffed.'

Li Peng listened carefully. It was the same with sending agricultural students. I had met some forty of these in the United States. A private inquiry conducted by Sam Noumoff revealed that not one of them had any notion of agriculture in China.

The pros and cons of the situation were being discussed by many educators, and Li Peng had been in charge of education for a while. He now looked at his watch. 'We still have twenty minutes. But we've ended our talk. Never mind, let's just chat.'

I discovered to my surprise that Li Peng was deeply resented, spoken of disparagingly, denigrated, by many of the intellectuals. 'Why?' I ask. No one can really give me a clear answer. Evasively, they say he has no talent, is devoid of intelligence, a very ordinary fellow, and that he was helicoptered up, to premier, above many more worthy people. 'He is protected by the old ones.' Certainly, Li is backed by the more conservative elements in the Party, versus the dashing reformists in a hurry round Zhao. But economists on both sides are battling each other. Li Peng is on the side of prudence, of cooling the economy, mastering inflation.

In September 1988 Zhao Zeyang gives an interview to American economist Milton Friedman. The latter then lectures economic institutes. He advocates *more* laissez-faire, especially on prices; letting prices find their own level, to stimulate industry; letting market forces impose their own equilibrium. Evidently he knows nothing about China. Li Peng is dead against this advice, and so is vice-premier Yao Yilin (also identified as a conservative by the western media). Both of them want more investment in agriculture. Agriculture is fundamental to China. But only 5 per cent of the total budget is committed to it. More money must go into agricultural projects.

Corruption grew, with coal hoarding by entrepreneurs, who bought it at the coal mine for 10 yuan a ton, and sold it in Shanghai, where it was scarce, at 100 yuan a ton. Sixty thousand 'briefcase' companies were set up with the help of Party cadres and their relatives. Using their inside knowledge, their connections, they paid no taxes, and smuggled goods from Hongkong. Ten thousand branches of such companies were in Hongkong itself. Others in Vancouver and San Francisco, and in Australia.

Peasants were sold bags of chalk with salt, instead of fertilizer, ruining their land. Some of them protested and wrote to the newspapers. The local Party man took revenge . . . There was another decline in grain production. Peasant families now hoarded grain, refused to deliver it to the state against 'blank paper'.

In every province, local Party cadres, administering a district or a county, give themselves the right to impose levies, raise taxes, collect funds for road upkeep upon buses and trucks passing the area.

This is laissez-faire with a vengeance. Inflation soars. On 1 May all subsidies for vegetables, sugar, eggs, and pork meat are cut, which sends the prices rocketing.

Panic buying begins. The stores are emptied as people buy, buy, buy anything they can store.

The usual juicy story circulates. Someone high up, living in Middle and Southern Sea, when told that meat had doubled, tripled in price, and was now too costly for most people to buy, has expressed surprise. 'Why don't they eat prawns? They are only 50 cents a *cattie*.' The said 'leader' buys at the special stores for high cadres. On the market, prawns are 6 dollars a *cattie*.

I cannot believe the story. It is too much like Marie Antoinette's: 'No bread? Let them eat cake', and probably just as apocryphal. But anger boils up.

Zhao Zeyang is photographed playing golf. The peasants are angry with him. Another rumour circulates. In an unmentioned province, peasants have gone to the ancestral graves of a certain renowned leader, and disinterred the bones of his ancestors. There is no worse insult, no greater curse, than to inflict this desecration.

In summer the leaders of Party and government meet at the seaside resort of Beidaiho. There they are photographed smiling, swimming . . . but behind closed doors, they engage in the most furious verbal battles. Thus it has been for some years, and 1988 is even more so. These conclaves are supposed to be secret, but now there are leaks, which will be traced to a personage in Zhao Zeyang's entourage. This leak, together with the rumours of an American foundation's lavishness towards Zhao's handpicked experts, begins – or rather amplifies – the erosion of Zhao Zeyang's position.

Just before the Beidaiho summer session, on 30 May, Zhao has stated that price reform should take place, that prices should be allowed to find their own level, giving full play to market forces. He is fiercely opposed by Li Peng and Yao Yilin, both in Beidaiho with him. The story of Li Peng's confrontation with Zhao is not known in its entirety, but a man I know, an expert in national minorities, with good connections, gives me some clues. 'Zhao said: "But what is wrong with high Party cadres going into business?" Li Peng then stormed at him. "I do not like to think that Zhao said such a foolish thing. If he has, then something very wrong has happened to his thinking. Who has influenced him in this manner? And why does his son, who allegedly dealt in the Hainan scandal, lead an easy life in America?" '

In the universities, students now drop out. Or they have to do extra work, to peddle goods, right on the university campus, to make ends meet. The joint salaries of their parents are not enough to pay the fees.

Every campaign in China always begins with criticism of a book, a play, an article.

It is a television serial, *River Elegy*, which becomes the trigger episode, launching the downfall of Zhao Zeyang.

River Elegy has been shown in full, sixteen episodes, seen by at least 100 million people. In it Chinese culture is described as bound, strapped, incapable of growth and change, medieval and destructive, because it is geographically imprisoned in 'the yellow earth' which gave it birth. China, it is hinted, should totally abandon 'yellow earth' and turn to another culture, that of 'azure ocean', open, innovative, exhilarating . . .

It provokes the fury of many of the First Generation, and even a good many in the Second (mine) and shock among the Third . . . it is lapped up by the Fourth. Just like the *Ugly Chinese*, many of the Fourth Generation revel in self-abasement, rejecting everything, and this grovelling is *modeh* (modern), fashionable. Zhao Zeyang has given permission to show *River Elegy*. He may not approve of it, he does not think that it should be taken seriously. But to the First Generation it is part of that eternal conspiracy which they unceasingly seek to expose. It is also a negation of all that they have fought for, believed in, died for. It is a call to become 'lapdogs of the West'.

I read the script, and I think it is fairly jejune and should not be made into a political case. However, it does become a political issue. The First Generation recalls Fang Lizhe saying that everyone now should be international, and allegedly: 'What's wrong if Americans run China?' Fang is prolix, and though expelled from the Party, he gives interviews to newsmen from Hongkong, from western countries, in abundance.

River Elegy is condemned. It preaches 'total surrender', it wants 'a new slavery' for the Chinese people. Zhao is criticized for condoning it, as well as for tolerating corruption, for the inflation due to hasty and ill-thought planning.

Deng Xiaoping will now arbitrate. Zhao will be given another chance. Cashiering him at this moment will have a bad effect. But no reform in prices will take place. There will be a modicum of controls reintroduced, for the total laissez-faire has wrought havoc. 'The economy looks like a thousand wild horses all pulling in different directions.'

Li Peng the premier, and Yao Yilin, take the economy in hand. An ungrateful, unpopular task. Retrenchment. Slashing down expenditure. No more capital investment in building. Return of heavy handed restrictions (there will certainly be a good deal of sabotage of the latter). Reorganization . . . And, above all, mastering the inflation.

In May of that year 1988, the students of Peking University organized a 'salon' to discuss world affairs. The word is frowned upon by a major reformist, Liu Xiaobo, whose iconoclastic excoriation of the system has made him well known. 'Salon . . . the word is tied to previous cultural aggression,' says he. The salon is not interfered with. It changes its name to 'democracy salon'. It takes place in good weather on a lawn in the open air, nearby is a bronze bust of Cervantes.

My Third Brother is a professor at the University. 'Fang Li Zhe goes there to talk,' says he. So do other dissidents, and also the wife of the American ambassador, who is Chinese, but speaks to the students in English. Hongkong magazines publish the speeches.

Third Brother does not attend the salon. He has too much to do. He is distressed because 'I have no one to take over from me in my department . . . I had five researchers, four have left, because the pay was too low . . . '

The gap which is taking place in some of the science departments worries Third Brother. He is hostile to the 'democracy salon'. He calls it 'fairly empty talk', but he is also very critical of the lack of intelligent discussion, and the arbitrariness among the Party cadres. He is, however, a patriot. He returned from the United States in the early 1950s, and he says: 'What kind of young do we have now, who prefer to eat the food of foreigners?'

We go briefly to Vietnam, Vincent and I, in the autumn. It seems to me that I must understand a little more about the Cambodian affair and also about Vietnam-China relations. Dinner, and a two-hour conversation with foreign minister Nguen Co Thach, whose French is perfect, manners exquisite, and who quotes from La Fontaine's fables. However, he seems somewhat misinformed about certain historical events, and I had to disagree politely with his version of the Long Nol coup (according to him, it is a Chinese plot, whereas everyone else in the world seems to know that it is an American one). A booklet is given to me, printed in the USSR, called *The Truth About Vietnamese-Chinese Relations for the last Thirty Years*. It is a compendium of denunciations, a hate book, at times verging on the phantasmagoric. I have read such imaginative outpourings in the United States, at the time that China was 'the enemy', the time before Nixon. I am not here to defend China. 'Of course, this is an old booklet, we are soon going to issue another one, it will be somewhat different,' says my guide, a very charming and intelligent lady. 'I am quite sure that Vietnam and China will renew their friendship one day,' I reply.

I already know that Mr Gorbachev is signalling to China . . . he is ready to come to Peking . . . and he will, the following May. I know that Vietnam has been told by the USSR that Russian aid will be cut, due to other commitments. The USSR will now want hard cash for what they send to other countries.

But Mr Nguen Co Thach seems to believe his own propaganda. He hates with a deep hatred the Chinese. I do not try to persuade him.

Back in China briefly, we fly to Chengdu for a Buddhist ceremony. My Third Aunt, aged ninety-three, died in her sleep, and is cremated at the Precious Light Temple near Xindu. The villagers of Xindu county have not forgotten my gift of ten years ago, when the floods had damaged their fields. The Party secretary is there, her hands full of presents from the villagers. 'We are doing very well now, building new houses,' says she.

The ceremony is videotaped by Sixth Brother, and when we return to his apartment he gives me the good news. Cousin Liu, the son of my father's eldest sister, has returned from Taiwan to Chengdu. He has come to visit his native province and his relatives.

Many hundreds of thousands of people from Taiwan have been coming to China in the last two years, to spend the Spring Festival, to sweep their ancestral graves, and to invest. Cousin Liu has been made welcome by the officials. He was at one time Chiang Kaishek's ambassador, well known for his virulent attacks on 'the red bandits', meaning the communist Party. But what do a few insults matter? Everything is changing, has changed. 'On both sides of the straits, all men are brothers,' say the officials. 'Our pulses beat at the same rhythm,' says cousin Liu. There is only one China, in her dense, unique diversity. 'We hope our honoured Taiwan compatriot will invest in Sichuan,' says an official. In Fujian province, which faces Taiwan across the straits, there are special concessions for investments by Taiwan businessmen. Two-thirds of Taiwan's 18 million inhabitants come from this one province of Fujian. Also many Overseas Chinese in the Philippines, in Malaya and Singapore. President Corazon Aquino has returned to visit her family (her real name is Xu), and so has Cardinal Sin. Cousin Liu has come to rebury his parents. He wants a good grave for his father, who died some eighteen years ago. There is a family meeting, and it is decided to purchase a piece of land on a hillslope not too far from Chengdu. There Third Aunt will rest, or rather her ashes. By her side Sixth Brother will place the small mementoes he has collected to remember his father by. I contribute several letters I kept, written to me by Third Uncle. We both admire the beautiful calligraphy, the style. 'The view is beautiful from the slope, it will please the venerated ones,' says Sixth Brother.

We now bring up-to-date the book of generations of our family. We are, Sixth Brother, and Third and Fourth, and Fourth, Ninth, Eleventh, Thirteenth, Fourteenth Sisters, and I, who now rank as Third Sister, the twenty-second generation of the family. The ideogram which begins the personal name for the next fifteen generations has already been determined. But will the young like the names chosen for them? They can, of course, always assume another name, keeping the consecrated family generational one, even if they do not use it. Now, says Ninth Sister, family ties sunder. The young refuse to care for the elderly . . .

'Do not worry overmuch. Even if they do not care now, the day will come when they will. One day our great-grandchildren will come to the mountain slope, to seek their roots. And that is also a kind of immortality.'

In November, the British Council in Hongkong invites me to give three lectures. It is their 40th anniversary. I speak of China. Of 'hasty and ill-advised' plans, of 'short-sighted projects'. Of the return of 'comprador bureaucratic capitalism' and corruption, corruption . . . I say this is not productive capitalism, but a satellite, parasitic phenomenon. I take the tapes to China and give them to the Friendship Association. 'This is what I said. You may not like it.' I find, surprisingly, a good many people agreeing with me. I am quoted in a magazine run by the Democratic League (one of the eight non-communist parties) in China.

In the same magazine I discover that a forty-year-old social scientist named He Xin, who seems to have made a mark in China, predicts 'a perilous situation' and 'an explosion' should things go on as they do.

How very curious that he, myself, and my two friends, Geoff Oldham and Sam Noumoff, should have come, independently of each other, to the same conclusion. 'How long do you think it will take before the explosion?' asks Geoff. 'Maybe one year, maybe two.'

I am also quoted, along with certain other intellectuals, as critical of the disparity between the coastal economic zones and the hinterland, warning that if the latter slip into poverty and backwardness while investments centre on the coastal areas, this will be very dangerous for the country . . .

There were 150,000 cases of corruption among Party members in 1987. We wait for the figures for 1988.

A number of lauded, publicized joint ventures, have now run into problems.

Perhaps because of the general morosity, and the Party infighting, Mr Lee Iacocca's visit in October 1988, despite months of preparation, was kept very low profile. Iacocca's book was a bestseller in its Chinese translation. But Mr Iacocca did not meet any top leader except Deng Bu Fang, the president of China's Welfare Fund for the Handicapped.

Wang Meng, minister of culture, and I meet again. He says something must be done about the publishers who refuse to publish serious, good writers, because of uncertain sales. The writer must contract to buy at least 1,000 copies of his own book to get printed. There is also a shortage of paper. The new-rich entrepreneurs hoard paper, as they hoard coal. There is a dearth of science books and educational textbooks for the schools. 'That's laissez faire, that's the market economy,' fumes an old writer.

Trouble in the countryside. The peasants now stockpile their own grain, refuse to deliver it to the state. Some villages organize themselves to resist the government procurers from taking the grain from them. Seeds, fertilizer, are far more expensive. It is calculated that even with the rise in price paid to the farmer in 1988 (48 cents per *cattie*) all he can get for one harvest is 20 yuan per mu of land . . . just enough to buy 4 *catties* of meat . . . for almost a year of work.

Vice-premier Yao spends hours and hours poring over figures. He warns that inflation might reach 50 per cent if retrenchment is not really effective. It is no use telling the people that inflation in Brazil is something horrific like 1,600 per cent, and around 300 per cent in Israel . . . what concerns them is their own food basket. 'There will be major riots if we don't stop the inflation,' warns Yao.

Retrenchment in capital projects in the cities means shifting back to the countryside some 30 million labourers. Back to the land. But the farms are too small. Hundreds of thousands gravitate from the poorer to the richer provinces, looking for work in the new townships, in the prosperous cities. Around 50,000 arrive in Guangzhou. They camp on the streets. 'We returned them to their own provinces by truck, by lorry . . . but meanwhile we had to feed and care for them,' says the vice-governor of the province to me. The railway stations are crowded with such campers, waiting for trains to somewhere. It is said that some women give birth in railway stations, and call their babies 'small locomotive'.

There is a new ditty in the streets. 'Oh, with ten cents in the time of Mao Dzedong we ate plenty, With a dollar in the time of Deng Xiaoping we starve.'

So ends 1988, year of the irritable Dragon.

Comes 1989, year of the Snake.

Eleven

FEBRUARY 1989. I lecture at Nankai University in Tianjin, Zhou Enlai's former college. His memory is kept alive with a museum, a bronze statue, and symposia held to study his diaries and papers. I had attended in the previous March a ceremony in Zhou Enlai's native town of Huai An, to commemorate his 90th birthday anniversary. There were no more than 2,000 people, and I was the only person from abroad (bar two stalwart American newsmen). No leader from Beijing. Because that was the way Zhou would have wanted it. No ceremony. He hated them.

The subject of my lectures is the history and development of democracy. Establishing discussion on the democratic process itself is important, and someone has to start thinking not in mob terms, but in an evolutionary, rational way, of *teaching* the young what democracy really means. The crux of the matter, of course, is the separation of the executive from the legislative. This, I know, is not going to happen very soon, in fact, it will take a long time. But it has to be done some day. I therefore also discuss the 'supervision' of the communist Party by eight non-communist parties, an idea started at the Hundred Flowers period by Zhou Enlai, backed by Mao, in 1956. Mao had propounded the 'mutual supervision' idea. 'Socialism . . . does not mean only one party,' Zhou Enlai had said – of course adding that the communist Party must be the leader party. I feel that the matter of mutual supervision as a first step, a preliminary towards exercising the right of democratic dissent, should be resurrected, implemented. 'Step by step. One must learn to swim before throwing oneself into the ocean.'

The lectures seemed popular, attendance increased every day. They were taped. I did not preach overthrow of the regime, it would bring chaos, and military dictatorship to follow. Opposition came from a young man who propounds the thesis of 'the leader of genius', or neo-authoritarianism. This is a theory which has found its way into many newspapers in the last few months. China has thrived when she was run by strong, able, wise men. China needs a strong leader to push the reforms forward. The 'four dragons' – Taiwan, Hongkong, South Korea, Singapore – prosper precisely because they are authoritarian regimes. Taiwan has been under martial law since 1949, and this is 1989 . . . China does *not* need democracy, but a strong leader . . .

I have heard arguments for neo-authoritarianism from several intellectuals. It is said that some persons close to Zhao Zeyang feel that Zhao could strengthen his position by sacrificing political reforms for a while.

The man is booed. I intervene. 'We are trying to educate ourselves in democracy. We should be able to listen to different opinions without booing. I do not agree with neo-authoritarianism. But I also disagree with those who think that "democracy", nebulous, anarchic, without discipline, without strong legal structures, is a cure-all for China.'

The debate is very animated. There are many questions. How could western nations claim to be democratic when at the same time they had colonies? A shrewd young woman asks this question. 'How long before we have democracy?' asks someone else. I tell him how, in 1956, I had said to Zhou Enlai: 'It will take twenty years before you in China know the meaning of democracy.' I add, 'I think it will take twenty more.' There is a chorus of groans. 'Maybe if we all work hard, and responsibly, we can shorten the period. But we must know democracy will not come through shouting, nor street demonstrations . . . it will come if we keep on strengthening legal structures, fighting corruption . . .'

'A wind is blowing through the world, and it hits China too. Let us hope it will be a breeze, not a tornado,' says one of the professors after the lectures. Everything has gone well. Another professor tells a joke. He has just returned from France, where he has been asked what he thinks of the French revolution of 1789. 'It is too soon to tell,' he had replied. 'It is only two hundred years ago.'

1989 is not only an anniversary for the French revolution, it is also the 40th anniversary of the People's Republic of China. Many intellectuals expect, hope, there will be a gesture from the government. An amnesty, or a pardon, for those jailed since 1979 . . . and that means Wei Jingsheng of Democracy Wall.

Some fifty scholars, together or separately, send letters. Among them astro-physicist Fang. Fang has scathingly denounced corruption, saying he knows of numbered accounts in Switzerland where money is stashed away by the 'crown princes'.

Wei Jingsheng has now been in jail ten years. He still has five years to go. My friend Heart of Ice, Bingsin, has signed a collective letter asking for amnesty. 'I felt it was the right thing to do.' Bingsin is revered and honoured. She always refused to denounce anyone, all through the Cultural Revolution. She and I remember a previous great amnesty in 1959, the 10th year of the People's Republic. In that year Zhou Enlai released several dozen Guomindang officers interned as war criminals, and also freed ex-emperor Pu Yi. He had invited Pu Yi and his family to dinner. He had also pushed the rehabilitation of many thousands of rightists that year.

But no reprieve came, even when there was a rumour that some members of the NPC, determined to exhibit a spirit of its own, also urged the government and Party to grant amnesty.

ABOVE, THERE IS NO POLICY.
BELOW, EVERY SMALL PARTY CADRE MAKES HIS OWN POLICY.

Another ditty. There is discord at the apex of the pyramid

of power. A discord which will grow, and induce a paralysis at the centre . . . with dire consequences.

President George Bush visited Beijing in late February. At a return dinner for his Chinese hosts on 26 February several dissidents have been invited, including Fang Lizhe and his wife. The Chinese expostulated, via diplomatic channels, when they saw the guest list. Apparently the American embassy staff in Beijing ignored this, and persisted in inviting the Fangs.

Had Deng Xiaoping, invited to the United States, and arranging a thank-you banquet for Bush, insisted on inviting the head of the Ku-Klux-Klan, or of the American communist Party, I wonder whether this would not have been undiplomatic. Everyone knows that Fang is *persona non grata*. However, the couple get themselves driven by a well-known American to the banquet, and are stopped by security guards. This incident is built up by the western news media . . . Deng's downfall from popularity in the United States begins. Geoffrey Oldham and I had already remarked that Deng had been too often on the covers of *Time* and *Newsweek*. 'Something is bound to happen to him . . . '

Some of the older intellectuals think that Fang Lizhe has behaved without national pride. 'To get an American to drive . . . he thought the Chinese guards would not dare to stop the car because it was American-driven.'

In the evening an Australian, Hanmin my American-Chinese friend, and I talk. Hanmin says he is bemused by 'an exalted, all pervasive conviction I find among the members of the American embassy here, that they *have* to spread America's brand of democracy and way of life in China.' But surely, this was to be expected? The missionary instinct has always been very strong among Americans. Previously it was the Bible, now it is democracy.

'Remember, Hanmin, both you and I owe our education also to this strong missionary instinct of the Americans. My university was founded by Henry Luce . . . '

There is another side to this concern for the souls of others. An unacceptable side. It comes under the heading of Big Business, or the Transnational corporations, preaching economic interdependence, a new internationalism. Very fine sounding, were it not all so asymmetric, in the end detrimental to the poor Third World, which goes on paying more and more to the Rich. 'Interdependence means some are more dependent than others,' says Hanmin, and the Australian and I laugh.

On 8 April an enlarged meeting of the politburo is to be held, to discuss the problems of education (which means discussing the problems of unrest in the universities, the festering defiance, violation of rules). Hu Yaobang emerges from his retreat, declares he will attend and speak at the meeting.

'He was in an agitated mood. He was always excitable, now he shook with impatience . . . he had scarcely slept the night before. After Zhao and Li Peng had spoken, he began. "I want to speak about the Party . . . " He was told the subject was education, but no one could stop him. He went on. Corruption, disintegration, loss of morale . . . "The fault lies with the central committee, with the politburo." He hit the table with his fist to emphasize his words, then suddenly stopped, crumbled, and fell.' He had had a heart attack.

Under intensive medical care in hospital he recovered, but on 15 April, early in the morning, suffered a massive infarct and died instantaneously.

The news was broadcast, and by afternoon wreaths appeared beneath the Monument of Heroes in Tiananmen Square. Couplets, posters, poems, plastered a wall of Peking University. Some of these posters were strangely hostile:

LAMENT HU YAOBANG

CURSE LI PENG

OVERTHROW DENG XIAOPING

Hu Yaobang had not been outstandingly popular with the students. Suddenly, he was made into a hero.

THE ONE THAT SHOULD HAVE DIED LIVES ON
THE ONE WHO SHOULD HAVE LIVED HAS DIED.

That night there was some bottle bashing in Peking University dormitories.

On 17 April the first student demonstration took place. Six thousand students marched with banners proclaiming: 'Oppose Dictatorship', 'Down With Feudalism And Autocracy'.

A young student, Wang Dan, made his entrée as student leader. It appears, from all records, including his own avowal, that he was advised, if not entirely directed, by the forceful, determined wife of astrophysicist Fang Lizhe. A petition was drawn up by the students, containing several demands, the main ones being 'rehabilitation of Hu Yaobang' and 'cancelling as incorrect the movement against bourgeois liberalization of 1987'. Later in the afternoon more demands were added, such as, that the government was to disclose the incomes, perks, privileges and bank accounts of the leaders and their children, to improve living conditions for the students, give more money to education, rescind the regulations on demonstrations imposed in 1987.

By 10.00 p.m., 2,000 students were in front of the main gate of Zhongnanhai, shouting through loudspeakers: 'Li Peng come out', 'Down with Li Peng'.

Why this hatred of Li Peng? He appears to have been, from the first day, a target for them. He was one of the architects of the retrenchment economic policy, but had not the students too suffered from the previous inflation?

For two days the main gate of Zhongnanhai was under continual assault by relays of students who tried to get in, but were restrained by the local police. Bottles and bricks were thrown, but there were no major casualties, and the police were unarmed. However, far from the scene, a girl returning from a theatre show died in a traffic accident involving a trolley bus. This was broadcast by the students, on loudspeakers, as an atrocity committed by the police. 'More than a thousand scholars fell in pools of blood' was

159

another highly imaginative story propagated on loudspeakers through the campuses.

On 22 April a funeral ceremony was held for Hu Yaobang in the Great Hall of the People. Just as had been done for Mao, Hu's embalmed body lay in state, to receive the homage of 4,000 high rank officials. He was praised in the funeral oration as a great revolutionary, a staunch Marxist, a statesman . . . eulogy as fulsome as that pronounced for Zhou Enlai. That day 10,000 students marched to Tiananmen Square, next to the Great Hall, and occupied it to mourn Hu Yaobang. They refused to leave the square unless their demands were received personally by Li Peng. 'Li Peng come out,' they shouted.

This is where Li Peng did not emulate his august predecessor, Zhou Enlai. He did *not* come out to talk to the students. Zhao Zeyang was asked by some of the members of the politburo to do so, to urge them to return to the campuses, but he refused. Zhao went that very afternoon to play golf, and the next morning flew to North Korea on a state visit, returning 30 April.

By 25 April, forty-six colleges and universities in Beijing announced class boycotts, and – apparently on the advice of Fang Lizhe's wife – the Autonomous Student Union (ASU) was organized that day. The three student leaders were Wang Dan, a flamboyant nineteen-year-old, Uighur, Wuerkaise, and the *passionaria* of the movement, the beautiful, vibrant Chai Ling. Branches of ASU were founded in thirty-four of China's universities within the next few days.

'This is no ordinary student unrest . . . it has organization behind it,' says Deng Xiaoping.

The mourning for Hu Yaobang is a pretext, because the young thought of him as a clown, made fun of him, were against him when he invited 3,000 guests from Japan. Why did he suddenly become a hero? 'There are black hands behind the scenes,' says Deng Xiaoping. Black hand means manipulator. And indeed there are, as will be amply proved, even by western observers sympathetic to the students.

A book entitled *Broken Mirrors*, several articles in a well-known magazine, *The Far Eastern Economic Review*, and a study by a French Sinologist, acknowledge that the students were being guided by certain intellectuals, and that their slogans were being written for them.

Even if this is true, and there was behind the scene manipulation, nevertheless the student movement was a genuine, idealistic surge.

Sinologist Jane McCartney, present at the time, had many interviews with the students. She writes: 'The student protests were not entirely spontaneous . . . they were indeed advised, counselled, guided. A certain academic, after stirring the students into action, then took a back seat . . . older intellectuals waited on the sidelines, sending out signals that they would be willing to help if asked . . . many of the slogans and watchwords of the movement came to the students via stage managers hovering on the edge of the set . . . '

A French Sinologist remarks: 'In the tragedy that followed some of the intellectuals who took part have an overwhelming responsibility.'

Unfortunately, these remarks were only published in 1991, two years later.

In the afternoon of 25 April, knowing that an editorial was going to be published defining the movement as 'turmoil', thirty members of the State Council, Education Commission, and Beijing Municipal Office, asked the students to hold a meeting with them at 2.30 that afternoon. The officials were there at 2.15. By 4.15 no student had turned up. At 7 p.m. Chinese television then broadcast what would become the editorial in all the Chinese newspapers the next morning: TAKE A CLEAR CUT STAND AGAINST TURMOIL. 'A handful of people have used student grievances . . . set up illegal organizations to seize power from legal student unions . . . This is a planned conspiracy, turmoil, which in essence, aims at . . . negating the leadership of the communist Party and the socialist system.'

161

On 26 April, the Union of Chinese Intellectuals (UCI) was formed, comprising the intellectuals supporting, advising, guiding, the student movement. The major proponents would become increasingly visible as time went on. 'There was an interim period of some two to three weeks when the intellectuals behind the movement remained marginal . . . gradually they plucked up courage to manifest themselves,' writes McCartney.

The students enjoyed facilities inaccessible to ordinary citizens and even to Party officials. Telephone calls to the West free of charge, fax machines placed at their disposal and manned by western sympathizers in at least one institution. 'Two of my western colleagues, foreign teachers in my Institute, handled all the faxes, paying foreign exchange,' a Chinese teacher employed at a major university in Beijing tells me. Encouragement from dissidents abroad, grouped under the Chinese Alliance for Democracy, came pouring in. The western press and TV, by their presence, their attention, and admiration, also greatly boosted the self-confidence of the young.

A sudden change took place in the slogans carried on banners by marching students. On 27 April the slogans read:

SUPPORT THE COMMUNIST PARTY

SUPPORT SOCIALISM

SAFEGUARD THE CONSTITUTION.

OPPOSE BUREAUCRACY; OPPOSE CORRUPTION; OPPOSE

PRIVILEGE.

The massed 30,000 students sang the Internationale. Apart from traffic jams (49 trolley bus lines blocked and 800 buses, affecting around 1.5 million commuters) there was no violence, and the police did not interfere. By evening the students dispersed.

Funds poured in.

The crowds were sympathetic, applauded the students, gave money. Liu Xiaobo, famous for his unorthodox views, flew from America into Beijing with a letter of encouragement from the Alliance for Democracy and around 8,000 US dollars. According to Mr Ma Xun, a capitalist with interests in Canada and Hongkong, close to student circles abroad, altogether more than 10 million US dollars, and 10 million Hongkong dollars, poured into the student movement in Beijing.

'The macro-climate abroad produces a micro-climate in China,' said Deng Xiaoping. He saw the event as part of the wave for democracy sweeping Eastern Europe. But he, and others in the politburo, denounced it as the outcome of a major conspiracy, the policy of 'peaceful transition to capitalism' once proclaimed by John Foster Dulles. This linked the student uprising not merely with discontent inside China itself, but also with a deliberate and vast destabilization scheme from abroad.

At this juncture, everything that could be done was done by certain western media to help and stimulate the student demonstrations. Voice of America increased its broadcasts to China to twenty-four hours a day, relaying any and every rumour that circulated.

A statement from the State Council was issued. It praised the students' patriotism. 'Fighting against corruption and bureaucracy, fighting for democracy, is what our Party and government endeavour to do.' But the Party could not possibly recognize the ASU leaders as sole representatives of the students, and ignore the legal Students Union. Wang Dan, Wuerkaise and Chai Ling refused to have any student representatives present other than themselves. They seem to have become inflated with their own success, particularly Wuerkaise (who in appearance much resembles Cohn-Bendit, the leader of the May 68 student movements in Paris). Wuerkaise became a cult figure for the Chinese students, as did Chai Ling. A TV snip shows Wuerkaise being carried like a king on a rug-covered litter, borne on the shoulders of his enthusiastic classmates.

On 1 and 2 May new demands, far more aggressive, were added to the original petition. This turned it into an ultimatum. Presented in the afternoon of 2 May, it demanded a reply by noon the next day. Each point had to be answered in writing, the answers attached to the petition document. 'This is an ultimatum . . . it cannot be entertained,' said the spokesman for the State Council.

4 May came. A day which had seen massive student arousal throughout China in 1919, heralding the onset of the Chinese communist revolution. That day some two hundred Chinese journalists joined the students in marching, demanded freedom of the press, the right to tell the truth as they saw it.

It was now rumoured that Zhao Zeyang, back from Korea, and who had first agreed with the 26 April broadcast and editorial, had now reversed himself. This appeared a clear encouragement to the students to continue.

The intellectuals involved with the movement became visible, among them representatives of a research institute, China's first private think-tank, run by an ex-Red Guard, now a prosperous businessman. 'The students are a front for us,' said another one time Red Guard, Wang Juntao, prominent at the time of Democracy Wall. 'We need the students . . . but we have to teach them what to say.' Some other now visible guides were members of the four think-tanks which Zhao had set up, and a representative of the Stone company, specializing in electronics and computers. As for Fang Lizhi and his wife, they never appeared at Tiananmen, though Wang Dan seems to have been in frequent telephonic conversation with the energetic and versatile Mrs Fang.

On 4 May Zhao met with members of the Asian Development Bank. He said that there would be 'no big turmoil', thus directly contradicting Deng Xiaoping. 'We must mobilize all the intellectuals to support Zhao,' said Yan Jiaqi, a historian of the Social Science Academy, who specialized in studies of the Cultural Revolution.

Crowd support dwindled after 4 May, and to revive public interest the ASU planned a hunger strike, which started at noon on 13 May. 'We shall fast to death,' said Chai Ling on the loudspeakers.

Gorbachev was due to arrive on 15 May. The hunger strike appears to have been timed to coincide with his coming.

The volunteers on hunger strike were to occupy the square, preventing the usual ceremonies of welcome to the distinguished guest from Moscow. It was a major provocation designed to humiliate the Chinese government and especially Deng Xiaoping. 'No government in the world will put up with this kind of behaviour,' fumed Deng. 'We want to put pressure upon the government through Gorbachev's visit,' candidly explained student leader Wang Dan.

A hunger strike in China has a far greater emotional impact than in France, or other western countries. This is because of the traditional fear of famine, the constant preoccupation with food. Hundreds of thousands of citizens filed to look with awe at the hunger strikers, to give money . . . 'not one of them must die . . . ' Doctors and nurses were mobilized. If any student complained of a headache after a day's fast he was immediately whisked off to hospital. The Chinese Red Cross was there, and ambulances. The latrines set up, which the students did not clean themselves, were cleaned by hospital staff.

The hunger strike appeared convincing evidence of determination, of purity of intent. The students wore head bands on which was written 'not afraid to fast until death'. 'The Chinese do not know about prolonged hunger strikes in India, nor of hunger strikes in France,' remarked a Belgian businessman who was present at the time. It was Wuerkaise who, standing on the steps of the Monument of Heroes, administered the oath to the volunteers . . . 'We are going on hunger strike . . . during these beautiful days of our youth, we leave the beauty of life behind us . . . ' The average length of the hunger strike per student was four days. Many were placed on glucose drips on the second day, all were under constant medical attention.

Wuerkaise, though he took the oath to go on hunger strike, was found eating a bowl of noodles at night, seated in the back of a car. 'I need to keep up my strength, because I am a leader,' said he. He added that he suffered from a heart condition, and therefore could not go hungry too long.

During the two days left before the arrival of Gorbachev, hundreds of leading academics, members of the Central Committee, the director of the Education Commission, went to plead with the students to return to their campuses. China had broken relations with the Soviet Union in 1964. This was the first time in twenty-five years that a Soviet leader had come to China. It was a visit of enormous importance. The Chinese government did not want to exhibit a display of non-power, of being subjugated by a crowd of youngsters.

A late night visit by the mayor of Beijing also proved fruitless. 'We hold our resolve until the end,' chanted Chai Ling on the broadcasting system erected by the students, in her beautiful, gripping voice.

Gorbachev arrived on 15 May, and the welcome ceremony had to be held at the airport, since Tiananmen Square was not available. His appointments were also delayed. The main avenue to the Great Hall of the People, next to the square was blocked. He had to enter through a back gate.

By then, many thousands of floaters were hanging round the square. Altogether one million three hundred thousand people from other areas had reached Beijing in that May. They swamped the trains, not paying for tickets. The train service, having no police of any kind, found it impossible to refuse them. Violence would have ensued.

Zhao Zeyang now committed a major error. He told Gorbachev that Deng Xiaoping had the final word on all decisions taken. 'The whole Party knows we cannot do without him.' This was supposed to be a state secret, and some observers felt it was an attempt to put the blame for the turmoil on Deng Xiaoping.

Some 1,500 newsmen and TV broadcasters were in Beijing

at the time, to witness Gorbachev's arrival, and the humiliation inflicted by the students upon their own government. Massive demonstrations continued all through his stay, with crowds of up to two or three hundred thousand. Cadres, journalists, hotel bell-boys, and a Christian seminary which marched under the banner THE LORD LOVES YOU participated. But more disquieting to the Party was the presence of young workers from the Capital Iron and Steel Works and the Jeep corporation. An Autonomous Union of Workers (AUW) was formed on 13 May.

Li Peng, on the morning of the 13th, spent several hours talking with the workers at the iron and steel works, but was unsuccessful in making them desist from their plans. On the 17th the Union of Intellectuals issued a political manifesto, penned by historian Yen Jiaqi, and attacking Deng Xiaoping. 'An emperor without an emperor's title . . . a senile and fatuous autocrat . . . rule by old men must end . . . the 26 April editorial must be overturned.' Zhao Zeyang appeared early on 18 May, with Li Peng, visiting two Beijing hospitals and the hunger strikers there. Zhao was now under heavy attack at meetings held by the Party. He offered to resign, but this was rejected. The disarray of the leaders was now very obvious. It was at this moment that some of the Long Marchers, including the diehard Wang Zheng, seem to have decided that the turmoil must be put to an end, and that the army must be used.

However, once again a meeting with the students was attempted on the afternoon of the 18th. The meeting was broadcast live on Chinese television. And it was there that Li Peng showed himself utterly unable to project an image of calm authority, to exhibit composure, or to handle the student leaders. 'These [the students] were . . . a rabble . . . barely out of their teens . . . even their clothing seemed to scream of disrespect', write the two English newsmen, Fathers and Higgins. 'Wuerkaise swaggered in . . . in a pair of striped pyjamas . . . Wang Dan wore a red headband scrawled with slogans . . . '

'Your intentions are good, but the situation is developing independent of your goodwill and your patriotism . . . social order is disturbed, disturbance has spread to the whole country . . . it is now impossible for us to sit idly by and do nothing,' said Li Peng.

He was interrupted by Wuerkaise . . . 'This meeting is not a little late, but much too late (Li Peng had arrived ten minutes late at the meeting) . . . it is not you who asked us to come for discussion . . . we asked you . . . the topic of discussion should be decided by us.'

Li Peng was sweating hard. His face glistened. His speech faltered. 'My youngest child is older than you are . . . none of my three children are involved in profiteering . . . ' He was again cut off. The meeting broke up. Li Peng had been made to lose face.

That evening, the decision to impose martial law was ratified.

On Friday 19 May, at 6.00 in the morning, Zhao Zeyang and Li Peng were shown on television, going to Tiananmen Square, climbing into one of the seventy-eight buses allocated to the hunger strikers, as it sheltered them better than tents would have done.

Zhao appeared greatly distressed, tears glistened behind his glasses. 'We have come too late, too late . . . you mean well, you wish the country well, but things are very complicated.' He knew what was going to happen, for on the night of the 18th Deng Xiaoping had called a large meeting, including the Long Marchers whom he had shifted out of power posts. He could not do anything else. There was no other way. The Party was in disarray, and in the newspapers, in the institutes, Party members were giving money to the students, were marching with them . . . The military commission, and several army commanders, were also present at the meeting when the decision was taken to proclaim martial law and to move army contingents into eight districts of the city.

It seems that seven army commanders disagreed with

using the army. I have seen a copy of a letter, purporting to be from these commanders, and filed in the New York Public Library, which has collected all documents pertaining to the Tiananmen story.

The intellectuals who were involved with the demonstrations were immediately alerted. On Friday morning they sent warnings, or went personally, to entreat the students to leave the square. The director of the Institute for Economic and Structural Reform, Chen Yidze, drafted a broadcast for the students, demanding that the inside story of the decision-making process, and the divergence of opinion at the meeting, be made public. Chen Yidze is one of the main leaders of the Alliance for Democracy abroad.

In the night of 19 May Chinese radio and TV repeatedly broadcast the decision on martial law. Yang Shangkun, the president, spoke and so did Li Peng. 'The patriotic enthusiasm of the students is not the target,' said Li Peng. 'But . . . a tiny number of people . . . incite turmoil.' Yang announced that contingents of the People's Liberation Army were to be moved to Beijing . . . 'This is definitely not aimed at dealing with the students . . . '

'Down with Li Peng, down with Li Peng,' shouted the students.

Li Peng would explain to a journalist on 25 May that martial law did not mean military control. It was not handing over to military authorities, and it only applied to eight districts in Beijing. A martial law enforcement body, comprising himself, Wang Zhen and two others, was set up.

Throughout that fateful Friday, the student leaders had debated the issue. Wuerkaise felt it was time to leave. Suddenly a number of the AUW workers arrived in trucks to Tiananmen to join the students. The AUW had issued its own ultimatum to the government. Unless the student demands were met unconditionally, they would call for a one day general strike throughout China. The government had to answer within twenty-four hours.

Rumours of an impending crackdown had spread, and again there were large crowds, which heartened the students. They now felt strong enough 'to rock the system', or in Chinese, 'to scale Heaven itself'.

Yet already within the student group there was bitter and venomous infighting, chiefly due to the pocketing of the money by a few leaders. But now the arrival of AUW workers made them feel so hopeful of success, that they began to plan for an alternative government. With the working class on their side, or so they thought, they could indeed overthrow the system. 'I could be a much better premier than Li Peng,' said one of the backers. Chai Ling spoke in her compelling way to the assembled students. There were tears when she said that some students were ready to immolate themselves by fire, as the Buddhist monks in Vietnam had done.

Students began to leave. They were insulted, some were beaten. Around 5,000 stayed on. The Health Department cleaned the heaped filth and excreta. They sprayed disinfectants and emptied the latrines.

On 22 May official news of Zhao Zeyang's suspension from all his functions was broadcast. On that day, the American philanthropic foundation which was identified as close to his entourage, sent notice that it was closing. It would no longer operate in China, and all funds were withdrawn.

Twelve

AFTER THE BROADCAST of 19 May night, contingents of the PLA started to move into Beijing from several directions. They were stopped at the outskirts by tens of thousands of residents and students. There was no violence. The crowds shouted: 'The PLA is the People's Army . . . the People's Army do not fight the people.'

In 1967 Mao had ordered the PLA to put a stop to the rampage of the Red Guards. They had done so with – according to reports – a minimum of violence. They did not shoot back even when shot at by the young Red Guards, who had rifled arsenals and used machine-guns in a thoroughly irresponsible manner against anyone, including groups of other Red Guards. The army had been a moderating factor, and now the people held up their children to shake hands with 'big brother soldier'. The officers addressed the crowds. 'We are not against the students. But we have to maintain order . . . '

The contingents did not attempt to force their way. They remained in the outskirts for some days. Appeals to the students to leave the square, to return to the campuses or to their homes continued. Two marshals of the army, and Deng Yingchao, Zhou Enlai's widow, sent messages and letters. These had some effect, for many students by then were leaving, including 3,000 from other cities who, Cultural Revolution-style, had taken trains to Beijing without paying ticket fares.

On 23 May the hunger strike was called off. The sit-in

on Tiananmen Square, as well as in front of Zhongnanhai, continued. The students set up their own inspection teams. Anyone coming in or out of the Party and government headquarters had to run the gauntlet of student investigation. 'I smuggled myself in under a disguise,' Jiang Zeming, erstwhile mayor of Shanghai told me. He had been called to Beijing to participate in politburo meetings. And to take over from Zhao Zeyang the post of secretary-general of the Party.

In seventy cities, more than 200,000 students were now involved. More disquieting was the presence of young 'workers', including the millions of floaters, among them unemployable former delinquents. The possibility of a mass upheaval triggered by the students becoming a great wave of violence and vandalism could not be discounted. 'Both sides seem to have been seized, at the time, with an uncontrollable escalation . . . something akin to a panic rushing forward flight (*fuite en avant*) says social scientist He Xin to me.

The PLA had changed. It was no longer the PLA of 1967. It was now a professional army, not a well-honed, intensively political and educative arm of the Party. The 'fish in water' phenomenon of the guerilla soldiers in the early days of the revolution was eroded. The young soldiers of 1989 were neither mentally equipped nor physically prepared to deal with city riots. They had been taught to fight with maximum of firepower against an external enemy. They had new, formidable weapons. Although Li Peng had mentioned the previous year the need for an armed police, methods of riot control seem to have been ignored.

'But what else could have been done?' say, defensively, those who feel that there was cogency and necessity in the use of the army. 'It was no longer simply student demonstrations. We were on the verge of a very serious mass upheaval.' They cite the violence, the vandalism, the arson, which took place in June.

Perhaps it will never be possible to answer this satisfactorily.

I, for one, stick to my conclusion. That the army should not have been called in because the students were already leaving, leaving in droves. By the time the tragic events of 4 June took place, there were less than 4,500 in Tiananmen Square.

An evident factor encouraging the students to pursue their sit in was the number of foreign correspondents and news media present. Many had remained in Beijing after the Gorbachev visit, and the students were the recipients of their continuous attention, admiration . . . excitement was whipped up when it flagged. The student leaders strove to remain the focus of attention. What greater seduction than to be a hero on TV? To be able to say 'My picture is being seen by millions of people throughout the world'?

Demonstration fatigue among the citizens became palpable by the end of May. Beijing crowds love a show. Beijing is a city where people like to loiter, to stare, to argue. They join in any gathering, however trivial. When a policeman stops a cyclist, a small crowd will gather, emit opinions. But now the show had gone on for forty-five days, and they were tired. There were transport difficulties and food shortages. Another large march was held on 23 May. DOWN WITH LI PENG, DOWN WITH DENG XIAOPING, ABROGATE MARTIAL LAW, LET THE BOGUS GOVERNMENT RESIGN . . . were the slogans. But there was a change in the composition of the student mass, bitter quarrels among those who remained. A western observer remarked that they 'cloaked their real demands in grandiose rhetoric', and that the outstanding grievance was poisonous infighting over money. Money had flooded in, but so much of it had disappeared in the pockets of a few leaders . . . or so the students continuing the sit-in complained. 'For the sake of great democracy, we must give up small democracy,' grandly said Wuerkaise, looking more like Cohn-Bendit than ever.

173

I think it is very unfair of some westerners then present to write, two years later, that the students were selfish, interested in their material wellbeing, cloaking their real demands in nebulous appeals for democracy and freedom. The two urges co-existed in them. The theme that the students were egotistical and self-centred is, however, held by a respected scholar, Lucian Pye, as well as by the famous dissident Liu Binyan. My own view is that those who pocketed enough money to be able to buy their way out were probably as described by Mr Pye and Mr Liu, but this cannot apply to those who went on, nor to those who later went to jail, because they did not have the 'connections' which the others began to establish, right after martial law was proclaimed, in order to make a getaway.

In the last days of May small army units repeatedly attempted to get into the city and reach Tiananmen Square. Some walked in, clad in plain clothes. Certain groups were able to reach important buildings, where they remained ensconced. Others were surrounded by crowds and rendered helpless. One such, of about 5,000 unarmed soldiers, jogged some 12 miles from the suburbs, reaching the Peking Hotel in an exhausted state. They were surrounded. 'Some had their uniforms ripped, a few were beaten,' writes one witness, but others aver that there was no violence, and that after some four hours of sitting and recovering from their jog, the soldiers withdrew.

But these repeated attempts induced in the military a sense of failure. Most of the soldiers, of peasant origin, felt confused. The students were 'patriotic', so continued to say the Party leaders. The people were 'brothers' . . . yet at the same time there was turmoil, sinister links, a counter-revolutionary plot . . . and the PLA was *not* welcomed, was jeered at . . . was being shamed. How long could this go on?

On 30 May the Goddess of Freedom (or Goddess of

Democracy) appeared on Tiananmen Square. Ten metres high, made of plaster of Paris at the Central Institute of Fine Arts, she was brought in by night in pieces, and was put together and unveiled with firecrackers and speeches. Once again crowds flocked, to look, and brought their children. A Hongkong support group arrived with 650,000 US dollars, and 2 million Hongkong dollars. A pop singer from Taiwan, Hou Dejian, who had joined the students, belted out many songs, and there was a fiesta atmosphere that night.

Several days before the goddess appeared, two of the three student leaders, Wuerkaise and Chai Ling, were arranging to leave. Chai Ling told an American correspondent that bloodshed might take place. She sought the help of foreigners to flee the country. Chai Ling did not warn the students that there might be bloodshed. On the contrary, she now placed herself at the head of a new emerging group of leaders. Another hunger strike was proclaimed. This time there were not 2,000 but only four volunteers, of whom three stated they would not fast longer than three days. The fourth was singer Hou Dejian, who could only fast forty-eight hours, for he was due in Hongkong the following week to cut a new record.

Chang An Avenue, the Avenue of Enduring Peace, runs straight east to west across Beijing, bisecting the city. It runs in front of Tiananmen Square, between it and the massive red-walled quadrangle which encloses the Forbidden City. It carries on westwards and 6 kilometres from the square passes in front of an exclusive area of multi-storeyed apartment buildings, known as Muxudi. Here live high Party officials, ministers, ambassadors. Next to the most important building of all, called Ministers' Building, is a flyover bridge.

It was here that the killing began.

Social scientist He Xin – who calls himself a political scientist too – was one of the eye-witnesses of that night's shooting. We had, without knowing each other, been quoted in the same non-communist magazine expressing our apprehension regarding the economic situation. He Xin had done something else. The day after the editorial of 26 April, calling the student demonstrations TURMOIL, he had penned a letter: A WORD OF ADVICE TO THE POLITBURO. He warned that 'inappropriate measures' were to be avoided, 'measures leading to a deepening conflict, more discontent . . . because then political reform and democratization will again be delayed.'

He Xin and I were both aware of the boomerang effect of student demonstrations.

As late as 1 June, He Xin tells me, high level meetings urging that no reprisals against any student or intellectual be taken 'save for a minute handful with ulterior motives' were still being held. Many intellectuals were present at those meetings, but before a consensus was reached, violence began. It began inadvertently, according to He Xin. 'It was triggered by an accident.' On 2 June, around 10.30 p.m. It had rained, the pavement was wet. A China TV camera group had borrowed a Mitsubishi jeep from the 5th corps of the police. The driver was drunk, he hit and killed three men on their bicycles. This happened on the avenue in front of the Muxudi apartments. Immediately there was a crowd, and it swelled into thousands, 'as if by magic' says He Xin.

But the crowd that night was not the usual crowd. Among them were men with chests bared, bandannas round their heads, carrying heavy clubs. They called themselves workers of the AUW, but many must have been floaters. 'The people are being killed. The army is killing people. The army is killing students', roared these men. A frenzy possessed the crowd. The 'workers' would not let the corpses be removed, but wanted to parade the dead bodies in front of Zhongnanhai Main gate.

'This was the trigger point,' says He Xin. It coincided with the decision taken to move the army into Beijing that night. Trucks and lorries filled with soldiers drove in along the intersecting roads, running north to south, cutting into the main avenue. The crowds flung themselves at the lorries, used road dividers to pen them in, slashed the tyres. Road blocks had been set up at some intersections, and these were now reinforced with empty buses.

There was already an encampment of AUW workers on Tiananmen Square. They had their own radio station, and that night broadcast repeatedly, urging armed resistance. Two hundred thousand people gathered on the square as the students announced another demonstration, to be held on 4 June.

On the square itself, in the avenue, the presence of people 'looking for trouble' was noted by two British newsmen who were there. From the radio station installed in Tiananmen Square instruction as to the best way of making Molotov cocktails against army tanks and armoured cars were issued by the 'workers'.

Fairly violent scenes now occurred at the blocked road intersections. At one, called Liu Bukou, army lorries were immobilized and rioters swarmed over them, snatching away rifles and machine-guns. The soldiers opposed little or no resistance. Snatching of guns, and some stoning, occurred at other crossroads. Stacks of weapons were triumphantly exhibited, and found their way to Tiananmen Square.

3 June came, with the soldiers immobilized, helpless. Lorries filled with men shouting 'Kill. Kill,' drove down the Avenue. They were armed with clubs, knives, Molotov cocktails. At 5 p.m. the radio of the AUW on Tiananmen Square urged the people of Beijing to 'take up arms to overthrow the government'.

'At no time did the students take part in, or encourage, the growing violence,' affirms He Xin. But they were helpless, unable to grasp that the worst was happening. 'The ruffians were now using the students, just as some intellectuals had done.'

At night Yan Jiaqi the historian appeared at the square to open the 'university of democracy'. He too seems to have been totally unperceptive, unaware of the growing violence, and its significance. Yan Jiaqi gave a twenty-minute speech, in which he stated that 'Li Peng must voluntarily resign, otherwise he will be brought to trial.' The students must not be afraid to die for what they believed in, he added. And then he left.

Yet five hours before this dangerous, irresponsible speech (dangerous to the students, which is unforgivable), the martial law enforcement group had broadcast a final warning. All citizens must leave the streets and keep away from Tiananmen Square. 'Stay home for your own safety and to avoid unnecessary losses . . . lawless acts . . . have infuriated the officers and men . . . these acts can no longer be tolerated . . . '

Again and again, booming away, from 6 p.m. for two hours came the warning.

No one among the crowds seems to have taken any notice. It was a fine evening, and people thronged out, in the streets, to see the show, to view some excitement – I do not understand, I say to He Xin. Why did so many not heed the warning?

'Because no one, but no one ever believed that the PLA would shoot.'

He Xin himself, an intelligent man, took his wife, and child on the pillion of his bicycle, as did tens of thousands of others. He went to watch what would happen. 'I had warned the government in my 27 April letter, if there were any victims, they would be looked upon as martyrs.'

Around 10 p.m. that night he with his wife and child reached the Military Museum, in the select Muxudi area. The soldiers were coming, they were advancing. Orders had been given that they *must* fulfil their mission. A large contingent was blocked at the flyover bridge by a barricade made of empty buses. There were around 10,000 people there. The crowd was hurling stones, bottles, bricks at the soldiers. The first contingent of soldiers did not carry weapons. They only carried white sticks, 'like the Japanese police', He Xin tells me. Probably stun guns. Some of the soldiers were hurt, their comrades dragged them away.

'This went on for some time. Suddenly there was a great big ball of flame, a huge explosion . . . after that, there was silence for a little while. The barricade of buses was on fire. And then more armoured cars rolled in, and that is when the shooting started,' says He Xin. 'Only a few scattered pings pings, at first, then again a silence, and then a lot of shooting, a lot . . . ' He Xin says he could not see all the details. And now it was late, and time to get the child to bed . . . they went home.

The two British newsmen, Fathers and Higgins, give the same description of the first convoy of unarmed soldiers, who tried for some three hours to cross the barricade under a deluge of stones, bricks, bottles and bits of concrete. 'They made their final unarmed assault at 11.15 p.m., and were then stoned by people behind the barricade.' Then someone threw a Molotov cocktail which set fire to one of the empty buses, and a wall of flame roared up.

According to another witness, who lives in Muxudi, and saw it all from her window, the 'bottle full of fiery gasoline' had been aimed at the soldiers' armoured cars.

The first convoy withdrew; new troops arrived, armed with Kalashnikov rifles. There were also tanks with machine-guns. They fired at the barricade, scattering the people in front of it. They passed the barricade, then began firing straight into the crowd behind the barricade.

It was by that time half past midnight.

'The largest number of people were killed here, at Muxudi,' says He Xin, 'the hospitals were full.'

The procession of armoured vehicles drove eastwards towards Tiananmen. On the way, one tank seemed to have engine trouble and stopped. Immediately the mob swarmed over it, pulled out the soldiers, beat them to death, then set it on fire.

There were also a few victims in the select apartments at Muxudi. 'The soldiers at first fired in the air,' says my friend Madame Wu, who worked many years for UNICEF, and lives at Muxudi. 'My cook was killed. She leaned out of our fifth storey window to see what was going on and was hit by a bullet . . .'

There were other deaths, for the soldiers, seeing lighted windows, thought there were snipers, and shot at them. No one had told them that this was a top residential district.

As the armoured cars and tanks continued towards Tiananmen, so they continued shooting occasional bursts at the crowds. The intention was to keep them far enough back so they could not throw Molotov cocktails.

Another witness, John Simpson, was with his camera crew near Tiananmen Square. 'It was half past twelve, the people knew the army was coming, they flaunted their weaponry, coshes, knives, bricks . . . ' A boy of sixteen rushed up to Simpson, wanting to be photographed. He opened his windcheater to show a row of Coca-Cola bottles strapped to his waist, filled with petrol and plugged with rags. Simpson saw a single army vehicle come driving erratically down the avenue. It was attacked with Molotov cocktails. Another one which followed was assaulted, the soldiers inside pulled out and bashed to death, their skulls beaten in. Simpson records that he helped, with a student who remains anonymous, to save one soldier . . .

The 4,000 students left in the square that night were isolated from these events. The AUW workers wanted to fight, using the weapons stacked at the foot of the monument. The students persuaded them not to do so. By 2 a.m. the square was surrounded by army tanks and armoured cars.

Hou Dejian and other students discussed with Chai Ling. They could not leave now. Once on the avenue, they would be shot or attacked. They had to negotiate with the army officers of the contingents round the square. Hou Dejian proceeded to do so, and some weeks later would give an accurate account of what happened. Around 4.30 in the morning the negotiations appeared to be concluded successfully. A directive was broadcast by the martial law headquarters. 'It is time to clear the square . . . the martial law enforcement HQ accepts the request of the students to be allowed to withdraw.'

The students filed out, carrying their banners, through a corridor left clear in the southeast part of the square for the purpose. But some stragglers were beaten rather savagely by exasperated soldiers.

Nobody died on the square itself. The lurid story of tanks mercilessly crushing 'sleeping' students is farcical, no one could possibly have gone on sleeping with the noise, the loudspeakers blaring . . . such fantasy only dents the credibility of reporting. Further stories of helicopters lifting cadavers off the square fall in the same category.

What happened was awful enough; extra horror does not need to be added.

For me, Hou Dejian the pop singer is a hero. He was arrested, then released, and is now in Hongkong. Because his story did not correspond with the dramatic, and highly fanciful, accounts produced at the time, he has not enjoyed the idolization showered on less reliable personages such as Wuerkaise, or Chai Ling, whose subsequent testimonies were overladen with passionate emotion, and not burdened by accuracy.

Official accounts have since been produced, dwelling upon the attacks to which the army contingent was subject, the number of vehicles burnt (some 500), the atrocities committed upon individual soldiers, disembowelled, burnt alive, eyes gouged out . . . These deeds also took place, but the deaths among the people of Beijing were very large, and they cannot, and must not, simply be brushed away. The official figure is 300 dead, but a figure of 500 is a fair estimate; 6,000 police and soldiers were injured too, and the death toll among the soldiers is estimated at 150. Among the dead were 36 students (some say 38) from 20 universities and colleges in Beijing. They were caught in the crowd in the avenue outside the square. Fifteen other students from outside Beijing also died.

This was 4 June.

And all of us, millions of us, carry the memory of it as a personal wound, an anguish which will not go away.

On 5 June Voice of America broadcast that astro-physicist Fang Lizhi and his wife had sought refuge at the American embassy. Neither of them had ever appeared at Tiananmen Square.

Thirteen

GRIEF, ANGER, DESOLATION are glib words thinned by use. Tiananmen Square, or as in China we now call it, 4 June, was a shock, a gash into our consciousness, so deep, so stunning, that it may never be entirely effaced among us: the Chinese in China, but also the millions of Overseas Chinese, those, like myself, who are also part of the world outside China. Even today I feel the wound, unhealed.

In my apartment in Lausanne the telephone rang, rang. Friends. Many wept. 'I feel I have no face left,' says a Chinese professor ringing from San Francisco. 'I weep and weep . . . ' says the wife of a Chinese diplomat in a European country. I too cannot stop crying, flat on my stomach, back in the seemingly unquenchable sorrow of total loss. Or so it feels, for many days.

But I do get up, go out, to send faxes to Beijing on 5 June, and on the following days. Indignant and long faxes. Rereading them two years later is as painful as was writing them. I have not shown them to many, only to two very good American friends, and two Chinese abroad.

Then come the newsmen, the hungry-for what-is-your-reaction people. One correspondent, representing *Paris Match*, I shall remember for his total honesty. He is the only one who, at the time, did not attempt to make me say things I was not saying.

In the faxes I sent I wrote bitterly, angrily. I quote only one sentence among others: 'A great opportunity to renew trust in the government, to build genuine youth participation, to get rid of festering corruption in the Party, has been utterly lost . . . this is a terrible error . . . '

'Self-inflicted wounds,' says Vincent. 'Why do the Chinese inflict these wounds upon themselves? It was utterly unnecessary.'

'All of China's tragedies are authored, directed, performed, and appreciated by the Chinese themselves. There's no need to blame anyone else,' Liu Xiaobo, a dissident, wrote this, and I agree with him.

For days the Chinese newspapers and other media seem utterly paralyzed. All news about China is handled by western media . . . when, at last, the Chinese press reacts, returns to life with explanations and justifications, they sound unconvincing.

To invoke an outside conspiracy – as is done – does not justify the action that was taken. It is possible that, indeed, there were plans and schemes by certain powers to destabilize China. However, no conspiracy from outside would be successful if, within China itself, there was not fertile ground for implantation. And certainly the amplitude, the scope of the whole movement, was far greater than merely a student demonstration.

Natwar Singh, secretary for external affairs of India, and my friend since 1956, telephoned me. 'I wonder why the Chinese leaders panicked . . . they could have waited a few more days . . . left the students to wallow in their own mess . . . so many of the young were already tired of the whole thing, they were leaving . . .'

By 15 June I knew that I had to go to China. Having expressed my views by direct faxes to the Chinese leaders was not enough. I must confront them in person. I would not do what astro-physicist Fang and his wife had done. Arouse the young, send them out into this dangerous and reckless undertaking, and then clear out under American protection . . . I must go, and go alone. I must go to seek out my friends. Many of them holding views which might now get them into trouble.

Letters came from various universities where I had lectured. The students were safe. In Nankai U. ten students had gone missing for a while. They were reported killed, upon which the Nankai students bought knives, and clubs, and were going to demonstrate on the streets . . . but the ten turned up, and Nankai U. subsided.

My decision to go to Beijing was not unique. An eminent Chinese physicist, Nobel prize-winner, went much before me, in July, and for the same reason. He had to speak his mind, and he had to do it face to face. Mrs Chennault, the Chinese widow of the late General Chennault, also went. Chennault had flown Chiang Kaishek's aeroplanes, he was totally anti-communist, and so is his widow. But she is Chinese, and in the last decade has commuted many times between the United States and China, to promote business, to create links of friendship, to discuss reunification with Taiwan . . . Mrs Chennault is influential, a friend of American presidents and secretaries of state.

The American Cancer Society vice-president rang me up. The society was booked for a trip to China. Was it safe? 'The problem is not safety,' I said. 'The decision must be yours. If you do go, make sure to tell the Chinese exactly what you think . . . ' 'You bet,' replied the vice-president. 'It is far more ethical, more courageous, to go and tell them . . . they will appreciate it. It is also more democratic to go and say: I want to hear both sides of the story.' This was my view, not inspired by desire for publicity, nor to endorse the – to me – disastrous action taken. Simply by an integrity which, at the time, seems to have been reviled and condemned by certain members of the French press, who had worked themselves into an almost hysterical mood against China.

This same press today continues to ignore the fact that France was the only western country to ignore all sanctions applied to China, its businessmen continuing to fulfil the contracts made with the Chinese. It is a very exemplary case of the left hand not knowing what the right hand does.

Geoffrey Oldham, angry, sorrowful, sent me a list of

queries to take with me, and so did other eminent university men. Geoffrey wondered whether Sussex University could go on co-operating in scientific projects with China. Graham C. Greene, director of the Great Britain-China Centre in London, worried about the fate of certain intellectuals he knew. I promised to look them up.

Most important of all perhaps, to me, is to make sure that there will be no wholesale purge, or 'rectification' of the intellectuals. So many of them, even if not involved, were sympathetic to the demonstrators when they demanded an end to corruption in the Party. And reading the Chinese newspapers which reach me from Beijing regularly every week, I detect only too clearly that there has been an editorial shake-up. Some of the most vituperative members of the erstwhile writing teams of the Gang of Four are once again emerging, to control the news media, and the wording of the articles is typical Cultural Revolution style.

Every catastrophe is also a new beginning. 'You can make a fresh start with your final breath,' wrote Brecht. The 4 June affair is not the end of China. But it is the beginning of what?

'But they will kill you, you have openly blamed them,' a friend says to me when I announce my intent to leave for Beijing.

'If you think so, then all the more I must go,' I reply.

29 August, Beijing airport. Intelligent Principle is there, and also Third and Fourth Brothers, and Fourth Sister's husband. Within the next two hours other relatives drop into the Peking Hotel room where I stay. And I am back.

I have been back so many times, so many times now. My life is a pendulum, oscillating, forever swinging back and forth, between China and the rest of the world. I re-enter that unbroken universe, from which I never really depart entirely. Although I am also other selves, increments of a variegated life, although grafted upon me are vestments of will and achievement won elsewhere than here, this is the place, the land, the people, the matrix, life-giving placenta. Without China I die. It is biological.

But I am very clear too that this is ancestors' land, a land of infinite potential for the future, but of countless fallbacks into the past. Ancestors' land, but also a land for the inheritors, the young, those that will come after us. And it is for them that I must be here, fall back as a star falls back into a black hole simmering a thousand suns to come.

In my province lies the Valley of the Dinosaurs, where the saurians bred many millions of years ago. There are deep salt wells in the valley, which explains their existence. Here they have left their gigantic bones. One does not have to dig deep to uncover them. And in cultures as well, archetypes and throwbacks occur, and not only in China. This is found everywhere and in Europe too, where a return to the prejudices and predilections of the past have emerged. Dinosaurs cohabit with computers, and in that first night back in Beijing, I dream of dinosaurs, I feel their presence, a whiff, the faint dream of a roar.

Beijing is the same, yet not the same. There is an undefined aroma of quiet dismay, and very soon people will talk with me. 'We never thought they would shoot,' they say. That is all. The treacle flow of bicycles along the avenues is orderly as always, there is in the wheel whirr a long patience. This outward composure does not denote hatred, but a certain disappointment. 'We never expected the soldiers would fire.' Soldiers, impeccably white-gloved, alert, are on guard at the main gates of offices and important buildings. They are polite, they deal ably with people who come up. There is no curfew. Food is abundant. Inflation has already been curbed. There is a stillness.

'It was all so badly handled . . . it was so . . . unexpected.'

The dining-room at the Peking Hotel with its mosaics I know so well is empty, save for fourteen Japanese businessmen and a dozen from Taiwan (or from Hongkong, or both). The waiters, the room staff, shake my hand. 'You have come.' 'Yes, I have come.' In this season of no-tourists, no travellers, this end of August into September 1989, perhaps my coming signifies that soon, others will come. The Friendship Association compound is unguarded. One of the department heads is noticeably (to me) absent. 'He is studying,' says Intelligent Principle. Studying is what many intellectuals in Beijing who became involved in the student demonstrations are now doing. They attend meetings and read documents and then each one will write a statement of no less than 3,000 words stating whether now their views are correct, and they have achieved unified thinking.

Many of these men and women implicated are Party members. Some will be accused (and western observers seem to bear out the correctness of the accusation) of having deliberately incited the students, guided them, told them what to do. Now they have to account for what they did and said. There are others who merely sympathized, contributed money. One of my friends has given something like half a month's salary. 'I felt I had to do it.' I spend some hours telephoning people I know. 'Are you well?' 'I am well, please set your heart at rest . . . ' 'Then perhaps we can meet, lunch, dinner?' They say 'certainly' or they say: 'Perhaps a little later, in a little while, in a few days . . . perhaps next time . . . ' Then I know.

I drop in on Gladys and Xianyi Yang. Xianyi has been seen on the BBC Television screen in England, saying the shooting was 'fascist'. They are at home, and by no means ostracized, there are the usual visitors, both from abroad and from China, coming in and out of their living-room. 'I thought I was talking with friends, I did not realize they were recording me, that I would be on TV,' says Xianyi. I shall meet western correspondents who feel remorseful because they showed students, intellectuals, speaking, and in their obsession with a scoop, they never thought of the danger when their images, their reports, would become evidence against the ones they interviewed. Nothing much happens to Xianyi, except that he has to leave the Party. 'No one understands why you joined in the first place,' we (I and others) tell him. The two have served China selflessly for decades. They have suffered during the Cultural Revolution.

In the East Peace Market where, as a child, I smuggled myself many an evening to watch the open-air Chinese opera – a child did not have to pay – the shops, the stalls, have a surfeit of goods. People do not buy. Perhaps they overbought during the panic days of last year, and this spring. At the Bank of China a woman director tells me that everyone is now hoarding money, because interest rates have gone up. 'Perhaps we shall lower the rates to make money circulate.' There are billions stacked in personal accounts in the banks. But the sluggishness of the market is undesirable. Retrenchment, introduced to cool down the economy, and the strictures upon the needless building spree which had gone on for some years are blamed for the goods piling up in inventories. Inflation is down to 7 per cent from 35 per cent the previous year, and by 1990 it will be around 5 per cent. Food prices are lower, and will be stabilized for a while, until the next cut in subsidies to grain and oil. But this will only happen in 1991, and will be gradual.

There is a lonely Venus de Milo in a curio shop yawningly empty of buyers. Venus made a grand entry in 1978, and hundreds, thousands of her, big and small, blindingly white, were in the stores. It was Western Art. It was Nude: it was modern. In January 1989 an exhibition of nude paintings was held in Beijing and thousands flocked to see it. But the models sued the painters. 'We agreed to be painted, but not to be exhibited.' The girls claim their reputations are damaged.

The discos and the dance-halls are full, and music pours out, music from Taiwan and Hongkong. The stars have introduced a new Chinese word, *qita*, the guitar. The street committees are busy on another clean the public latrines drive. There are still 8,000 or more of them, for the old houses in the *hutungs*, which are no longer dusty, but tarred, have no plumbing. Aged men walk their birds in the birdcages and there are bird concerts, and except that there are no tourists, all strives to be as usual.

L., my old friend, comes to see me. We have gone on long journeys together, and we have also had many long talks, unguarded talks, in which I can unburden myself, say anything that weighs heavily upon me, and find it lightened by the saying. It is particularly useful to talk with L. before seeing anyone high up in the government or the Party, for no leader wants to be caught unawares, he wants to have some notion of the questions that will be asked. I bring up a host of disagreeable comments, and L. nods, nods, closing his eyes the better to listen, and says: 'Constructive criticism is always helpful, even if the time is not ripe and the manner not appropriate.' We can do nothing about the ripeness of time, except to wait, and sometimes, oh wonder, the time is ripe quickly, in a matter of days. But the appropriate manner in which a topic is brought up is important, and L. simply by being there and nodding and putting in a remark or two helps me fashion my style of address, expunge my temper, articulate more clearly what I want to say. I tell L. that it is outrageous to ask grown men to write a 3,000-word self-examination. Would it not be better to understand the roots of their discontent instead of smothering it into a forced acquiescence with the 'correct' view? Then I start on bourgeois liberalization. 'Merely to use such words as b.l., to condemn something or someone, does not address the issue. It does not really correspond to anything scientific, or proven . . . it is just a label seized and stuck on certain things. And as for the word "counter-revolutionary" (L. knows that it is a word I have been fighting against and will continue to battle against as being imprecise, unbased on fact, unscientific, a calumny very often . . .) 'It makes me want to throw up,' I say and L. simply closes his eyes. 'So much harm has been done with this word, hurled at anyone who dissents . . . in the past, so many people were dubbed counter-revolutionary . . . and then the policies changed, and they were rehabilitated, but so many years wasted, so many persons shrunk, stunted in spirit, and all for nothing . . . a waste, a waste . . .

'And what is this rumour I hear about sending 4,000 intellectuals to Sinkiang? This is stupid, besides being savage . . . it will greatly harm China . . . ' 'It will not happen,' says L. 'It is merely the suggestion of certain people. It will not take place.' Of course both he and I know who these 'certain people' are. Of course I also know that Deng Xiaoping, backed by the new man from Shanghai, Jiang Zeming, and ex-carpenter Tianjin Mayor Li, has totally refused to contemplate a massive political purge or sending scholars to border regions. 'This is dinosaurian,' I say. I have, in my mind, also labelled a certain person. Labelled him the dinosaur. To an American newsman who later comes to interview me I openly and loudly condemn the person by name. The American is bright and also careful. He will not write the name down.

In 1957–58, when the rightist purge came, intellectuals were sent to hinterland provinces, and that is why so many scientific institutes and universities grew up there, and today are doing well. I have met these courageous and patriotic men and women. One can tell by their accent that they are not local. When they say 'I came here in 1958' then I know what happened to them. Now they are honoured, consulted. And Deng Xiaoping will never repeat again what was done then, under his aegis.

'In 1949 China began in earnest its first industrial revolution, the one that the West started in the late-eighteenth century. Now we have another technological revolution coming to us before the first has even been ended. Knowledge is coming as an avalanche, and we can no longer havoc our pool of scientists, send them here or there at the whim of a Party official . . . '

'The unfortunate 4 June happening', I say in my most diplomatic style, 'affects the young abroad. We have a hundred thousand youths abroad. Many will now stay, not return . . . they say they are afraid, and who can blame them for feeling mauled in spirit?'

I point to a Chinese newspaper article which contains the sentence: 'Not a blade of poisonous weed must remain . . . all must be extirpated.' 'This is true Cultural Revolution phraseology . . . how can this language still be used today? How can it be tolerated?'

The important thing is to find out the best way in which to set the case *for* the intellectuals. I have written a long, a very long memorandum. I give it to L. I also give it to some friends. It will find its way.

Miniskirts are in. By 1990 they will be seen everywhere. Now they are spotted, as unconcernedly the girls walk about, and I am glad that no puritan movement is on.

Heart of Ice, Bingsin, ninety years old, is unaltered, ivory young face and lovely voice. Her daughter Tsing is once again splendidly aglow with incandescent fury. She tells me what happened to some people she knows. Not jail. No arrests, that is only for those deeply involved. But for the marginal sympathizers (and there are so many) the meetings, the harassment. Her account gives me a view of the extent of the implosion. In one school, when asked how much money each individual had given, one man truthfully replied 'one dollar'. He was the only one of seven teachers to have given money to the students, so the other six ganged up on him in true 'burrow infighting' style.

Xia Yen, all of ninety-one, sits in a wheelchair and tells me how anguished, how torn with grief he is by '4 June'. He says it was wrong, wrong . . . Another man, a former ambassador, tells me, 'Even Mao listened to criticism . . . but now some people won't listen to anything.' These men are not young. They are First Generation (Xia Yen) and Second Generation. I shall meet many others, and so I realize that this is not a generational phenomenon. It is *not* only May '68 in France. It is far more.

'But it has not involved the peasants, and only very very few young workers in the factories,' an ex-diplomat tells me, now studying social problems.

Junjian, my good friend, was wise. He did not participate, did not listen to the siren song on Tiananmen Square.
He bought food, and closed the gates of his house. 'I knew
from the very beginning that some people were behind it
all,' says he. 'There was deliberate provocation, enormous
provocation . . . something *had* to be done.' But, he says,
'In the beginning the government was too soft. That is
because the Party, the government were divided . . . no one
could really *decide* what was to be done. And then later, the
reaction was much too harsh.'

'The whole affair was badly handled, first weeks of
hesitation because the Party was split, then later a decision
taken in haste,' says someone else. Yet others say: 'Of
course there were elements of conspiracy. We have all the
evidence of outside interference, outside intervention. Look
at the money that poured in from abroad . . . '

'The students were used . . . used as pawns in a power
game . . . one day this will be realized,' says a high official
whose son was involved in the student demos.

I attend the funeral ceremony for Zhou Yang, who died
some ten days before my arrival. Zhou Yang, known as a
Stalinist in his younger days, in the end spoke of humanism, warned against alienation, pitched himself against the
thunder of wrathful dogmatists. He is to be honoured as a
staunch revolutionary, a true Marxist, and the ceremony is
held at Eight Talisman Hill, where in neat rows lie the urns
containing the ashes of those men and women who forged
the China of today.

The hillslopes are dotted with gravestones, and among
them is my father's, who lies next to Agnes Smedley, the
American writer who fell in love with China's revolution.
Long lines of mourners, most of them intellectuals, stretch
in rows along the avenue leading to the pavilion where Zhou
Yang's embalmed body lies, in a glass coffin, awaiting our
ceremonial three bows. His face is painted, showing more
colour than when he lived.

In the crowd I perceive Wang Meng. No longer minister of culture, but who has been on holiday, and looks tanned and fit. We greet each other happily and he assures me that all is well, is well . . . 'I know my friends abroad have been worried about me but there is nothing to worry about . . . we must meet and talk,' says he. We do, later, and he talks chiefly about royalties in Italy and other countries, for his books are translated now.

After bowing to Zhou Yang's remains I walk to my father's grave. He was no revolutionary. Always a sense of poised dubiety inhabited him, whether in religion or in politics. 'It's all man-made . . . and what is man-made must be examined critically . . . never can it be all good or all bad.' He only believed in railways, railways for China, and he built them for decades. He used to write bits of poetry on slips of paper, and bury them in his flower-pots. Perhaps that is why his flowers thrived so extraordinarily well. I remember one line of poetry, in his strong Sichuan accent:

Only the clear wind filling his sleeves

An honest official, father explained, at the end of his life, had no treasure, had amassed no gain . . . only the emptiness of wind swelling in his sleeves. The large sleeves of the gowns of those days were used as pockets.

I speak to Papa, lying quietly under the gravestone. I too, shall have only the wind in my sleeves at the end.

On 1 September, I spend three hours talking with the new secretary-general of the Party, Jiang Zeming. Later I shall write up the interview and publish it in Hongkong, and also in a book which will appear in London in June 1990, entitled *Tigers and Butterflies*.

Jiang looks like a happy, prosperous businessman. He has almost an American verve about him, fitting clothes, quick and ready laughter. He is reassuringly full of cheerful asides, and free of any tendency to plug doctrine. He puns, he jokes.

He comes from a family of intellectuals, his grandfather was a famous painter from the city of Yangzhou, a city renowned for having bred scholars, artists, and erudite officials, through the centuries. He was educated at Shanghai's best school and universities and his English is good.

Jiang Zeming represents the new breed of Party men, the new generation coming up in the hierarchy. The intelligent, well-educated technocrat. There are now a good many like him. I shall spend the next two years (1990–91) seeking them out, discovering them. For they are the future, the men and women who will run the country when the present First Generation has passed away. Already, in many areas, power is passing slowly into their hands.

Jiang Zeming was trained as an engineer in telecommunications, and has written a book on the information and media revolution. He is bilingual, in touch with world events. He gets swiftly to the point. Discussing first the 1986–87 student demonstrations in Shanghai – 'they were far more difficult to cope with than in 1989 as far as the student element was concerned'. Crowds rose in Shanghai to block the railway tracks, and a train was set on fire by unemployed workers, that floater element – around a million in Shanghai as well. The mob attempted to stop a train, six people were run over, hence the attempted arson. A hundred and sixty-six people were arrested, and three were shot. 'None of them were students,' says Jiang. He quotes Deng's phrase: 'The macro-climate abroad has produced this micro-climate in China.' Eastern Europe is changing, however, perhaps there will be second thoughts in certain countries, after a while,' says he mildly. He compares the return of the kings of France after the French Revolution of 1789, and Napoleon, to what happens in the USSR to-day. The kings came back 'and everyone thought the past would return, but it could not, then there was 1848', says Jiang. What happened in China was a first paroxysm, 'an initial attack seeking to destabilize the system'. He hinted at evidence of outside interference - 'we have all the evidence' and 'the Americans know it'. In fact some Americans were about, and George Bush's brother, 'a friend of mine', says Jiang, would soon arrive in China (he arrived two days later).

We got to the heart of the matter. There would not be a purge of intellectuals. Jiang was most firm and clear on this point. I remind him of 'unfortunate' phrases in some articles in the newspapers, leading one to expect the worst . . . there are reports of thousands arrested. Yes, says Jiang, because turmoil was bad in about thirty cities large and small, and that makes a lot of turmoil and a lot of people involved. In Chengdu 'your provincial capital' there was three days of rampage, vandalism, pillaging, breaking of windows, ending with the burning down of a large supermarket. There was also violence in Xian and in other cities. Some intellectuals and students had been arrested for their direct involvement in a plan to overthrow the system. 'But we shall be very careful. We shall strictly examine each case . . . it may take time, but it must be done.'

Jiang Zeming is a reformist, but not a 'soft' reformist, which means selling China to the big western companies. He is for political reform, but insists that this can only be done in an atmosphere of social and economic stability.

He agrees with me about the lamentably inefficient information media in China, and we spend some time picking out the most glaring outrages to commonsense and to veracity. He goes much further than I in spelling out that verbal terrorism is no way to deal with problems.

After seeing Jiang Zeming, I have two hours and dinner with vice-premier Yao Yilin on 9 September. I have seen him several times before, and he knows that I was critical of certain economic policies practised by Zhao. But he also knows that 4 June is weighing heavily on my mind. 'The action taken was a strategic victory but a tactical defeat,' says he. And this is a phrase of enormous significance. I shall ponder it for many weeks.

The simplistic – and knowledge devoid – shorthand of 'hardliner' and 'soft' reformist, does not apply to China, although it is true that, in my simple imagery, there are dinosaurs, and computers.

Jiang Zeming, without army backing, will have to deal with the machiavellian complexities within the Party itself. He will have to deal with the past, the past so present, as it is today in Europe. When I see the *Newsweek* cover, with the Tsarist emblem, with the Orthodox Church resurgent, I think that I dream. Europe too – and America backing the past instead of a future for Europe – is going backwards emotionally. Will China do the same? I see already traces of this. In the young, who fawn upon the western people they meet, who adopt a slave mentality, denigrating their own land, just to please, to please . . . To please a lordly West. China too is caught within this web of emotional returns, as well as a hunger for going forward.

I see a great many people, and am able – modestly – to adjust a few problems. I know that abroad the downfall of the present regime is ardently desired, and would be seen as a great victory, a triumph for democracy . . . But is it true?

For anyone who knows China well, it is not so. It means civil war and chaos for a long time . . . and with hindsight, in June 1991, seeing the chaotic state of certain countries in Europe who go begging for money, I think that, perhaps, China will find another way, her way, to reform the system. Perhaps I shall be proved wrong, but I have a hunch that I may be right. The doctrine of chaos, so akin to Taoism, teaches us that reality is not a series of logically connected events, but a succession of random encounters. Continuity is the flux of change, upon which we imprint hindsight logic.

And so 4 June, Tiananmen Square, and what happened there, cannot be the end, but the beginning of something which has to be done, which will now have to grow. This is historical inevitability. And I know my people enough to know that they are learning, learning the lesson.

Thus is history fashioned, not through smoothly connected, logically categorized events, but through mindless confrontations and deplorable violence.

Had the students kept quiet, nothing would have moved. Now I know in my bones, before anything is said, that some process of change will be initiated.

And this happens precisely at the time when the western sponsors of these students are abandoning them, are calling them foolhardy, and full of themselves . . .

Pawns. Pawns to be rejected when no longer useful. Useful for what?

Fourteen

BACK TO CHINA in the spring of 1990, again in the autumn, and yet again in April and May of 1991. Searching for facts, for reactions, for developments, and also for the successors, those who will take over within the next decade. I believe they will come from the provinces, from other cities, even from remote border areas.

1990 is meant to be a grim hard year for China, with economic sanctions, diplomatic boycott, refusal of loans by the World Bank and other organizations. China is expected to crumble. So say a good many China experts. She will not be able to stand the pressures, the economic pressures . . .

But this does not happen. The country copes. Retrenchment, reorganization, stricter controls . . . stagnation perhaps, but inflation is drastically reduced from 35 to around 5 per cent. Moreover, in that autumn, the Asian games are held in Beijing and are extremely successful.

No more soldiers in the streets in the autumn. Everything apparently back to normal. I write apparently, because there are differences. It is more difficult for western newsmen to approach Chinese intellectuals now. I think this new stricture will only maintain resentment with the few intellectuals regarded by westerners as 'valid', and 'well informed'. Simply because they occasionally relay titbits of rumour, of gossip.

Forty thousand Chinese students in the United States have been given prolonged permits, to remain in the USA. This has depleted China's universities, colleges, research laboratories and hospitals of much needed expertise.

Great publicity, support both financial and moral, star treatment, has gone to the students and others who have fled abroad. They are the focus of media glory. Chai Ling is received by a very famous family. Wuerkaise appears in London in a most expensive suit, his girlfriend in an opulent fur coat. The Alliance for Democracy is set up. It receives, at first, a great deal of money. Investigative reporter Liu Binyan, with his usual fierce integrity, refuses to join the Alliance, denouncing the money grabbing and petty squabbling which swiftly lands the Alliance in disrepute. Nevertheless, he predicts that this generation will be the one to bring about a great change in China; the reign of the 'octogenarians' must end. Octogenarians do die, but somehow I do not see them replaced by the dissidents abroad, although I hope they too will play a part in China's future. But the change will come from within, from those in the Party, and in the other parties, the non-communist parties, from the intellectuals, the middle school teachers, from China's countryside. The student movement was precursor of inevitable change. And now the time to seriously tackle political reforms has come.

Since the expected young trainees have not returned, Third and Fourth Brothers, approaching seventy, do the work of the absent younger men in their departments. Sexagenarians, septuagenarians, even octogenarians, come out of retirement, volunteer to work again. 'We must serve the people. The people cannot go hungry in body or in mind. We do not agree with some of the government's actions . . . we too condemn corruption. But this is our land, and we do not run away.' Someone has a mordant phrase. 'The runaways are merely the cultural pets of some western politicians.' Cultural pets. Too often we in the Third World are conscious of the patronizing stance, the unctuous voice. He puts it more crudely. 'Lapdogs. Some prefer to become lapdogs . . . for a quiet, comfortable life abroad.'

I feel very sorry for the students when, by the end

of 1990, and in 1991, I read articles, even in a respected economic magazine, allied to the *Wall Street Journal*, clearly depicting the debacle of the Alliance abroad. Revealing that money is no longer forthcoming to sustain it. I feel more sorry than ever for these youths, and their dreams.

Junjian feels sorry too, for he likes the young people. 'Aiiah, children, such children . . . they had their heads turned, inflated with self-importance. They will return one day. We should welcome them back.'

In the spring of 1991, I hear that three major dissidents have sent messages indicating that they would like to return on condition that no legal action be taken against them. I also hear that the wife of a prominent dissident has already returned to her family in China . . . she suffered a total collapse. Chai Ling, beautiful as ever, but now divorced (her wedding, on Tiananmen Square, inspired a well-meaning French author to write a book), does not too badly. She cradles in her arms a little dog wherever she goes.

There is a comic attempt to send a boat, carrying the replica of the Goddess of Democracy, on a voyage from France to China. It leaves France amid salvoes of rhetoric and emotion, and finds no welcome in Singapore, nor in Hongkong, nor even much of a welcome in Taiwan. It is not allowed to stay in Japan. The fanfare is suddenly muted, the 'event' becomes non-event, erased, forgotten by the very people who sponsored it. Meanwhile, despite the sanctions, French businessmen continue to do brisk business in China, and all contracts are honoured.

The Berlin Wall fell in late 1989; democracy swept over Eastern Europe. With relish some newspapers predict that now, now, China will fall . . . but this does not happen. Deng Xiaoping says it. 'It is the old comrades who intervened in good time.' This is a hard admission for him to make, since he had been the architect of rejuvenation, had tried to make the First Generation retire.

One still hears and reads about the conspiracy theme. About 'peaceful transition to capitalism'. Even if there has been meddling (and apparently there has been) I agree with vice-premier Yao Yilin. 'We must distinguish between outside and inside causes . . . it is the inside we must concentrate on. The economic situation led to massive discontent . . . that is why so many ordinary people sympathized with the students . . . we must have no illusions about this.' Hence his phrase: 'A strategic victory but a tactical defeat.' The debate still goes on, within the Party. Deng Xiaoping does not lose heart, though the two men he picked to push reforms have both been accounted failures. He will try again.

Deng Xiaoping is now reviled by the students, who call the regime 'patriarchalism', which it is. Confucius is still alive in the minds of all of us, in the minds of Party members as well. It always surprises me that some western Sinologists, who in their writings urge Chinese youth to fight for democracy, at the same time eulogize that obdurate authoritarian, Confucius.

Deng will not give up opening to the world, or economic reforms. 'The heart of the matter is in the Party itself,' says he. 'The responsibility for what happened on 4 June lies with the Party.'

This frankness has cleared the air, re-established a certain poise. Alas, the Cultural Revolution pundits have returned in force to the newspapers. They leech onto the dinosaurs.

The Party will celebrate its 70th birthday on 1 July, 1991. Already in 1990, it is quite clear to me that there must be, there will be, some attempt at political reform. Step by step. Every step will encounter resistance. There will be the usual deviations, distortions, machiavellian acrobatic twists at which the Party men are so proficient. But it will have to come.

In the spring of 1990, at a lecture, I say to members of the Political Consultative Committee, to members of the Democratic League: 'I think the time has come to be more active for political reforms.' In the spring this is still unclear, but by autumn all the signs are there.

Thus begins the healing process. What was jagged, wretched, unbearable wounding, has become scab, fibrous tissue, still painful, but a continuity. We must heal, we must go on. In order to change. We must weep for the innocent dead, those caught in the shootings of that dark June night. But we must walk forward.

I meet again former Tianjin mayor Li Ruihuan. He is now promoted to the Centre in Beijing, to the politburo. He must take in hand, remould the apparatus of propaganda, the whole structure of the information media. A horrendous task. Li, an ex-carpenter, is so intellectually alert that he puts many an intellectual to shame. He talks with the speed of a machine-gun, but with a precision of thought which is entrancing. His words are accurate pellets, each one of them meaningful, and he never seems to catch breath.

'We harboured many illusions. We harboured the illusion that the communist Party was still loved, that the army was welcome as fish in water among the people. We had not realized that times had changed. We did not take preventive action in time. This total unpreparedness has cost us dearly . . . we became extremely passive . . . until it was too late. We must reassess all that has happened, keep cool heads. There is still a great deal of emotion about . . . we must acknowledge our errors.'

Thus, without saying it, Mayor Li is saying what Yao Yilin the vice-premier had partly acknowledged, but Li has put it on the human plane.

'The intellectuals are very important. We cannot accomplish our modernization without them. We have neither honoured nor valued them enough. This must change, and quickly.'

Li deplored the way the Chinese media failed altogether in the crisis. 'We have never overhauled our public relations system. We felt we did not need to do so, the western press was writing such laudatory articles about us . . . we got very smug.' He probably thinks back, as I do, to Deng Xiaoping on the cover of *Time*, being Man of the Year. 'We did not realize the power, the tyranny, the changefulness of the media . . . their impact, and how minds are manipulated.'

Li Ruihuan is now in charge of setting up better editorial staffs, for what is written for Chinese consumption and for the outside. I say 'good idea', but it is a question of total communication, and style of writing, for both inside and outside China. Sitting with us is a serene and dignified gentleman, who has run the propaganda department for many years. He is so dignified, so urbane, that I have a shrinking feeling he will not change. I speak of translation. The urgent need for good translation. I am already, on my own, giving prizes for good translations, every year. I know the problems. But I think Li will encounter the hardest task of all. It is easier to change the economy than to change the minds of the people encrusted in the propaganda ministry, in the culture ministry. Wooden vocabulary, insisting on a word for word, clumsy, 'correct' translation rather than an interpretation of the meaning of a sentence. And many more silly rules, which I mention. Li Ruihuan smiles. The dignified gentleman half smiles. I think Li is going to have the most difficult task of all in China.

Among the writers, the game of official chairs continues. The officials named at the Fourth Congress are out, and an older batch of writers, previously displaced, is in.

Some of the young writers go into a passive resistance stance. They will not write. After all, their salaries are secure. Shan Rong tells me that now she paints. 'The time is not appropriate for writing.' However, in 1991, a year later, she seems to have recovered, and is very active among 'amateur writers', newly created groups.

My friend Liu Xinwu has dinner with me. He is no longer editor of *People's Literature*. He and Shan Rong earnestly discuss the gradings of writers into the four categories which I have previously mentioned. Somehow I feel both of them want to be category A. But Junjian, who likes young writers, who does not attempt to become an official, tells me that the young are idealistic, and do not care about A B C D. 'They usually work at other jobs.' Jiang Zeming will pick up this idea. I am happy when amateur writers are publicly honoured a year later, leaving the official literocrats in the shade (temporarily).

A Marxist theoretician, heavily browed, swarthy, drops in for a chat. 'China must proceed from reality. The reality is that she cannot operate a western-type capitalist system. But economic reforms have already created a massive change in the relations of production. It is therefore necessary to rethink *totally* the matter of dealing with the economy.' He hints that the old type of Marxism is outmoded 'but some of the older comrades have very little scientific background. They spout phrases they only comprehend partly.' We think of the same person as he talks, but of course we do not pronounce the name. 'We may not like to admit it, but the First Generation, the octogenarians, belong to an epic. Though they do not understand modern economics, they do understand danger to China. They smell it. And despite the tragic events of 4 June, they have kept China together, and spared the people much worse horrors.' It is a bitter paradox of history, says this beetle-browed, quiet-spoken man, that with the wave sweeping the USSR, the latter will have many troubles. And China 'could not have coped with the chaos, the immediate famines . . . we would have reverted to a military dictatorship of the worst kind . . . have you noticed how easily, how swiftly, democratic countries accept military dictatorships provided they proclaim themselves anti-communist?' He leaves with a parting sentence. 'If we have good harvests this year, and reduce inflation, and pull the economy together, we have another chance.'

At the house of an ex-ambassador, we debate the American Foundation, called the Soros affair, since a Mr Soros was in charge of it. Here we are free to say anything, and one person energetically denies that there ever was any attempt at corruption from the multi-million dollar foundation established by Hungarian philanthropist Soros. However, I have received contrary material, notably from a Canadian university. My friend Sam Noumoff, two years back, had debated at Party schools the activities of the management training institutes funded by the foundation. Of course no one can blame a capitalist for altering, or trying to alter, the manner in which enterprises are managed. There has been, there continues to be, much debate on this point. In 1991, in an interview in the *New York Times*, Mr Soros recognizes that his strategy of influencing management training has succeeded in Eastern Europe, but failed in China. 'There was *no* conspiracy among the intelligentsia,' say some of the friends round the ex-ambassador. 'All that happened was quite spontaneous . . . ninety per cent of the people who participated joined because they saw no solution to the problems of corruption and inflation . . . they marched, they demonstrated . . . it had really nothing to do with trying to overthrow the government, nor with democracy.'

The usual parallel is drawn, between the Cultural Revolution and the student demonstrations. 'I think it is time we should study the Cultural Revolution again. The powerful impetus it gave to youth by proclaiming Great Democracy.'

Democracy. *Min Ju.* The People are Masters. 'But to many it means do just as you please,' says the ex-ambassador. A young man, who seems very frightened, says: 'I hear that soon, soon, there will be another Cultural Revolution.' We all smile because, at the moment, and despite the rhetoric, this is more improbable than ever.

'It was very badly handled.'

Everyone says it, including Vincent's masseur.

Vincent has had a mild stroke, and is recovering well. He enjoys massage, and acupuncture, because round the bed where he lies being pummelled by a diminutive man with muscles of steel and wonderful hands, everybody talks, talks . . . it is like a small tea party round his prone body, and the massage lasts two hours. Time for a lot of talk.

'Silence is more dangerous than talk. Words hidden in the belly are concealed daggers.' There is talk, not furious, but disconcertingly frank. 'It was very badly handled.' We leave it at that.

Among the intelligentsia, however, many bellies are still stuffed with unspoken words. The intelligentsia's stance of mutism is deliberate. Passive resistance. But when not on public show they talk a great deal.

I read out of Deng Xiaoping's works: 'A revolutionary political party does not fear the people's cries of protest. What it fears most is their silence.'

'It was very badly handled . . . no one really tried to understand the Fourth Generation . . . now we must try again.'

To begin with, each university student will do a spell of a month to three months in the army. Also go to the villages, the poor areas, on investigation tours.

'The young were divorced from China's reality', everyone now says it. Since this was obvious for some years, perhaps a little reality will help. But the main thrust should be their involvement, their participation.

Vincent lectures on India to a famed institute for international relations. He is asked what his country does when 'social unrest' occurs. 'In all the socialist countries, whenever there is an internal problem such as riots, one sees the tanks go in, the army display all its apparatus. This happened in Hungary in 1956, in Prague in 1968.' (It happened again in Lithuania in 1990, in Moscow on 29 March, 1991 when 50,000 soldiers and hundreds of tanks were used to prevent a demonstration.) 'No socialist country,' says Vincent, 'seems to have bothered to learn about crowd control, which uses different methods from attacking an external enemy.'

'Your husband has given us most valuable, most valuable, views,' says the director of the institute to me.

Mr Qiao She is in charge of security. He has the thin, aristocratic face of a professor of philosophy, and was trained as an engineer.

We talk about torture.

I have received letters from England, from Canada, alleging that two students have been tortured, boiling water poured on their hands. Would I check?

I duly check with Mr Qiao She. I have other questions, regarding some individuals who have been arrested, notably the husband of a certain writer. The latter has asked me to intercede.

'But you cannot assume responsibility for this man . . . you have never met him,' remonstrates Intelligent Principle. 'Of course I am not trying to interfere with *the Law*,' I reply, sounding righteous, remembering the brush-off I received ten years ago over the Wei Jinsheng case. 'But as a fellow-writer . . . ' This passes muster. Then another problem arises. The writer says, 'I know that if *you* ask, he will be released.' I have to remind her that this is precisely the kind of influence, connections, that we are supposed to fight against.

Mr Qiao She meets my queries head on. 'Yes, we do have cases of torture. Many of the police and security men are young recruits, not always well trained. There are strict orders against torture . . . but at local level, you know how difficult it is.'

I know. Above there is a policy, below there is a counter-policy.

'Every effort must be made, that the innocent should not suffer unduly,' I say. Mr Qiao She nods. 'There is a difference between formal arrest and detention. We will investigate each case. But it takes a long time. Like everywhere else, the police are eager to produce "results". And investigations mean each time also investigating the investigators, to be sure there is no connection, acquaintance, link [and I think, but don't say it, possibly bribing too]. The teams are sometimes balked. Evidence is difficult to get at.' He cites the case of a man who right after 4 June was brought in, accused of having killed a soldier. Three witnesses said they had seen him do it. 'We questioned them at length . . . we were going to pass judgment.' Fortunately some bright security officer did further research. The alleged culprit had been at home that night, he was accused because one of the three resented him, wanted revenge, and had persuaded the other two. A neighbour in the same courtyard had seen him at home, but had not dared to talk. 'It took nine months,' says Qiao She.

I remember an ugly story which happened in my own province some five years ago. A woman had dared to go to law, to reveal a case of extortion and theft by a couple in her village. The couple, and their relatives, seized the girl, and buried her alive.

'We are still very feudal,' says Qiao She. 'Do you think I want to punish a lot of people, keep a lot of them in jail? That would not be good for China . . . the fewer the people punished, the better. I don't want the jails full . . . it is very bad for our reputation, very bad also for our security units. I want to release as many as possible . . . but the families of the dead soldiers are asking for revenge . . . they want the criminals who killed their sons punished . . . that is why we are taking a very long time.'

It is possible, sometimes, to get at the truth with 'mass co-operation', says he. That is why telephones, hot lines, so that people can report, have been installed. It preserves their anonymity, keeps them safe from the vengeance of relatives of the arrested. 'This has a very bad press in the West,' says Qiao She. 'If there is a better way, of course I would like to know it.'

Law is so new, such a new, strange concept. Witnesses fabulate even though now the crime of perjury is punishable. The husband of my writer friend is released in spring 1991. His family telephone. I emphasize that it has nothing to do with me. Many other intellectuals are released, including the man who brought money to the students from the

United States. But Wang Dan, and others active in leading the student movement, receive jail terms. I feel sorry for them.

Astro-physicist Fang Lizhe and his wife lose prestige, because they are safe, and some say: 'Had Fang been a true Chinese intellectual, he would have offered himself for arrest, begged for the release of the young whom he and his wife advised, guided, directed, through that fateful spring of 1989.'

I go to Shanghai to see the popular mayor, Zhu Yongji. He talks on radio, on TV, to the people. He has charisma, he is clever. He is shaping a colossal project, no less than the rehousing of the 12 million people of Shanghai, the building of a vast new economic zone, in Pudong, across the river. Zhu will go to America, to Europe. He is dubbed 'the Chinese Gorbachev'. Which he is not. But he is a reformist, and I anticipate that he will rise swiftly. He does, becomes vice-premier in 1991.

In Sichuan I meet bright young men, their origin solidly peasant, but proficient, energetic, very much in touch with world affairs. I go to Guangzhou, the southern province which is doing fabulously well, where there was scarcely a ripple that June. The governor Ye Xuanping is the son of Marshal Ye Jianying, whom I saw in 1977. Here the prosperity in the countryside is startling. Wealthy villages become townships. There is however a major subject of complaint. Thousands of peasants from poorer inland provinces come here to seek jobs. They try to break into the Shenzhen economic zone as well. 'What do you do?' 'We spend some money feeding them, then we transport them back to where they came from,' say the businesslike administrators of the province. I go to the Zhuhai economic zone, and there meet some of the ablest young scientists in China. I see very well run factories. 'We are establishing links with inland provinces, they come here to learn . . . each province also wants its own economic zone,' says the Party secretary (another man who will one day have a good deal to say in the running of China).

The lobby of the beautiful Lakeside Hotel in Fuzhou, the capital of Fujian province, is crammed with Chinese. Chinese families, complete with children. The hum of voices drowns the splash of the huge fountain which dominates the lobby's centre. In the dining-room one solitary westerner waves his arms, trying to be noticed, to get service. The place is aroar with Chinese gustily eating, noisily talking, laughing. I go to the lift and there am recognized. In Nike shoes and miniskirts bouncing girls hop round me, dance up and down with American-type spontaneity, want autographs. 'Where are you from?' I ask as I sign. 'We are from Taiwan . . . you must come to Taiwan to visit us.' They are here on holiday, complete with parents and grandparents. It is the anniversary of The Mother.

I had noticed, early in the morning, doing my usual inventory of the space in which I temporarily reside, the little altar. Behind the shopping area. A small statue, wreathed in a red arch, spent red candles on both sides, and a gift of oranges on a plate in front of it. Heaven's Empress, Queen of the Seas. The Mother.

In the year AD 960 a girl was born to the Lin family in Futien, a small district of this province of Fujian. Sixth daughter of her family, she was mute, but had a canny knowledge of water. She could dance upon the waves, and save the fishermen in peril, and find the corpses of the drowned. She was reckoned a benevolent witch, and at her death, aged twenty-eight, a shrine was erected to her. In the course of the centuries her cult grew. Emperor after emperor, to satisfy the people, elevated her in rank. For in China, it is an imperial edict which determines godhead. Thus she became Empress of Heaven and of the Oceans. Her temples are everywhere through South China, and in Macao and in Hongkong, and in Southeast Asia and also in San Francisco. Out of Taiwan's 18 million people, 12 million come from this single province of Fujian, and worship The Mother.

A million people from Taiwan will come to Fujian province this year to visit The Mother's temple. A young historian reminds me that night that it was in a shrine to her that Zhou Enlai, in 1927, when pursued by the armies of Chiang Kaishek, took temporary refuge. It was there that he consecrated two famous men as communist Party members, in front of the altar to the goddess. 'Most appropriate,' says he. Now Fujian province has been designated as a special zone with privileges for the investors from Taiwan. 'Our brothers across the Straits come back every year to visit their families and their native villages,' says Lin Tsing, former ambassador to the United Nations, now in charge of relations with Taiwan. Lin Tsing has a great heritage. It was his great grandfather, Lin Tsexu, who publicly burnt 50 tons of opium imported by Great Britain into China. It was in 1840, a hundred and fifty years ago.

I lecture to about a thousand people, and there are many many questions: about Eastern Europe, the USSR, and of course democracy. Afterwards I receive books, many books, about The Mother. It is quite evident that Taiwan will reunify with the mainland one day, under the 'one country two systems' formula. Taiwan's material prosperity today is certain, but the future is not so bright. Taiwan businessmen realize the danger. They are only an appendage of western economics, they know their own vulnerability *vis-à-vis* the gigantic, and so capricious, so wayward power, the United States. Already Fujian province, hitherto starkly undeveloped, is changing, changing with bewildering swiftness. And the Taiwan businessmen do not talk democracy. There has been no democracy in Taiwan, but martial law for forty years. Only in the last two years has a democratic process begun. By 1991, not only is Taiwan investing in the Mainland, but Chinese companies, government backed, are investing in Taiwan.

Ninth Sister and her husband are prominent members of the Democratic League in Sichuan province. They are now energized, reactivated. They *must* recruit new members. The Overseas Chinese League members, and Common Front organization adherents, join us in several meetings. Talk. Talk. Very useful and 'constructive' as the Chinese say. Some eighty non-communist 'democratic personages' are being promoted to vice-ministerships, to vice-mayoralties. What if this is only a show, and still no power of discussion, of withholding their opinions, of propagating views that are different, is given to them? 'It is not a question of fighting for power, but of working towards a real consensus,' says Ninth Sister's husband. He is establishing schools in the foothill areas. In Liangshan, the Cool Mountains, where live the Heaven-born Yi people – those forever garbed in black, with charming twisted turbans upon their heads – the League runs a university for civil servants. The graduates are reckoned excellent. 'Democracy must start with education at the base,' says Ninth Sister's husband.

For the past six years the structure of a civil service, apart from the Party bureaucracy, has been initiated and already civil servants emerge, full of talent. Another anti-corruption drive takes place. Two ministers, found guilty, stand trial. This is popular. Then a movement called 'the housewife's basket' begins. It means that food must be available, at stable prices. The cost of meat, vegetables, is lower than in the previous year and by the winter of 1990–91 inflation is down to 3 per cent.

A renewed drive to set up Lei Feng, the angelic soldier, as a model takes place. 'I have spent the summer working voluntarily in a village. My mind has changed . . . I understand Lei Feng,' writes a young man who says he has attended one of my lectures. I still find it difficult to reconcile myself to the saintly Lei Feng. Other models are written about. Scientists, teachers, other intellectuals, who have devoted their lives to the people, who are patriotic. There are now 500 women mayors in China, many of them in their early forties or fifties.

When I return to Europe some of the friends of China,

who emotionally – and sometimes politically – had conceived intense, uncritical affection for the country, are still bitter and say that democracy has failed in China. The truth is that it has never really been tried. I think back to the phrase used by Vassar-educated president of Fudan University, Madame Xie Xide: 'Hope is a path that needs constant treading to keep it a path.'

I hope. But I see clearly that democracy cannot be imposed by outside interference, by influence, however benign or not so benign, and by imitation. I agree with a friend from Singapore who writes: 'Any precipitate change will only lead to a military regime, to a return of the warlord era, to chaos. It is better for China to evolve slowly than to evolve wrongly.'

One can only go on trying, *with* the Chinese people, with the democratic parties in China, with the reformists in the communist Party, with the young, the Fourth Generation.

In early summer 1991, after the Gulf War, many western governments re-establish normal diplomatic intercourse, and business as usual. Despite attempts at restrictive measures and a lot of noise in the United States Congress, China can only try to carry on, to attempt change without another frightful backlash.

The economic debate continues. It has centred for over a year on two major items, the village township enterprises, and the functioning, or rather dysfunctioning, of the massive State plants.

The village township enterprises (VTE) are the private sector. This sector has grown very swiftly and now represents over 30 per cent of the total production of the country. But some of the men in power are against it, as for instance vice-premier Yao Yilin, because the VTE compete with state enterprises for coal and cotton, silk and steel. This has led to a large black market in raw materials, to hoarding, to profiteering, so that coal at 10 yuan a ton at the pit head in Shandong Province is sold at 100 yuan in Shanghai. But it is not possible to retrench this sector now. It is too valuable. It brings immediate benefits, assures a flow of light consumer goods, ensures work and livelihood for many millions. And it is the instrument whereby urbanization, the creation of new townships, is taking place. A good many peasants go into these VTE relieving the pressure on unemployable rural labour.

In every third world country there occurs massive swamping of the cities by the millions leaving the countryside. The VTE are preventing the problem from becoming unmanageable in China.

By 1991, although denied the subsidies and protection given to state enterprises, the VTE will do far better than the latter, and this is reported by the state statistical bureau (also by *China Economic News* No 9, March 11, 1991). It is obvious that China is diluting her socialism by introducing 'capitalist' methods and principles into the economy.

There must be a combination of market forces and free enterprise together with macro-planning, state control over essential, strategic resources. No country in the world exists without some measure of control over the levers of the economy. Total laissez-faire (as advocated by certain western economists and Sinologists) is unrealistic. It will only ensure total vampirism – to profit Big International Business.

But what about state enterprises? What shall be done with them? To talk about 'privatization' at the moment is also nonsense. One third of the total government expenditure for industry goes into subsidizing these helpless mastodons of another era. 'What can be done about them?' two former ambassadors, our friends, ask Vincent and me over a cup of tea. 'There is no way out,' reiterates writer Shan Rong.

I decide to ask the prime minister, Li Peng, some direct questions regarding market forces, and state enterprises.

'Some Chinese intellectuals do not like Li Peng and say it openly,' an Indian diplomat tells me. 'But I think he is an appropriate man for these transitional times.' I know that Li

Peng is not liked. This hostility dates back to his accession to the premiership in 1987–8, much before the student demos. Perhaps it has to do with the cuts in education which occurred while Li Peng was in charge of the Education Commission. But today, retrenchment and reorganization, though responsible for sluggish markets, have certainly choked off inflation, at least for a while. The issuance of 'blank sheets' to the peasantry has stopped. China has reaped the largest grain harvest ever, 420 million tons, 13 million more than in 1984, the record year.

I tell my good friend L. that I do not quite understand the hostility. Two university professors have told me that Li Peng is 'insensitive'. A third one says: 'He spent his childhood in an orphanage in the USSR . . . this has stifled in him the art of communication . . . he has no empathy.' A young woman journalist – one of those who wear a permanent look of grievance upon her face – shrieks at me: 'Why do you want to see him? He is stupid, stupid . . . ' I ask her why she thinks so. 'Do you know him personally? Have you any specific complaint against him?' 'No, no, but . . . ' 'Is it because he is reckoned conservative, on the side of the older power-holders?' 'Perhaps . . . ' In the end, she says, 'It's because he couldn't stand up to the students when he met them, Wuerkaise, and Wang Dan, and others . . . ' I remember the scene broadcast live on TV in May 1989. Li Peng completely rattled, stammering and sweating. I remember the arrogance of Wuerkaise. 'I must meet him to try to know him better. One short hour in 1988 is not enough.'

Li Peng and his wife, a charming, unaffected woman, invite us to dinner. Again I realize he has no charisma, does not know how to please, does not put people at ease, is stiff. But he is full of facts, and delivers them in order, one two three four, as if reading a statistical report. However, as dinner progresses, he relaxes, even cracks a small joke. 'I find it extremely difficult to be a prime minister . . . luckily, at home, my wife is the premier . . . so I can relax.'

Madame Li Peng smiles, her husband smiles at her, they look at each other and the warmth comes, the caring . . . this man *is* capable of very deep feeling, but he is hidebound by shyness, and suddenly I sense in him a still frightened, lonely youth, uncertain of himself. He is a good family man, he is uncorrupt, none of his children have privileges or is a 'crown prince'. Perhaps that is why people find him dull.

We talk of the state enterprises. Li Peng says they cannot at the moment be disbanded without millions of workers (some 60 million or so) becoming unemployed. 'You see the situation in some East European countries, where there is 50 per cent unemployment reported . . . we could not stand it here.' Even if these mammoths work inefficiently – or not at all – they act as storage containers, and it is cheaper to pay the workers even for *not* working than to have social crises. For the aggregate salaries come only to 10 per cent of the total sum expended. These hives of torpor are therefore safety areas, and it is possible for the time being to go on carrying the load. Li Peng tells me of a ship plant in Dalian, employing women welders only. 'Why women welders? They *asked* for the job, it is better pay . . . but we could dispense with 80 per cent of them. But then what? Discontent, social unrest . . . and the problems of modernization of plants would still not be solved.'

People talk of human rights . . . but suddenly I think that, with this policy, China is being far more careful of human rights than many a capitalist company throwing out workers, simply because they want to show better earning figures.

We talk of the continuing pressures on China; the greatest problem of all. 'We are having another baby boom . . . the multitude of babies born during the first years of the Cultural Revolution, 1966 to 1969, when there was no control, are now new parents.' Of the threat to abrogate the most favoured nation clause, which means heavier duties on Chinese imports into the USA: 'This will hurt Hongkong far more than it will hurt us,' says Li Peng. 'There is much talk of human rights, but the first human right is not to starve, and today many nations are facing famines . . . perhaps the wealthy people in America forget this.' He agrees that there are 'deficiencies and mistakes' in procedure, especially in law, in China. 'But we do try hard. However, we shall never give up the country to chaos, to misery, in the name of capitalist freedom.'

'China is an immense laboratory for the third world, the developing countries. We are trying out experiments, in so many areas, so many ways . . . we have to invent a new pattern for ourselves,' I say, and Li Peng looks fixedly into space. 'There is now some measure of economic stability, and so we can begin to think of other reforms,' says he. On the previous day he had announced to an Australian delegation that political reforms were now being contemplated. 'We have to invent our own system, combining market forces with overall planning.' In the ten-year plan (1990–2000) economists envisage a mixture, with a private sector, a collective sector, a mandatory planning system in energy, transport, raw material resources. State control of the country's essential resources cannot be abrogated. 'The reforms seem to some people contradictory to stability, but stability will not be endangered if we proceed gradually, as we are now doing with cuts in subsidies. Also with the currency. No sudden devaluation, but gradual adjustment.'

Beginning May 1991 there will be a cut in subsidies of grain and oil. 'This will not affect purchasing power too much. The pattern of food buying has changed. Some years ago 80 per cent of food purchases were grain and a little oil. Now this is down to 38 per cent. People buy more meat, fruit and vegetables. The effect will not be so great, although of course there will be price rises in these items.' Thus Li Peng. The dinner ends and we leave.

Some western newsmen call Li Peng 'the butcher of Tiananmen'. True, he announced the imposition of martial law, since he was the prime minister. But the decisions taken were not his, although he does not seem to have opposed them nor protested when the order to shoot was given. 'A total lack of imagination, of vision' reiterate some of the intellectuals who ask me what the Premier and I talked about. It will take a long time for this tragic error to be forgiven or forgotten. One day, of course, the Party will have to reappraise the whole scenario. Meanwhile Li Peng will carry on, whether disliked or liked. There is in him a capacity of endurance not to be belittled. It is perhaps precisely his lack of glamour and charisma, the colourless tenacity which he projects which, in the midst of the new chaos shambling our world, is necessary for a while.

Wuhan. The university is beautiful. Its site borders a lake. It dates back to a 'self-strengthening school' erected in 1883 by one of China's earliest reformists. 'The international law department only began in 1980, thanks to Deng Xiaoping,' the jurists, lawyers, professors, cosily sitting with me in a room with a lot of sofas, tell me. 'The special department which you have asked to talk to, concerning research in Hongkong, Macao, Taiwan law was set up in 1982. You have asked how the different law systems, under the "one country, two systems" provision can be handled. This is a crucial problem.'

From Wuhan, from the international law department, jurists have gone travelling to many countries, the United States, Canada, Sweden, Switzerland, France, England, Germany, to study how law was handled and applied in these countries.

Within China itself, Law began in 1980. The problem of a) enacting law b) interpreting law c) administering law d) applying the law, is an endless one, and Wuhan University is leading – with other universities following – in this fascinating transformation of people's minds from Tradition to Law, from Party Edicts to Law . . .

Only in 1982 were laws made against bribery and corruption, and they were 'strengthened' (which means that they were given some muscle) at the end of 1989.

We spend a whole morning talking, talking, and I learn so much, so much more, of the work done here, its enormous value for the country's future. To begin with, the fact that in 1997–98, China will be faced with three different law systems: one in China, one in Macao, one in Hongkong. And later Taiwan. How will this be managed? A young jurist back from Switzerland invokes cantonal law and federal law in that country. But can this be adapted to China?

There is the major problem of 'investigation teams', and their role in law enforcement within China itself. I raise the all-embracing question of defining in law what is meant by the words: 'counter-revolutionary'. I have carried for some time a small crusade of my own against these words, writing memoranda against them, saying they are dangerous words because they can mean anything and they mean nothing. They condemn, without evidence. 'We are working right now on this problem,' say the jurists. And I am glad that once again my bones did not betray me, that I was part of that enormous symbiosis which is China, the people, what is within their minds.

The words 'counter-revolutionary' must no longer be used as a valid accusation. What is 'adverse' or 'nefarious' to the state must be defined in legal language. Must be based on the constitution. Evidence must be forthcoming. The constitution maintains the right to object . . . All this will be submitted to the National People's Congress later in 1991 . . .

This evokes from me another topic, which is the word 'individualism'. In the Chinese political dictionary, it is a 'bad' word. I have – and so has Intelligent Principle, and other friends of mine – debated against inflicting on the word the political meaning of selfishness, egotism . . . 'it is entirely a mistranslation of the meaning of individualism. Both Mao Dzedong and Zhou Enlai were individualists, since they went against the tide of those days,' I say. There are other words, phrases, to be overhauled, purged of political mishandling. This means revising the dictionaries. 'This work has already begun,' a jurist says smoothly.

A little bit of history follows. 'There were only nine of us in 1979: in 1979 only two students applied to study international law, but now we have 150 and several Ph.Ds. This year, 790 applications. Law is getting more popular in China. So much must still be done to teach the notion of law.'

Teaching law to the people.

I see it. In Fuzhou, capital of Fujian province. On the streets. A crowd, a motley one, young and old, urbanites and peasants, jamming a wide street, thousands of them. Between a theatre and a new supermarket. Is this turmoil, a protest demo? I wedge in and find there are fifty or more tables aligned along the sidewalk. At each sit men and women surrounded by people. What is it? 'It is our open law court,' says the Fujian government representative with me. 'Every Thursday and Tuesday and sometimes on Saturday we hold open law court in the street. Anyone can come, anyone with any problem. There is no charge.'

There are at least 3,000 if not more people in the street, some of them queue in front of the tables, others wait. 'Some complain of thefts, burglaries, others of housing problems, people not paying rent, or wife-beating, or adultery, some come for divorce procedures, and sometimes we have criminal cases reported . . . anything.' At each table sits a lawyer, with law students. Security men hover, taking notes for the criminal cases. 'We started this in 1989, it is very popular,' says my guide.

Open door law. Law taught on the streets. An old woman pulls me by the sleeve. She thinks I am a lawyer. She complains that her son is unfilial, for he takes his wife out on weekends, leaving her alone to cope with their child. 'I am the mother. This is not fair to me.'

'We listen to every complaint, grievance, question,' says a young lawyer. 'We try to settle as many cases as possible on the spot. If we cannot, we refer the cases to the appropriate

courts. This avoids waiting a long, long time in the courts.'
It is also a very good way of teaching recourse to law. 'A lot
of people come to listen . . . it also helps to teach them, to
spread the idea of law,' says the young lawyer, who hurriedly
gets back to his table where a queue has formed.

A middle-aged teacher from Honan province writes to
me. 'Please ask the university students to come to see us
. . . we are searching everywhere for teachers, for doctors,
for our villages. Where does democracy begin, if not with
us and with our needs?'

Talks. Meetings. My days are filled with meetings. Back
in Beijing, I call on the head of the Democratic League, Mr
Fei Xiaotung. He is very well known. He was dubbed a
rightist way back in 1957–58. He is famous now, and
active. 'In China democratic parties were formed through a
historical process of consensus and participation . . . thanks
to Premier Zhou Enlai. But the final decision always rests in
the hands of the communist Party, and this is the result of
our history. The democratic parties cannot contest power,
they must share in consultation.' Fei Xiaotung has a round
face, round nose, exudes benevolence, a kind of constant
hilarity. He is a man of undoubted patriotism, a corpulent
Talleyrandesque personality. 'The middle road,' says he,
'the middle road is the road for China.' He quotes, of
course, Confucian themes. He makes the point that democratic parties should be consulted before any big decision is
taken. 'But what is a big decision, what is a small one? No
one has as yet decided on that.' He says that now there is
a new sense of responsibility. Some of Premier Li Peng's
latest speeches were 'discussed with some contestation' by
the democratic parties. He repeats what everyone says, that
before any meeting of the NPC, the members should be fully
acquainted with the themes to be debated, and have had time
to prepare their own options. 'At the moment, opposition
to any decision depends on the political atmosphere, hihi,'
laughs Fei Xiaotung. There is no legal concept of what

opposition really means. 'We must have our own initiatives, our own conduits, both upwards to the power-holders, and downwards to the people. A reinforced right of supervision of any scheme, and the right of protest.' The Democratic League, under him, groups 100,000 high-grade intellectuals. No, says Fei, he does not think that there should be more at the moment, nor does he agree with my suggestion to extend league membership to Overseas Chinese. 'At least, you should extend it to Taiwan, Hongkong, Macao,' I say. Fei laughs and laughs. 'As honorary members,' says he. I feel that events will outpace the well-meaning man. Mr Fei Xiaotung is pleasant, but I do not think he will fight very hard.

A test case will be presented soon to the NPC. Not only the controversial 'counter-revolutionary' theme, but also the Yangtse Three Gorges dam. To build or not to build? Some years ago it was simply regarded as an executive decision to be taken, but opposition was so strong that now it is to be referred to the NPC. I interrogate two governors, one of Hubei province, one of Sichuan province. The Hubei governor is all for the dam. The Sichuan governor is totally against. It is not true, says the latter, that 'only a few hundred thousand people' will have to be moved (as says the Hubei governor). It will be millions. A whole city will be drowned. And worst of all not one watt of electric power will go to Sichuan, though it is here that the dam will be built . . . but Hubei province will get electricity, and so will the cities of the coast. The lake formed by the dam will provide, through a canal, needed water to the arid cities of the north, to Beijing the capital . . .

In 1991 Zhou Enlai reappears in the newspapers, as a model. It was he and his wife who organized, maintained, the non-communist parties of China. Zhou Enlai wanted them, sought to work *with them*, to run a government with many non-Party men and women, to obtain a large consensus. This was the idea behind the Hundred Flowers movement of 1956, conceived by him, backed by Mao . . . and which foundered the following year.

It will not be easy to start again in China, but neither will it be too difficult. China is changing, is changing. Change will come from the Chinese people themselves. They are not supine; an under-the-skin alertness tingles in them, a sense of waiting for change. People talk to me. Not only intellectuals, whose views, however lofty, may not be representative. But taxi drivers and waiters, shop assistants and bank employees, tailors and antique dealers and plumbers. Not one of these, whose life is better than it was ten years ago, wants violence. But all want an end to corruption, and more participation in decisions taken by high authority.

However, it may be that change through the imposition of an absolute peremptory western model will be tried. The 'right of interference' is brandished now by certain western countries. A formula invented by France, relished by the United States. The right to interfere in the name of human rights dominates the councils of the West. This will bring about, in China, an increased stiffening, and, perceptibly now, reliance on the army.

But I point out that corruption in the Soviet Union did bring down the communist regime. 'Corruption was utter and widespread. And in China, too, there is corruption. If China's Party does not stem corruption, then it will also collapse.'

The outcome may not be a democratic regime. It seems far more possible, for some of my friends almost inevitable, that it will be a military dictatorship.

Summer 1991. The total disintegration of the Soviet Union, the most catastrophic floods for the last half century in China. The two events coalesce, merge as one, in the minds of millions of Chinese.

Very few men and women, however civilized, are immune to belief in omens, predictions, presages. The faith in astrology exhibited even among recent occupants of the White

House is not abnormal. In China floods have always augured changes of dynasty, the overthrow of The Ruler. Of course this happens, as the waters engulf the fields, the villages, swallow millions of hectares into a new ocean. 'Heaven has manifested its anger . . . the rule of the communist Party is over', clamour some magicians, star-gazers, and even some intellectuals.

'From mid-May to mid-July we had an amount of rain equivalent to two years,' Tsui, director of the National Committee for Natural Disaster Reduction, tells me. He handles funding, clothes, food for the millions driven from submerged areas. He shows me on a map the affected regions in Central and East China, particularly the provinces of Anhui and Jiangsu, 100 million people.

'All the rivers overflowed, some of the lakes were so engorged they doubled in size, thousands of villages were wiped out.' The notorious river Huai, known for its rampages since the twelfth century, provoked the greatest disasters. Mao Dzedong, way back in 1951, had laid down an edict: The Huai River Must Be Tamed. This was done, in those years of willing enthusiasm, and during the Sixties and Seventies there were no great floods. But now, in the 1980s, due to land privatization, there has been massive neglect of water conservancy. Its budget was cut down by two-thirds. There has been heedless, thoughtless destruction of wooded hillslopes and forest. Denudation, loss of top soil, all along the Yangtse River is responsible for millions of tons of silt brought down every day, raising the river bed all along the river course. Add to this a growing population in the prosperous lower reaches, the building of villages on low level ground close to lake and rivers . . .

Writer Dai Houying, my spirited friend, who dared to contradict a French Sinologist, and says she will never again be translated into French, has gone to the flood areas. At first she thought the reports exaggerated. Now she has been there three weeks, and she is stunned. It is worse than anything she imagined.

225

Ten million people had to be evacuated urgently. Twenty million hectares of fields were covered in water. The army was mobilized, used thousands of flatboats to move the stricken population. There were around 3,000 deaths. One hundred thousand medical workers are there, for the risk of epidemics, cholera, typhoid, is high. 'We tried to be ahead of the onrushing waters. We had to protect threatened cities, so we deviated the floods, and evacuated the people ahead of time,' Tsui tells me.

Now the people must survive the winter. There will be food distribution for the next eleven months. 'We hope that the next harvest in North China will come before the frost . . . people say that there is always early frost when there are floods, but we hope not . . . we hope it will keep warm till after 22 September,' says Tsui. 22 September is the 15th of the lunar 8th month, the day of the Moon Festival. 'Another ten days after that, and that means 50,000 tons more of grain.'

In the Buddhist temples, in the temples dedicated to Great Yu, the man who tamed the floods of China more than 2,000 years ago, candles burn, and incense spirals heavenwards, to pray for a few more days before the first frost. The villages must be rebuilt, moved from low ground to hillslope, or raised on earth platforms. 'It means redoing the whole landscape for at least twenty million people or more . . . it will take three years,' says Tsui. How will all this be paid for? Massive donations come from Hongkong (100 million US dollars), from Singapore and Taiwan, and Overseas Chinese. Very little from the rest of the world, where news of the floods has been played down, or ignored. China is not in fashion. China is to be condemned, to be found fault with . . . 'It seems that having exorcised the Empire of Evil, the Soviet Demon, the West now needs to fabricate another Demon, China,' writes my friend Chen. 'For all their beautiful words on human rights, they exhibit little compassion for the Chinese as *human beings*.'

I ask Tsui whether there will be assurance that the money given will be well used. 'We have thought of this. The people won't tolerate cheating, pocketing funds . . . ' There have been executions of looters who tried to rob the stricken villagers. The government is not taking chances. No money will be sent directly, not even to provincial governors or heads of counties. Everything will be controlled through a central board, accountable and publishing their accounts openly.

This cataclysm has given the people in favour of building the Yangtse Gorges Dam another opportunity. They insist the dam is more relevant than ever. In this case it is not true, for the disaster happened well below the projected dam site, and is due to neglect of water conservancy measures. The dam will cost now 27 billion dollars or more. It will take twelve years before electric power is generated, and meanwhile locally needed funds will be tapped, cuts instituted in other projects, to finance the dam . . . yet on the other hand a massive programme for water conversancy is to be launched. This will also need money, urgently. Voices once again are raised in protest against the dam. A renowned expert says, 'We all know that other threats are looming. For all we know, the "new international order" promised is going to be a merciless, brutal confrontation between North and South. Throughout Asia, whatever the regimes, this is very clear. And China is a main target for fragmentation, for disruption . . . ' 'We are asked to exercise no protectionism, to open wide our markets, but in western countries the governments help industrial plants, subsidize them, protect their own markets,' a Malaysian economist tells me, attending an economic conference in Beijing. 'Have you noticed how they talk of freedom, of democracy, but never of equality, never of fraternity,' says an Indian businessman-cum-philanthropist.

Not all among China's top intellectuals are moved by the tragedy which has occurred. In the living-room of a western diplomat, a small group of top professors are gathered. Floods are on my mind, the stricken villagers huddling in makeshift tents on dykes, queuing to get their daily ration of grain. I talk of it, and meet cold stares. 'I have given half a month's salary, that is enough,' says one of them, haughtily. 'If I were you I would not meddle in politics, stick to writing fiction,' he adds. 'I'll only go if I'm given fitting transport . . . an aeroplane, just like the prime minister,' chuckles another. They seem very pleased with their brilliant demonstration of heartless disdain for their unfortunate fellow-men. Perhaps they think this will impress their foreign host? They are, of course, thorough democrats, all in favour of freedom, hoping the government will tumble. Perhaps, perhaps, these intellectuals will then become ministers in a new setup, and their honour, much aggrieved during the years, be restored. And to hell with the flooded millions, hanging on in the drowned fields of China.

General Secretary Jiang Zeming is tired. He has lost a good deal of weight since I last saw him in September 1989. He has been travelling a great deal through the land, and through the flooded areas. He has also been sitting up nights, holding meetings to study that other earthshaking event, the break-up of the USSR. But when I use the word 'another volcanic upheaval' he gently corrects me. 'We were prepared for it a long while ago . . . but not at the speed with which the whole structure disintegrated.'

Strange to say, it is not China, but India, which is economically hard hit. India had friendship and defence treaties with the Soviet Union. India supplied the USSR with many consumer goods, in return obtained military weapons in great amount. 'Our trade with the USSR was almost nil,' says Jiang. He also reminds me that it was China which tried to condemn the Soviet Union's interference in Hungary in 1956, and did mightily condemn the Soviet army's irruption into Prague in 1968. 'We are not altogether surprised,' he repeats. He too knows that now China is a target for fragmentation, in the name of democracy. 'But we shall not give in . . . we shall not again become colonized in the name of democracy.'

And then, because this is a friendly chat, we talk of poets and poetry. Jiang Zeming quotes and quotes, he is enamoured of the great poets. He writes for me a poem written in AD 1210 by Lu You, dedicated to the latter's son:

> Death abolishes ten thousand cares
> But still my heart will sorrow
> For the nine provinces apart
> The day our armies will have made all well,
> Do not forget to tell my soul
> Beyond the grave.

I shall reciprocate with a poem by Robert Frost:

> Ah when to the heart of man
> Was it ever less than a treason
> To go with the drift of things
> To yield with a grace to reason
> And bow and accept the end
> Of a love or a season?

The time of the robber barons is back in a world where the moral and ethical component of politics and economics has totally disappeared. Greed is the supreme god, and all social restraints to keep greed in check have been discarded. And this will also come to China. It is already there, among the young and the ambitious . . .

But I do not accept an end to love, to hope.

Acknowledgments

My heartfelt gratitude to the hundreds of people in China who have talked with me, shared their thoughts, doubts, emotions, without restraint. They cover a wide range, from peasants and workers and enterprise managers and Party cadres to university professors and students, waiters and shopgirls, and the new 'yuppies' making money out of free enterprise.

My thanks also to the Association for Friendship with Foreign Countries, my hosts since 1956 when I returned to China. Since then I have made sixty-eight trips to China and my hosts put up with all my demands, and never interfered in any way.

I must also mention non-Chinese friends who have helped me with their own perceptions and concern; Graham C. Greene, Geoffrey Oldham and John Gittings. John's book *China Changes Face* (Oxford University Press, 1989) is a valid work, which I greatly appreciated. I also thank Michael Fathers and Andrew Higgins, whom I never met, but whose account of the events of June 1989, *Tiananmen: the Rape of Peking* (Doubleday, 1989), helped me to work out the timing of those days, a timing so essential for exactly recording what happened in these tragic days.

I thank several Chinese eye-witnesses, among them Mr He Xin, who was present with his wife and child, Ms Wu Quanheng, and others.

History is a perpetual resifting of appraisals. This book may help to evaluate China as she really is, a country emerging from a difficult past, and which must find her own way to the future.

Han Suyin